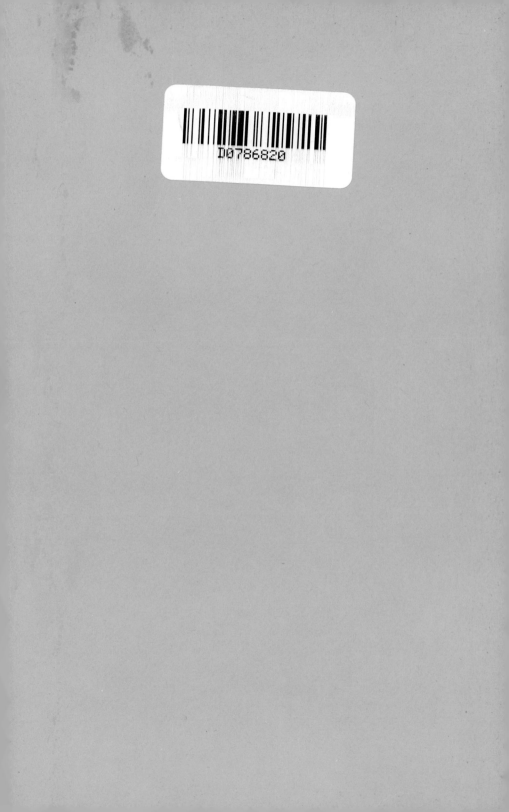

Judy Holliday

Judy Holliday

by
Will Holtzman

G. P. Putnam's Sons
New York

For Don, Ev, Linda and Gene

The author gratefully acknowledges permission from the following sources to reprint material in their control:

Mulligan Publishing Company, Inc., for "Friendly Neighborhood Dump" by Judy Holliday and Gerry Mulligan, copyright © 1965 by Gerry Mulligan, (ASAP); and for "I Want Something Lovely (to Happen to Me)" by Judy Holliday and Gerry Mulligan, copyright © 1965 by Gerry Mulligan. All rights reserved.

Mulligan Publishing Company, Inc., and United Artists Music Company, Inc., administrators, for "A Thousand Clowns" by Judy Holliday and Gerry Mulligan, copyright © 1965 by Gerry Mulligan. All rights reserved.

Stratford Music, Corp., owner, and Chappell & Co., Inc., and G. Schirmer, Inc., administrators of publication and allied rights for the Western Hemisphere, for "The Party's Over" by Betty Comden, Adolph Green and Jule Styne, copyright © 1956 by Betty Comden, Adolph Green and Jule Styne. International copyright secured. All rights reserved.

Library of Congress Cataloging in Publication Data

Holtzman, William. date.
  Judy Holliday.

  1. Holliday, Judy. 2. Moving-picture actors and actresses—United States—Biography. I. Title.
PN2287.H613H6 1982   791.43'028'0924 [B]   81-15826
ISBN 0-399-12647-3   AACR2

Acknowledgments

Biography is by nature a collaborative venture. I was blessed with the best of collaborators. I wish first to thank: Gerry Mulligan, Heywood Hale Broun, Ruth and Jim Buffington, John Houseman, Alec Wilder, Jack Lemmon, E. J. Kahn, Jr., Max Gordon, and Peter Lawford. These people gave freely of their busy time, which is a measure of their love for Judy.

Judy was fortunate to have been associated with many of the most gifted people of our time. My gratitude for their unselfish assistance: Patrick O'Neal, Al Hammer, Jerome Robbins, Herbert Greene, Anita Loos, Leonard Bernstein, Goodman Ace, Betty Comden, Adolph Green, Martin Charnin, Jean Stapleton, Joseph Campanella, Hal Linden, Neil Simon, and Maureen Stapleton.

It would have been impossible to know Judy without first knowing of her family and background. For their invaluable insights, my thanks to: Max Liebman, Sylvia Regan Ellstein, Nat Lefkowitz, Susan Ray, Pat Highsmith, Phyllis Lynde,

Algernon Black, Dr. and Mrs. Fred Raucher, Barney Josephson, Catherine Jones, Larry Siegel, and Sam Arens.

I owe a special debt to Lee Israel, whose generosity added immeasurably to this book. Thanks also to Willis and Shirley Conover, Ralph Roberts, Rogers Brackett, John Bowab, Ruth DuBonnet, Robert L. Green, Judge Simon Rifkind, and Gloria Steinem.

My appreciation as well to: Joan Hackett, Steve Allen, Jayne Meadows, Garson Kanin, George Cukor, Gale and Hester Sondergaard, Molly Frank, Frances Kramer, Katherine Hepburn, Elizabeth White, Lucille Kallen, Patti Karr, Alfred Drake, Mary Louise Wilson, Jack and Madeline Gilford, and Saul Chaplin.

There were many friends and associates who helped me along the way. I could not have written this book without their encouragement and guidance: Lisa Drew, Cheryl Crawford, Lynne Lipton, Andra Georges and Tim Shepard, Evie Goldich, Janice Rusin, Brian Firestone, Ellen Kutten, Ellis Amburn, Mel Berger, Biff Liff, Jeanine Basinger, Seth and Orren Gelblum, Brian Skarstad, Louise Beach, Maizie Ragan, Kathy Sulkes, Katie and Binky Fine, Anne and Ed Jamieson, Nate and Pat Pearson, and of course, Pearl.

I wish to thank the staffs of the Lincoln Center Library Theater Research Collection, the Library of Congress Motion Picture Section, the Academy Library, and the Federal Bureau of Investigation Freedom of Information-Privacy Acts Branch.

As always, my love and thanks to Sylvia Shepard, who somehow gets me through these things and makes it all worthwhile.

Will Holtzman
Wilton, Connecticut
September 1981

1

~~~~~~~~~~~~~~~~~~~~

Washington, D.C. March 26, 1952

It was a little like Judgment Day. You walked down long marble halls with impossibly high ceilings and the acoustics of a back-lot Bible epic. It was an architectural exercise in political proportion. Like God, the government missed nothing—your jittery breath, your thoughts, the fall of your pumps on the Simonized floor. So you play along because it's too comic to be real but too real to laugh. You walk into Room 457 and wonder if you dressed right, then realize it doesn't really matter, since those men with the pinhole irises see through you anyway. The Committee has its wardrobe of two-piece gabardines and grim sanctimony. They are the self-styled holy men who have arranged your personal Judgment Day and will now raise the ghosts of your past.

"Do you solemnly swear that the testimony you are about to give in the matter now pending before the subcommittee of the

Judiciary Committee of the United States Senate, will be the truth, the whole truth, and nothing but the truth, so help you God?"

"I do."

The senator turns things over to his staff director, Richard Arens, a lawyer with a hard jaw and a no-nonsense monotone straight out of *Gangbusters.* "Name?"

"Judy Holliday."

"Your name is Judy Holliday as a stage name, is it?"

"Yes," her voice flutters.

"A professional name?"

"Yes," she says firmly but diffidently.

"What other name have you used in the course of your life?"

"Judy Tuvim. T-u-v-i-m." Translated liberally it is Hebrew for "holiday." Arens acts as though Holliday were not a stage name but an alias. He seems especially eager to establish that she is Jewish.

There are more preliminaries. She was born in Manhattan, educated in the public schools, graduated at fifteen and ranked her class. She repeats the early show-business litany of nightclub work in an act called the Revuers with Betty Comden, Adolph Green, Alvin Hammer, and John Frank.

Arens interrupts, "Did you list Adolph Green?"

"Yes, I did."

"Who was the manager of the act?"

"There wasn't any manager," she corrects, though she mentions a recent phone conversation with Betty and Adolph, just to show she's been doing her homework.

Arens is not well-versed in the very entertainment field he means to purge. Judy does what she can to educate him.

Arens thinks he detects a mea culpa. "What made you think that you might have to answer questions about appearances and endorsements that you had made while you were a member of the Revuers?"

She answers squarely, "Because that is how the whole trouble started, with a book called *Red Channels*, and I have been asked so many questions; people have been very curious to know how I got into it, and I tried to clarify my position for the last year."

Red Channels is the hardback blacklist put out in 1950 by an ex-advertising man and his two ex-FBI partners, the same men who first published the weekly watchdog newsletter *Counterattack*. Subscribers to *Counterattack* receive a running commentary on who in show business has an untidy political past to launder, along with names and addresses of network, studio, and advertising executives who might hurry the process along. *Red Channels*, in turn, is a kind of redhunter's *Reader's Digest*.

But it's the Catholic War Veterans who have really gotten to Judy. For all the unseen treachery of the others, these are the visible bullies and tormentors. Their pickets have been after her off and on for two years now. She sees them in her dreams. She shudders at the sight of a high-school marching band.

Arens is unmoved by her plight. He advances his first accusation in the damning clinical language of the day. "Well, now, I put it to you as a fact and ask you to affirm or deny the fact, Miss Holliday, that in 1941 you were a part of the unit known as the Revuers, one of the entertainers in a party given by the United American-Spanish Aid Committee?"

Judy lets a little of the air out. "You mean I should say 'yes' or 'no'?"

"Yes, if you have a recollection."

"I don't know."

"You have no recollection?"

"Yes."

This is becoming a bit burlesque for Arens's taste. He presses on. "Now, I put it to you as a fact and ask you to affirm or deny the fact that on November 30, 1946, you marched in a picket line in front of Pier 53 in a strike sponsored by the waterfront section of the Communist party?"

"I don't know anything that I ever did sponsored by the Communist party," she answers directly.

The senator from Utah, Watkins, tries to ascribe motive. "You did not go simply because someone told you. Did you not go over of your own free will? Did you not ask questions about it?"

"Very often I was asked to do so many things in so many different places and for so many different causes that they would sort of slip away from me." She pauses. "What was it?"

"That was in 1946," Watkins answers.

"What was it for, strikers?" she asks.

Arens fumes. "I do not want to be in the position of testifying, I want to be in the position of interrogating you." Truer words were never spoken. This is Arens's show and he will not be upstaged. He takes a cheap shot. "What can you tell us about the incident that you were in? Were you in a bathing suit or what?"

"It was cold."

"With whom did you have your photograph taken?"

"With striking people."

And so the sparring goes. Judy wearies but gives no ground.

Arens then determines that she signed a letter to *The Nation* protesting the Peekskill riot on behalf of Paul Robeson.

"What investigation did you conduct in order to ascertain what the facts were before you sent this letter?" he demands, knowing fully that Judy was subpoenaed on the basis of second- and third-hand research and newspaper and magazine clippings that could not have carried a high-school term paper. Her hard-won success as an actress is now imperiled by such flimsy stuff as this. But these contradictions do not slacken his interrogatory momentum. "Did you not have any friends that were Communists?"

"Never," she answers too eagerly.

"Alvin Hammer, however, refused to testify before the House Un-American Activities Committee as to whether or not he was a Communist?"

"That is correct."

"Adolph Green and Betty Comden, with whom you were associated in the Revuers, have Communist-front records; do they not?"

"No."

Watkins offers her a second chance to name them. "Are you sure of that?"

"I am as sure of that as I can be of anybody that isn't me." Judy has just dropped a syllogistic gem. She may be frightened to death, but she will not name names.

Arens lists more organizations. The titles start to sound alike, Cultural Conferences, Committees for World Peace. "Had you not seen in the newspapers the articles respecting the Communist fraud, Communist peace fraud, the Communist fronts?" Presumably the same papers where she read of the Peekskill riot.

"I think I have to explain, as silly as it sounds, my way of reading the newspapers. I go to the theater section and I read it. Sometimes I read the rest. Now, no, now it is not true, but at that time it was true. Now I read the papers. At that time I was interested in the theater news and audition notices and puzzles." She could do the *Times* crossword in the time it takes Arens to lace his shoes. Still, she apologizes, "I am probably not a good citizen, because I don't read the news, or didn't." To say nothing of the rest of the country's casual newspaper readers who could tell you Ted Williams' batting average or the price of hamburger but couldn't find Seoul on a map.

"Have you been affiliated with the People's Songs?"

"I gave them a dollar after much nagging and pestering. I dislike folk songs intensely." Her tastes run more to classical, jazz, and show tunes.

Watkins injects a somewhat fatherly, cautionary note. "A person would be expected to know the organizations to which he contributes money?"

"Yes."

"You watch it now, do you not?"

"Ho, do I watch it now," she answers in her best caught-necking-in-the-parlor style.

Encouraged by that slight admission, Arens puts forward a vaguely genetic theory of Communism and asks about Judy's late Uncle, Joe Gollomb. "You knew, of course, and you know now that he was a Communist?"

"He was a very radical Communist. I don't know whether he was a member of the Communist party." He was, but only for a short time. Uncle Joe's politics tended to be transitory, even trendy. Judy was no red-diaper baby.

"He was employed by the *Daily Worker*, was he not?"

"Yes, he was. Then he had a change of heart and became a rabid anti-Communist. But I had broken away from him. He was a very domineering man who wanted me to be a writer and would keep at me and badger me until, well, you know a child has no defense against an adult who is insistent and aggressive. He would make me feel very unhappy most of the time."

"He was your sort of intellectual mentor, was he not?" Arens asks, quoting from a *Life*-magazine story.

"He wasn't really," Judy repeats, "because I would have nothing to do with him. Every time we got together, we fought vehemently."

Uncle Joe had no children, nor did Judy's Uncle Harry and Aunt Maude. Judy was not just the only child of Abe and Helen Tuvim, she was the only child among childless aunts and uncles. Following her parents' breakup they all placed demands on her, but it was Uncle Joe, the would-be Svengali, who was most demanding. He had worked as a teacher and journalist and gained prominence as an author of high-school adventure novels geared for a teenage audience. Even the most avid anti-Communist would be hard pressed to find political content in these harmless books. Judy's parents and relatives were mostly Greenwich Village socialists, part of a Jewish subculture that was as cultural and social as it was socially conscious. They were ardent trade unionists (her father had been an organizer) and for the most part staunch anti-Communists.

Arens abandons that line of questioning and asks about Judy's husband of four years, a classical musician turned recording executive, David Oppenheim. Thinking perhaps of Leonard Bernstein, he asks if they have friends who were Communists and who talked the party line.

"My husband's friends talked either music or records, and my friends talked show business." They were, by and large, politically aware though hardly doctrinaire proselytizers.

Judy then explains her newfound awareness. "I have had my eyes opened like they have never been opened in the last year by Columbia, by lawyers, by people that I have hired to investigate me. I wanted to know what I had done."

Watkins finds that interesting, if not admirable. "You hired people to investigate you?"

"I certainly did, because I had gotten into a lot of trouble."

"Who has tried to persecute you?" Watkins asks, blamelessly.

"I have had my contract threatened, and I have been picketed. One was the Catholic War Veterans who picketed me three times in New York City. The signs read 'While our boys are dying in Korea Judy Holliday is instead defaming Congress.' That was one of them which is so terrible and wrong that I naturally was very upset by it. Another one said that 'Judy Holliday is the darling of the *Daily Worker.*' Then they had leaflets saying that I was a Communist."

The Committee is not terribly distressed by this news. Obviously there are pickets, and then there are Pickets. Watkins wants it made clear that Judy is no less guilty for her casual association with front groups. "Of course, what you have said in effect here is that you, on most of these, your answer has been no, that you were not connected with them in any way."

She realizes the repeated denials are doing her no good and offers a consolation prize. "I can tell you plenty that I was connected with."

Watkins perks up. "What ones that are under suspicion?"

Judy refers to a one-minute recorded statement she made against censorship, refusing however to say who had asked her. Why did she make the recording? "To be used for the Stop Censorship Committee, the book banning."

"Who is banning books in this country?" Arens wants to know.

"Books have been banned in Boston."

"Those are licentious books, are they not?"

"Some of them have been proved not to be licentious." She is extremely well-read. He is out of his depth.

Arens wisely changes course. "What do you think about the McCarran Act?" That is, the legislation passed over Truman's veto, requiring the registration of Communists and their organizations, the establishment of a Subversive Activities Control Board, and even a provision for possible emergency detention of subversives.

But before Arens can get an answer, Watkins elbows in. He's a nuts-and-bolts man, more interested in naming names than in tedious politico-philosophical exchanges. "You said you could tell me about a lot more, and you have named one."

"I don't say 'Yes' to anything now except cancer, polio, and cerebral palsey, and things like that," Judy jokes, only antagonizing them further.

Watkins repeats, "I am very much interested if there were a lot of others that we have not heard about."

Judy reconsiders. "I guess there aren't a lot of others."

Her counsel, Judge Simon H. Rifkind, intercedes. "I am willing to tell exactly what our investigation shows, if that will help you."

Watkins admonishes condescendingly, "If we need you, Judge, we may call you as a witness," adding, "but I want to know what Miss Holliday knows." He then lays it on the line. "I am wondering whether she was really a dupe and just signed out of the goodness of her heart or whether she was associated in these movements. That is why I am going to let him ask you what you think of the McCarran Act, because it is important that we know," thus circularly allowing his counsel to save face.

"I don't know what the McCarran Act is," Judy admits.

Arens helps her out with an example. "Do you think that Communist organizations ought to be required to register?"

"Yes, I do, that is all part of knowing what they are about."

And so he is quickly back to probing her connection with such presumed organizations. She is still elusive on the general questions. Arens tries to nail her with a specific. "Do you know a lady by the name of Yetta Cohn. C-o-h-n?" Something about Jewish names seems to require spelling.

"Yes; she is my best friend for about twelve years."

"And how did you happen to know her?"

"I met her at a house in the country, Mount Tremper, New York."

"What is her occupation?"

"She is a policewoman for the city of New York."

"Has she had anything to do in any respect with your signatures and affiliations with these Communist-front organizations?"

"None at all."

"Has she ever counseled with you on this?"

"No; she has no interest in that sort of thing." Judy tries to anticipate and defuse his next question. "I was told that she was a Communist."

This floors him. He has spent the better part of the morning trying to get her to name just one name, and then out of the blue she seems to casually toss off this information about her best friend. Arens cannot believe his good fortune. "I beg your pardon?"

"I was told she was a Communist."

"Who told you that?"

"Mr. Bierly, who was investigating me and my friends."

"Would you kindly identify this Mr. Bierly?"

Judge Rifkind enters the spelling bee. "B-i-e-r-l-y. He was an investigator employed by the Columbia Pictures to look into the past record of Miss Holliday."

"He was a former FBI man, was he not?" Arens asks coyly.

Arens is no stranger to the name. Bierly was a charter member of the outfit that put out *Counterattack* and the notorious *Red Channels*. He was a pioneer in blacklisting for profit. But then business tapered off—even if you imagine a Communist behind every tree, there are only so many trees. For a variable fee he began clearing many of the same people he had fingered. Bierly took the plunge into free-lance investigating and clearing, and at present was on the Columbia payroll and doing quite well. In fact, he cleared Judy, whom he had besmirched in the first place through *Red Channels*. He had mastered the art of selling the virus and the serum.

Judy is less concerned with Bierly than with clarifying her slip about Yetta. "The only way that I can figure out that anybody would say that she is a Communist is because she knows me, and they say I am, because she is the most blameless creature, the most patriotic and honest creature that I know, and she is not only a member of the police force but she has been promoted to be the editor of the police magazine and I have full confidence that the police force of New York investigate their employees rather thoroughly, so that I think there is not only no basis for this but that it is a dreadful thing that she should be even mentioned simply because she is penalized by knowing me, and I am penalized by knowing her, and it just never ends anywhere."

Curiously, Arens lets it drop at that. It probably has less to do with the impassioned speech than his sense that Yetta is not good copy. He's more interested in Judy's protests over the indictment of the Hollywood Ten.

"It was presented to me as something about underdogs," she explains. "All right, I have been a sucker for that, I usually say 'Yes.'"

Watkins wants to know what has happened to change her thinking, when the change took place.

"I don't know," she replies. "There were so many things that happened. When I began to realize that there were such things as spies and people working against the country. I don't know when it was, but I know that the whole tenor of my thinking changed considerably in the last two years."

If Watkins is looking for a single patriotic epiphany, he won't find it.

Judy is now visibly upset over the exchange about Yetta. If only as lip service to protocol, Arens asks for the record, "Miss Holliday, during the course of your session here with the

Internal Security Subcommittee, have you been treated courteously and fairly?"

"Yes." She could scarcely say no.

Watkins won't be denied his own grand conciliatory note.
"You are not saying that because of any fear of coercion?"

"No." She could scarcely say yes. "The fact that I am nervous
is not because of this, because I get nervous whenever I get a
parking ticket."

"If you are nervous," Watkins observes, "I have not noticed
it, because I think you have conducted yourself very calmly in
my judgment." Maybe he has grown blasé about this business.
Maybe the lord high executioner hears sparrows while he
sharpens his ax.

At Judge Rifkind's prompting, Judy explains that the other
organizations she referred to earlier were associations of a
benign and innocuous sort, such as Stage Door Canteens, the
VFW and USO. She has performed gratis for servicemen, given
money to the American Legion and the Catholic Church.

"The thing we are interested in is what influences are being
exerted in this country to get people who are in a position to
influence public opinion, what influences are doing that,"
Watkins states humbly while at the same time displaying a
certain obsession with influences.

"If you are a Communist," Judy reasons, "why go to a
Communist front? Why not be a Communist? Whatever you
are, be it."

Watkins now has the foil he's wanted all along. "The idea is to
infiltrate and persuade people." He continues, "If you are an
example of what has happened, or whether you were a
conscious agent, is one of the things we are trying to determine.
In effect you said here in a way that you just did not
understand."

"I understood what was told to me. I wasn't responsible not
to look behind it."

"In other words, you did not check up on these requests. As a matter of fact, all of these happened just purely as a coincidence that so many of these people came to you?"

"It sounds terrible, but that is pretty much it," she says, aware that he is essentially sanctioning her presentation as a dupe.

Watkins is content to leave it at that. "That is all."

Judge Rifkind asks if Judy may read a prepared statement. There is a good deal of wrangling over that, with Arens implying that Judy's political change of heart has been motivated by a possible loss of work. Certainly that is a factor, but it is no mere vanity. The pressure on Judy has been in direct proportion to her rising fame since starring as the archetypal dumb blonde, Billie Dawn, in the movie *Born Yesterday*. What should have been a professional springboard has gone flat with rumors of Communist complicity. Fame is a tricky currency—you have to spend it while you've got it. Arens understands this. He is building a Washington career on headlines by calling luminaries such as Judy. He is very much a part of political show business.

Judy affirms the obvious. "All that has to happen to me is that I get publicity and I am through. But I am not simply turning tail because of that. I have been awakened to a realization that I have been irresponsible and slightly—more than slightly—stupid."

The Committee accepts this, despite their awareness that Judy's 172 I.Q. places her well within the genius level. That makes the admission of stupidity all the more savory. They are uncomfortable with the fact that Judy is an intelligent, independent working woman. By portraying her as gullible and easily misled, they minimize her modernity while at the same time asserting their male authority and moral superiority.

Judge Rifkind's patience with the committee is wearing thin. "Mr. Chairman, will you let her read that statement?"

She reads carefully from a prepared text. She denies that she was ever a member of the Communist Party and states her opposition to the methods of Communism:

*   *   *

I believe in personal freedom and that freedom should be restricted only to the extent necessary to maintain order and morality. I believe in the dignity of each man and woman. I believe that each human being is entitled to an opportunity to make the most of himself. I dislike regimentation. I do not want the government to shape my career or the career of any other American.

Having been brought up with people of the theater, I very early acquired an aversion to censorship. I early learned to be opposed to the persecution of minority races and religions. In order to give effect to my beliefs I have on occasion contributed to or identified myself with organizations whose principles seemed to coincide with mine. Some of these organizations are now cited as subversive. At the time of my association with them I had no knowledge or suspicion that any of them were subversive. I joined them because I was motivated by idealism and good faith, and I believed that the organizations were devoted to the principles which they publicly represented.

Naturally, like many others, I have since become more alert to deception and misrepresentation on the part of organizations which pretend to favor a worthwhile cause. On a number of occasions, I have recently learned, my name was used without my permission or even my knowledge.

I will continue to accept my responsibilities as a loyal American citizen and to give such help as lies in my power to worthwhile causes designed to further and protect our American way of life.

Hoping to trip her up in the substance of her prepared statement, Arens asks, "What is it you abhor about Communism?"

"I hate the idea that you are dictated to in what should be the freedom of your own life; that you are told how to think and what to think and that you are policed in your thoughts." She could just as easily have been describing the present ordeal.

"How about the materialistic philosophy of Communism?" Arens asks, waxing metaphysical.

"I don't know what you mean."

He puts it bluntly. "Do you believe in God?"

"Yes I do," she replies, fighting to stifle her indignation.

"Are you a member of a church?" adds Watkins. He is a Mormon elder.

"No," she says with restraint, wanting to point out that people of her faith attend temple or synagogue, not church. She detects an anti-Semitic edge to these questions.

On Judge Rifkind's lead, Judy inquires about the bulk of the presumably incriminating evidence which Arens has so far failed to produce. Arens turns on her with the fury of the infallible. "You are not suggesting that I made this up, are you?"

"No, I am not," she allows, "but a great deal of the material that you have there has been gathered from sources which have been proven to be not reliable." Later Kenneth Bierly would admit that much of the information in *Red Channels* had been gathered haphazardly and without the least formality of verification. But redhunters are more concerned with faith than facts. They work backwards from the evil monolith of Communism. They define themselves by opposition, they demonstrate true faith by decrying heresy. That is why so many of these hearings have been ritual instead of material. They know the answers before they ask the questions. They're not here to uncover new information, they're here to impart old truths. This is catechism. And like the stern knuckle-rapping nun, they will drill you until you get it right.

In the Committee's eyes, Judy has sinned politically. As bad, if not worse, she has sinned socially by being a free-thinking outspoken woman. The Committee's code is order and conformity; women are supposed to be wives and mothers, not supporters of progressive causes. She will have to moderate her views if she ever hopes to attain a state of political grace.

Still Watkins wants her to know they are compassionate men.

"If we had had this hearing in public, you know what would have happened. If we had let that happen, you would have had television and many other things."

"That would have been my last appearance," she acknowledges.

"We are trying to protect people and their rights," he continues, "and not doing any more damage than has to be done." If we ruin you a little, be thankful we don't ruin you altogether.

"I appreciate that enormously," she says, at last finding the rhythm of repentance.

Watkins goes on, charmed by his own pious eloquence. "We do not like to quiz you, that is the job, unpleasant as it is." Apparently she's supposed to feel sorry for him.

The senator permits himself a parting piety. "I do not know whether this will ever be made public. I am not the one to decide; it will be the full Committee. It may or it may not be, but we try at least to keep all those things in the executive session a matter of confidence." Watkins warns, "We take it that you are going to observe the same rules; you are not going to release anything about this?"

"Release anything?" Judy answers in disbelief. "I would rather die."

"Your statement, there . . ." So that's what's bothering him. He will have no leaking of noble sentiments as implied violation of the Committee's sanctity. "We have had witnesses come in and make a statement and then release it," he cautions.

She is a quick learner. She understands the implied threat: if she were to represent herself publicly as guiltless, they would be obliged to advertise her sins. She will say nothing in public of the hearing. "I would be digging my own grave."

The Committee is recessed. It is 1:10 and Judy has been in there since 10:30. For someone who violated no law, was a part of no conspiracy, she has just been through hell. She is a woman of dignity who has been made to look ridiculous. She is a woman of social conscience who has been made to look like a bleeding heart. She is a proud working woman making her way in the world who has been made to feel that she's risen above herself. But for all the insults and indignities, she did not betray her friends. She has lost work because of this controversy and may yet lose her career. She will not lose her self-respect. Judy is exhausted and frightened. She is two months pregnant.

That night, Judy calls her good friend Woodie Broun, who with Sam Jaffe and her husband, David, had stayed up with her two nights before, discussing the prepared statement.

"Woodie, maybe you're ashamed of me, because I played Billie Dawn. Well, I'll tell you something. You think you're going to be brave and noble. Then you walk in there and there are the microphones, and all those senators looking at you— Woodie, it scares the shit out of you. But I'm not ashamed of myself because I didn't name names. That much I preserved."

Without warning or explanation, the Committee released Judy's testimony the following autumn. Her name and number were still in the Manhattan phone book. Judy, who by then was nearly eight months pregnant, received phone calls from total strangers: "I hope your baby is born dead." "I hope you die in childbirth."

2

Judy was six when Abe left home. He had just returned from two months in Europe, where he toured as a promoter for an Austrian soccer team. The trip was not all business. Toward the end of the tour, Abe was joined by a woman friend whom he had known back in New York.

Abe Tuvim was never a model of convention. A Socialist, he fled to Mexico in 1917 to avoid the draft. He returned to New York in June of that year and married Helen Gollomb, which some friends considered yet another draft evasion.

Abe lived by his wits. He did not have a job, he had deals. Abe was a good talker with contagious enthusiasm. He had an ear for opportunity, an eye for likely backers, and an instinct for the angles. He was six feet tall, broadly built, and darkly handsome. He had deep-set eyes, a full head of hair, large cheekbones, and even larger ears. He was born in New York in 1894. His father was in the produce business. His brother was active in the labor movement and the Socialist party. Abe was a socialist of sorts, though his thinking was more romantic than realpolitik. He enjoyed the company of women.

Helen was born in St. Petersburg in 1889. Her family left Russia when she was four and settled in New York's Lower East Side. Her father was a craftsman, her mother, Rachel, a stern matriarch who ruled the family with unchallenged authority. There had been five children. One son died in infancy before the family moved from Russia. Another son, Louie, died in New York in a boating accident. Harry was the youngest, Joe the oldest. Helen was the middle child and the only daughter.

A short, dour woman with hard eyes and a quick temper, Rachel closely monitored her children's lives. Harry attended Cooper Union and became a chemist for the city's Public Works Department, rising in time to chief chemist for the Manhattan borough. Joe graduated from City College and went on to an M.A. at Columbia before teaching in the city schools with a certain reknown at De Witt Clinton High. He left teaching for writing and moved from paper to paper as reporter, correspondent, and drama critic. He worked briefly as a scenarist in silent movies for Vitagraph and Universal, which carried no literary distinction. After that Joe found his niche as a novelist for teenage boys, with a succession of books taken from his experiences at De Witt Clinton. Both Harry and Joe possessed strong egos that brimmed often into egotism. Both remained ambitious and oddly unfulfilled. Harry wanted to be a writer; Joe, whose following was faithful if mostly adolescent, wanted to be a better writer. Both men adored their mother.

Helen feared Rachel. She had been granted little independence as a child and became a dependent, somewhat fragile adult. Helen never went to college and was kept close to home, where she was especially susceptible to Rachel's moods. After the father died, Joe installed himself as the man of the family and followed his mother's example in overseeing his sister's life. Joe became the family sage. He had a measure of success, he was a part of Greenwich Village bohemia, and he moved among the city's intelligentsia. The family made much of Joe's accomplishments, though never more than Joe himself. Joe was the family's ticket into the literary and theatrical circles of the East Village, an elite Jewish subculture of the teens and twenties. The family returned the favor in a kind of hero worship, although Harry's worship was tinged with envy. To varying degrees, everyone ran Helen's life.

Helen was not unattractive. She was of medium height, with a wide warm smile, timid eyes, and her mother's substantial nose. She was unpretentious, unsophisticated. She had a ready laugh and laughed readily at her own offbeat views and incessant malapropisms. She liked to tell and hear stories. Helen was a passable pianist, intelligent without true intellect, and modestly political-minded. Her interest in the socialist labor movement was chiefly by example and osmosis through Joe. The height of her interest came when she briefly dated David Dubinsky, founder and leader of the International Ladies Garment Workers Union.

A more broadly based secular version of the ILGWU was the Rand School of Social Science, which maintained headquarters on East Fifteenth Street. It consisted mainly of a library and adjoining rooms for meetings, seminars, and classes. Above all, it was a gathering place for Village socialists, and though the Gollombs now lived far uptown on East 106th Street, Helen joined Joe downtown.

The Rand School was where Helen first met Abe, almost five years her junior. After a brief courtship, they were married on June 17, 1917. When Abe moved into the Gollomb flat, Harry and Joe had already moved out, Joe to live with his writer wife, Zoe Beckly. Rachel remained imperiously behind. She was ill-impressed with Abe's suave manner and scant socialist credentials. She disapproved of his fitful employment and looked down on his family, whom she considered the social and intellectual inferiors of the Gollombs. What small peace Rachel left the newlyweds was disturbed by Joe, who became protective of his sister to the point of nuisance.

If Rachel disapproved of Abe, Joe openly disliked him. In

truth, the two men were not unalike. They had the same build and coloring, although Joe's chin jutted in a kind of self-assured frown, whereas Abe's putty face seemed barely to hide some friendly joke. They had compatible social consciousnesses and moved in many of the same Village circles, though Abe was more on the fringe than his brother-in-law. They shared an interest in show business, as well as lingering reputations as womanizers. But Joe had education and money, and Abe had neither. Joe had status and Abe had none. The real wedge was Joe's overinvolvement in Helen's life. Whatever Abe's shortcomings, he would not be bullied or scorned. Though Helen adored Abe and hoped he would help free her from Joe's domination, she remained passive and did not openly take sides. All the while, Rachel stood on the sidelines, cheering Joe and heckling Abe.

The tension might have eased when Abe and Helen took an apartment in Sunnyside Gardens, a model community which the City Housing Corporation sponsored in Queens. Unfortunately Rachel went with them, and Harry and Joe were never far off. On June 21, 1922, Helen gave birth to a daughter, Judith, at the Lying-In Hospital on East Twenty-second Street. Abe was overjoyed, but if he thought this would help establish his family as a separate entity, he was wrong. Joe and Harry were childless. Their participation in Helen's life intensified with the birth of Judy. Rachel's matriarchal hold tightened with her one grandchild.

The wonder is not that the marriage eventually disintegrated, but that it endured as long as it did. For all the meddling, Abe and Helen had their moments together. They remained active at the Rand School and became habitués of the fashionable Café Royale.

Located at the corner of Second Avenue and Twelfth Street, the Royale was styled after a typical Viennese café. It was owned by a Hungarian Jew named Zofmarie, who served a tasty but heavy Hungarian cuisine. The real attraction was the clientele. Café Royale was a watering hole for the Jewish literati and the

Yiddish theater. The intellectuals occupied one wall, the theater professionals the other. Camp followers and browsers braved the middle ground, which often was a free-fire zone for polemics and histrionics from either side. One wall was done up in darkly paneled woods and looked across at a large mirror where actors and actresses often groomed and preened. With such patrons as Paul Muni, Jacob Adler, and Molly Picon, Café Royale came to be known as the Second Avenue Sardi's and it was later the inspiration for a Broadway play by H. S. Kraft called *Café Crown.*

Joe introduced Helen and Abe to the Royale, but Abe was soon a figure there in his own right. This was the domain of talkers, and what Abe lacked in formal education he more than made up for with drive and charm. Abe and Helen became regulars and often brought Judy along. She was a cherubic sight among the flamboyant types there. At four she barely reached their knees. She was chubby and round-faced, with enormous eyes and a pixie grin that could be had for the coaxing. She had trouble with her L's and preferred not to talk. She adored soft things and slept with a swatch of fur. She was uncommonly at east among adults, but that had its drawbacks. While Judy developed quickly intellectually, she seldom saw other children. On those rare occasions when there were people her age around, she tended to see them as unwanted competition for the adult attention that was otherwise solely hers.

When Judy was five a reporter friend of Abe's dropped by the apartment one Sunday with his daughter. She was Judy's age, though cuter and more outgoing. The little girl became the center of attention. Judy withdrew to a corner and pouted. Abe was not long finding her.

"Do you want to go for a walk?" he whispered.

Judy nodded and took his hand. When they were a few blocks from the apartment, Abe stopped and knelt down. "You feel bad because she's getting so much attention, don't you?"

"Yes I do," she answered.

"I know, that happens," Abe explained, mindful of the

neglect he felt living in Joe's shadow. "Look, Judy. We all go through things like that. She may be getting a lot of attention now, but we all have qualities that don't always show up right away. You'll see. You'll come out just fine."

Judy's chubby cheeks slowly widened into a smile, and she gave Abe a big hug.

Abe and Helen loved Judy fully and affectionately. Abe was especially proud of her, and when he brought a Jewish soccer team to Yankee Stadium for an exhibition game, he named Judy the mascot. She sat proudly on her father's knee. She wore a floppy beret, high laced shoes and knee socks, and a homemade skirt that tied at the neck and was embroidered with a Star of David and the Hebrew symbol for life. She looked like a Jewish Buster Brown.

Later that summer Abe and Helen rented a place in Sea Gate, on the western tip of Coney Island. Rachel was there. A small trolley ran nearby, and for some reason Judy became fascinated with the tracks. Something in their shininess attracted her. She was told of the danger and instructed repeatedly to stay away from the tracks. Judy was strong-willed and ignored the warnings. It was decided that Abe would have to give her a spanking. More likely the idea originated with Rachel and filtered down through Joe to Helen, who notified Abe. That was the usual chain of command. Abe was no disciplinarian, but it was easier to comply than resist. Besides, Judy was testing them, and no amount of friendly persuasion would keep her off the tracks.

Judy got the spanking, and though it was hard to tell which hurt worse, her pride or posterior, she was holding nothing back. Just then some friends showed up and found Judy sitting on a couch and sobbing. Rachel sat across from her on a chair, and when the friends came in, she looked coldly at Judy, then turned to them with a faint grin and said, "She got it good." Judy seemed to make note through her tears.

Assimilated as the Gollombs were, they had many old-world habits. The family was everything. There was no privacy to speak of, no decisions made large or small without consultation with the elders. Judy found adult acceptance, true, but at a price. She had several parents, or, what with the constant compromising of Abe and Helen's parental autonomy, none. Joe in particular was very fond of Judy, but with no child of his own, he seemed determined to make her over in his image. He convinced her early on that she must become a writer. While other kids were off playing, he gave her books to read. It was almost as if she were a bit of applied social science, the great hope of the Gollombs. The family embraced her, nearly smothering her in the process.

Abe grew distant. There was no hope of courtesy, let alone respect from his in-laws, and yet they were always around, underfoot, judging him and offering unwanted advice. Helen had never stood up to her family, and so was powerless to defend her husband. Friends of Abe's who came to dinner were struck by an unsettling scene: Rachel silently brooding, Helen fluttering around birdlike preparing dinner and enumerating Joe's successes, and Abe ignoring all but Judy, who scurried about happily oblivious. Anyone who knew Abe knew he could not endure this indefinitely.

Then a curious thing happened: Joe started showing up at the apartment with attractive available lady friends. He had always been remote and aloof with Abe. Now he was very eager for him to meet his friends. Rachel's complicity went no further than silent ratification; this was Joe's brainstorm. Helen was naively unaware as always, but Judy, with no more than a child's intuition, sensed her uncle's scheme. Joe baited the hook but he might have saved the effort.

Around this time Abe was seen at the Café Royale with another woman, a close friend of the family. At first the Royale regulars thought nothing of it. This was a large, boisterous place which fed on a steady diet of local gossip—hardly the spot for an illicit rendezvous. If Abe was there with a married woman, it must have been for no more than pleasant conversation and a quick cup of coffee. But when Abe and the woman returned repeatedly, the Royale was soon buzzing. Oddly, the two were quite open about the time they spent together there. Equally odd was the fact that Helen knew, or at least thought nothing of it. Though Joe suspected something, he kept it to himself.

Abe was invited abroad by the Austrian government. He toured with a soccer team and was back in his element. He was meeting and charming people, organizing, operating, promoting. Much as he missed Judy, he was glad to be free of the domestic claustrophia which Helen had come to represent. He could be himself again without some in-law peering over his shoulder waiting for him to do wrong. He could be a big man, not some anonymous brother-in-law of Joe Gollomb the writer. That existence in Sunnyside seemed a world away when he met his woman friend in Europe. She was not an outstanding beauty, but she was lively and bright and imaginative. She was also married, but that didn't concern Abe at the time.

Abe came home, got his things, and moved out to a flat in Manhattan. Helen went to pieces. She was hysterical for days; all the long-suppressed fear and pain swept through her like a tide. Joe could have warned her long ago of Abe's rumored infidelity, but then Helen might have taken him back, and that would never do. The break had to be abrupt and irreversible. Joe took a calculated risk with Helen's mental well-being so that the family might be rid of Abe. They protected Helen beyond her own need for protection just to add to their sense of importance and mission. Their cruelty was no less than Abe's, perhaps more.

A strained calm followed the crisis. Helen became severely depressed. She cried frequently and was unable to cope with the trivia of day-to-day life. The family looked after her but refused to take her to a doctor. Psychology was akin to voodoo, and there wasn't much a physician could do. The family looked after Helen as best they could. The family saw to Judy's basic needs, but nobody thought to explain events in terms she could grasp. That had been Abe's job.

It was like losing both parents. Abe was gone, and until the depression passed, Helen might as well have been. Abe had been Judy's friend and ally, and yet the Gollombs made it clear that he had caused Helen terrible suffering. It was grossly insensitive to turn Judy against her father. A six-year-old cannot dislike a parent without deep feelings of confusion and guilt. By telling her these things, it was as if the family had handed Judy an emotional bomb and told her to go play quietly. Judy did what she could to defuse the thing: she generalized. Her father wasn't the problem, men were. They left you and made you sad. Helen's breakdown was not as easily explained away. In the absence of adult comfort, Judy got the idea that Helen was now her responsibility. This agony had come and could come again. Judy must see to it that it didn't.

Helen's depression deepened, and she spoke of suicide. Harry's wife, Maude, took Helen to Atlantic City, and the trip seemed to do her good. At least she stopped threatening to kill herself. Joe decided that travel was tonic and arranged a European vacation for Helen, Rachel, Judy, and himself. Joe was charmed with the grandness of his gesture, and when he found he was a bit shy of the necessary cash, he refused to let Harry help out. This was Joe's show; he borrowed the balance.

The four of them left New York on May 15, 1929. Helen indulged the family penchant for writing and kept a diary. She could barely contain her excitement:

Is it possible that it is I who is moving away and not the pier of thousands of faces and waving handkerchiefs? Yes, it's I. Oh, what a thrill. Next to Judith's cheek against mine a minute after birth, this is the greatest.

I kidded Joe for making it possible for me to get this thrill. A kiss to Mother. If ever I was grateful to her for giving birth to me, it was when I was gliding down the bay. Joe took us all through the salons, decks, and each seemed like a dream. Then bed.

The slip was more syntactic than Freudian. They woke with

the breakfast bell the next morning and Judy promptly threw up. Joe was right behind her. Helen and Rachel went down to breakfast and were joined later by Judy and Joe for lunch and a stroll around the deck. There was dinner and another stroll. Helen kept her eye out for single men and was prepared to flirt, but the opportunity never presented itself. The remainder of the voyage was uneventful. They arrived in London after a week at sea and checked in at the Imperial Hotel with its spacious rooms decorated in deep grains and brass. Judy was intrigued with the bellboys, who were no taller than she, though in fairness to the bellboys, she was tall for her age. Judy thought it would be a good idea to take one aside and dress and undress him like an overgrown doll. Rachel scolded her.

In just under seven days Joe gave them a Cook's tour of London. He had traveled extensively in Europe ten years earlier, stringing stories for the New York *Evening Mail*. He rated himself cosmopolitan and was now eager to show off his expertise. He couldn't have asked a better audience than Helen.

They went shopping on Regent Street and marveled at the brightly colored silks and shawls at Liberty. They took in the British Museum, Westminster Abbey, Parliament, Hyde Park, Buckingham Palace. And they ate. Joe wined and dined them at Simpson's and Cheshire Cheese, where Helen was more impressed with the service and atmosphere than the food. Judy kept pace with the grown-ups. Since infancy she had been a good eater. Joe was delighted with Helen's obvious pleasure and told her, "Wait till we get to Paris!"

They got to Paris on a Thursday evening, May 30. With perhaps some self-conscious ecstasy, Joe gushed, "Paris! Paris!" Helen was initially less enthusiastic. The traffic and noise reminded her of New York. She felt like going back to London, but she could not disappoint her brother. With a little effort, she was eventually able to work her rapture up to Joe's level.

They made the rounds of Paris cafés and restaurants, and each of them gained five pounds. On Sunday they visited Versailles, and Judy ran among the fountains. Joe wanted to go

on to Berlin, but Helen was entranced with Paris and declined.
The following Sunday they visited Sainte Chapelle and Notre-
Dame. Helen was overcome:

It was so beautiful and interesting! Why didn't I collect a
better vocabulary so that I could do justice to what we see.
How I miss expressions and words. I feel dumb compared
to my enthusiasms.

The change in her outlook was more than Joe had dreamed.
She was happier than he could ever remember her being. And if
the circumstances were temporary and storybook, there was still
no trace of the depression that had haunted her. Joe could
congratulate himself, and did.

The trip had been a revelation for Judy. She was most
impressed with the simple fact that she was among adults and
touring abroad. If Europe meant so much to Uncle Joe, it must
be a mark of great prestige. Certainly it was the center of many
of the finest writers of the day; Hemingway, Pound, Fitzgerald,
Joyce. More important, she believed that her mother was well
again and could be kept well. The secret was knowing when and
how to please her. This did not erase the bitter memory of the
recent past, but did make it bearable.

The Sunday before they were due to leave for home, Joe took
his ladies to an old haunt, De L'Arvanne, situated on a
waterway. After dinner Judy and Helen rented a boat. Judy
rowed. The sun settled toward the horizon, and the two of them
drifted, watching barges pulled by horses on the shore.

3

~~~~~~~~~~~~~~~~~~~~~~~~~

She wasn't much to look at. Her fair curly hair had grown dark and lank. The soft adorable pudginess gave way to preteen gawkiness. She didn't have the elbows and angles that promised statuesque beauty, but the big-boned broadness of a Slavic peasant girl. She was not especially comfortable with children her own age. She was not interested in boys. But Judy Tuvim was a rising academic star at P.S. 150 in Sunnyside.

At ten she took the standard Otis Intelligence Test. Her I.Q. tested out to a remarkable 172, well within the genius level. This pleased the family no end, and since Judy's parenting had in many ways come to be a committee affair, each took some credit. As far as Joe could tell, his niece was coming along nicely. Not only was she bookish, her tastes ran to the literary. While the other girls were reading *The Bobbsey Twins*, she was reading *The Brothers Karamazov*. She didn't have much interest in Joe's recent works, which were cashing in on the detective vogue as a hedge against the deepening Depression. The important thing was, she was reading, and reading is a precursor to writing.

Her first written work was a school play called *Tuckers' Christmas*. When Judy announced she would play the lead, her classmates complained and asked why. "I will play the lead," Judy explained, "because I'm bigger and I've been to Europe." So much for schoolyard reasoning. During a later performance, Judy in her role as the mother, summoned her children, "Come here, my children!" Five of them rushed over, and Judy fell on her butt. It was all handled with great aplomb, but the obvious moral was that even big, well-traveled playwrights can be brought down to size.

Judy became a member of the school literary club, which put out the 1932 edition of the *Sunnyside Spirit*, commemorating the bicentennial of George Washington's birth. It was not the most exhilarating theme for even an elementary-school literary magazine, but the writers coped. The centerpiece was an abbreviated play in three acts entitled *The Return of George Washington*, an imaginary excursion by the Founding Father into 1930's America. There were twenty-one scenes, each written by a different sixth-grader. Judy, the only fifth-grader among the playwrights, wrote the prologue in precise if somewhat precocious prose. Other literary milestones lay ahead.

"How can I assist in keeping the streets, parks, and playgrounds clean and wholesome?" This was the question posed to 375,000 high-school and junior-high students in a citywide essay contest sponsored by the State Chamber of Commerce. There were three divisions: high school, parochial high school, and junior high school. Judy won the last of these.

Awards were presented in a ceremony at City Hall. Judy's family was proudly among the three hundred audience members. After a succession of tiresome civic-minded speeches by the superintendent of schools, the president of the Chamber of Commerce, and assorted clergy, the winners read their essays. Judy wore a simple black dress with a lopsided scarf, and a fashionably short peek-a-boo hairstyle. Despite a case of nerves,

Judy read well and received a forty-dollar cash award for her efforts. She was photographed with the other two winners, and the picture ran in all the major New York dailies. Joe's protégée seemed well on her way.

Judy completed P.S. 150 and Queens lost whatever allure it held for Helen. Helen took a flat on Manhattan's West Side near Harry and Maude's place. With Rachel newly ensconced, the family knot tightened. Joe's marriage had long since gone by the boards, and Judy was now well within reach. He kept after her, telling her what to read, how to think. Joe had a brief flirtation with the Communist Party, which ultimately turned him bitterly anti-Communist. His writing had temporarily lost its audience, and by way of partial compensation, he became obsessed with Judy's progress. But Judy was feeling the restlessness and rebelliousness of early adolescence. As much as she wanted to please her uncle, he was getting on her nerves. She started seeing more of Abe.

The move from Queens made Abe more accessible. Judy paid him regular weekend visits, sometimes returning with a suppor check for Helen. In addition to other enterprises, Abe was doing public-relations work for the Musicians Union, and while he was not exactly rolling in money, he was able to contribute to the household he'd abandoned. Harry picked up the remaining financial slack.

Abe had had his ups and downs since leaving Helen. The woman for whom he first left would not divorce her husband. They saw each other sporadically and later had a brief business partnership. Friends learned to gauge the status of the relationship by Abe's mood. When they were together, he was glowing; apart, gloomy. Even after it was clear that the relationship had no future, Abe gave no thought to reconciliation with Helen. She was more embedded than ever in the family orbit, and that was all the deterrent he needed. And yet, neither moved to finalize the separation with divorce. They could hardly be avoiding it for Judy's sake—she had endured enough for a dozen divorces. And if there was once the fear of a hysterical relapse,

Helen had sufficiently recovered to survive what would have been a mere legal formality. In separate ways, Abe and Helen were lonely and lost. They would always have that bond. Unhappy as the marriage had been, it was more easily ignored than legally dissolved. It was the closest either would come to a full, fulfilling relationship. Divorce would only have underscored that pathetic truth.

For a lonely man, Abe kept busy. It seemed to Judy he had a different ladyfriend every Sunday. They weren't pickups; they were nice, attractive women who chatted and fussed over Judy, which was precisely what Abe wanted. He was proud of his daughter, and sometimes he showed her off like card tricks. She could dazzle them with her fancy talk and quick mind. She could flash the sunny smile that transformed an otherwise ordinary face. But Abe was not particularly perceptive. His fatherly solicitude blinded him to Judy's growing resentment of his female companions. More than them, she was starting to resent him. The memory of her mother's breakdown was as vivid as if it were yesterday. He seemed carefree, while Helen was careworn, and that seemed unfair. And as often happens with separated parents, Abe tended to overload the time he spent with Judy, with the result that the visits became busy and oddly impersonal. Like Joe, Abe needed Judy to fill a certain void in his life. Judy was running short of patience for both men.

There was one friend of Abe's Judy liked. Sylvia Regan had known Abe at Café Royale and was a dinner guest in Sunnyside. She was working at Labor Stage when Abe was hired to organize and promote a World Labor Athletic Carnival at Randall's Island off East 125th Street. Abe not only wangled office space at Labor Stage but also borrowed Sylvia from her boss for the time it took to stage the carnival. The two of them spent a great deal of time together, and while they were never intimate, they did date for several months.

The event was supposed to do for various labor unions what the periodic musical revue *Pins and Needles* did for the members of the ILGWU—that is, show off the more gifted union members to their fellow workers and the general public. Of course, Abe's promoter instincts told him that musical comedy had more inherent audience appeal than a swarm of sweaty athletes on a remote East River island.

He started by hiring a consultant named Abel Kiviet, a world-class runner as well known for his athletic prowess as for his clothes-designer wife, the very chic Madame Kiviet. With Abel's help, Abe brought in some of the better-known track-and-field stars of the day, including Jesse Owens. On the strength of these and other names, the carnival received plenty of play in the press. The event drew a large crowd and was a resounding success. The amateur athletes of the labor unions had their day in the sun, the unions their favorable publicity, and Abe a feather in his cap. Abe could promote snow in Siberia.

Judy attended the carnival as a favor to her father. Where sports were concerned, she had little ability and even less interest. In late summer of 1934 she was much more interested in the coming school year. Judy met the admission requirements for Julia Richman High, an immense all-girl public school on East Sixty-seventh Street. She was leaving the somewhat provincial middle-class safety of P.S. 150 for the uncertainty of a big-city school with students from every part of the social and economic spectrum. Her many achievements at Sunnyside had come effortlessly. Here the competition would be stiffer.

Catherine Jones taught English at Julia Richman. Jonesy, as she was known to students, also handled the editorial class which put out the school literary magazine, the *Bluebird*. Judy attended both classes, and Jonesey was instantly struck by her charm, warmth, and poise, to say nothing of her conspicuous intelligence. Judy was self-assured and quietly mature, with none of the conceit or phony sophistication that some of the other girls exhibited.

The *Bluebird* was sold for twenty-five cents at the main building and at the four annexes on Fifty-first, Sixty-sixth,

Seventy-fifth, and Eighty-sixth streets. The editorial group was responsible not only for the magazine's content but also for its sale and promotion. Jonesy asked if Judy would be interested in public relations. She eagerly agreed—after all, it ran in the family. The staff decided to use the old Broadway warhorse *Fashion* as a publicity device. Judy was part of a small troupe that toured excerpts of the show around the main building and annexes. She was assigned the part of a French maid, and much to Jonesy's amazement, came up with a convincing French accent and flounced around the stage with a delicacy and lightness that belied her indelicate size. Jonesy, who had worked in the professional theater herself during the twenties, imagined she was seeing a real actress at work. Judging by the ease with which Judy plugged magazine subscriptions after each performance, she was every bit as much a promoter as she was an actress.

There was no fault to be found with Judy's work in the editorial group, and she was given a 100 for the term. When the principal discovered this, she reached Jonesy and asked how a perfect score was possible. Jonesy explained, "She's good, she's better at this than I am. What else could I do?" The mark stood, and though Judy's work in English class was nearly as good, it was far less punctual and she received an 85.

Judy wasn't the only Tuvim making a theatrical splash that year. Abe was taking a plunge as a songwriter in a Broadway show with the title of *Africana*. It was the brainstorm of Donald Heywood, who with some help from a school teacher named Almarez Camara constructed an operetta having to do with the conflict between a traditional tribal king and his reform-minded Oxford-educated son. Heywood handled the libretto, music, and direction, but brought in an associate director, Charles Adler, son of the Yiddish theater's Jacob Adler. Abe Tuvim was chosen to help out with the lyrics. Abe didn't have much experience, but he worked cheap.

The curtain went up on *Africana* at nine o'clock sharp on November 26, 1934. Heywood conducted the overture and took his bows. Seconds later Almarez Camara appeared at the back of the theater wearing a brown fur coat and a white muffler. He walked purposefully down the aisle and engaged Heywood in an argument. The cast was stunned, but the audience assumed it was part of the play. Abe stood by shaking his head in disbelief as Camara snatched a chair from the orchestra pit and brought it down firmly on Heywood's head. The critics ran for cover and the intruder was subdued and removed from the theater. Clearly the worse for wear, Heywood resumed the show. At eleven o'clock the curtain came down on the first act. Few people stayed around to see the second.

The critics agreed that the altercation had been the best part of the show. *Africana* closed after three performances. Judy missed the show but had a good laugh when her father told the gory details. Abe's infatuation with Tinpan Alley was undiminished by this minor setback. He went on to write a handful of published songs, including the spicy "The Way You Pleasured Me Last Night."

Judy was flourishing at Julia Richman. She continued to excel in her studies, and for the first time made friends her own age. There was Barbara Baer, better known as Bobbie or BB. Bobbie was round and dark-haired and a tireless talker, less adult than Judy, but far more radical in her thinking. She was effusive, whereas Judy tended to be silent and sometimes sullen. They were best friends.

Judy met Pat Highsmith in autumn of 1935. Pat was six months older than Judy, with a similar subtle dignity. She was gentile and feared Judy and Bobbie had more in common for their Jewishness. But the three of them were fast friends, meeting each noon in a school corridor where they shared lunch and literary ambitions. Judy was still advanced in her reading, but unlike some of the other bookish girls, she never flaunted titles like some badge of intellect. She was developing other interests, and, besides, the reading had largely become a means of escape at home among family. She continued to experiment with writing, and in 1936 the *Bluebird* ran a poem of hers, "Twilight and Snow."

> Sleepy snow is falling noiselessly
> From a slate-gray sky.
> Layer upon layer,
> Patiently, it falls,
> Weaving a compassionate blanket
> For the mournful
> Barren earth.
>
> Dusky twilight sinks
> Over the alabaster scene;
> And the infrequent rooftops are clothed
> Of evening.
> Twilight and snow . . .
> Enveloping the world.

The "mournful" and "barren" were less literal expressions than indications that the poet had more than proms and pimples on her mind. Judy and Bobbie were unconventional in their dress, and with Pat were self-styled schoolgirl bohemians. They liked to spend time in the Village, in the vicinity of Pat's family's place on Bank and Grove. At fifteen they would snack at the Grand Ticino restaurant on Thompson below Washington Square. More than once Judy finished a plate of veal parmigiana, announced, "I think I could eat another one," and did just that. Sometimes they would choke down dry martinis at the Jumble Shop on Eighth Street. They were very sophisticated.

During her junior year, Judy was named editor of the *Bluebird* and with all due gravity conducted a talent hunt:

> In a school teeming with over eight thousand enthusiastic, alert girls, there must be much hidden writing talent

waiting to be "discovered." The process of weeding out these girls, and helping them realize and develop their potentialities, we called a "talent hunt." Probably the factor most important to success in later life is the directing of youthful energy into constructive and worthwhile channels. Thus the *Bluebird* hopes to encourage the talented. We begin this encouragement by telling you a little about our "talented."

She then touted her finds with all the import of a Maxwell Perkins unearthing young Hemingways. She was not above cronyism.

Once in a long while we are privileged to have in our midst a girl who has true talent and a great gift for writing. Such a girl is Barbara Baer, elected this term to literary editorship of the *Bluebird*.

Later that year Judy and Bobbie awarded Pat first prize for her short story "Crime Begins." She would go on to success with her first novel *Strangers on a Train*.

Judy's home life had changed relatively little. Not long after taking an apartment on West Seventy-fifth Street, Helen found work with the WPA teaching piano at the Henry Street Settlement on the Lower East Side. The settlement had an international reputation for its work among the poor. It maintained a medical staff which saw to the problems of the sick and the aged. Social workers fought for better housing, recreation, and education in local slums. With the addition of its own theater, which gained prominence as the Neighborhood Playhouse, the settlement also became a cultural center. It was not as aggressively political as the Rand School had been, but the atmosphere and aims were similar and only slightly less to the left.

Helen enjoyed her work at the settlement. She was able to improve and share her knowledge of the piano. She liked the company of her young students, and they very much liked her. Pat Highsmith studied with her and parted a few months later better versed in Bach. Pat knew little of Judy's family and nothing of Helen's breakdown. In fact, she found Helen to be calm and confident, in sharp contrast to the tense, irascible Rachel she had met during rare dinners on the Upper West Side. Helen was out in the world making friends and contributing to the family finances.

But Helen's independence had its limits. At home Rachel still supervised everything from meals to Judy's wardrobe. Rachel's control and dour presence left her daughter childlike in many ways. Helen had no real concept of money. She was forgetful and distracted. At best she was part of an adult hierarchy consisting of Rachel, Joe, Harry, and Maude, which acted as Judy's joint parent. At worst she was a constant concern to Judy, in ways almost her child. Judy had long been aware of her mother's vulnerability. She remembered Helen's threat to kill herself when Abe left. Judy became protective and in that sense joined the others as part of the lifeline upon which Helen had come to depend.

On the other hand, Judy was a typical adolescent, full of anger and antagonism for her parents. Abe's absence and Helen's dependence complicated an already difficult phase of growing up. Judy learned to withdraw into herself. It was a way to shut out her parents and all the other intruding adults without actually physically removing herself. It won her privacy but brought her loneliness.

Judy found release in reading, but her interests turned steadily toward theater. No one quite knew where this fascination came from. Joe had always preached literature, and Abe's Broadway experience was a formidbale flop. Possibly Judy's old visits to the Café Royal drew her to the liveliness and glamour that surrounded theater. Or it may have been that the intrinsically social side of theater appealed to Judy, who was not social by nature. Writing is a solitary art, and Judy had all the self-enforced solitude she wanted for now.

Whatever the motives, Judy became less involved with the *Bluebird* and more involved with the drama club. As her Julia Richman swan song she signed up for the annual senior show and became its director. At Judy's urging, this was the first musical senior show, something of a satirical, topical revue, with the usual intramural in-jokes and spoofs. It was a sizable undertaking, and Judy brought it off calmly and professionally.

The experience was bracing for Judy. As graduation approached, she wanted to take a closer look at professional theater. Schoolwork had always come easily to her. It had no relevance, no excitement, and most of all, no challenge. Judy was only fifteen; college could wait—if need be, indefinitely.

Helen was beside herself when Judy revealed her plans. Helen regretted her own lack of a college education, and anyway, Joe had not one but two degrees. Judy's feelings for her uncle were at an ebb, and for all she cared, Joe could have been the dean at Vassar, that wasn't going to budge her. Helen pointed out that Pat had been accepted at Barnard. Judy said that was fine for Pat, who meant to pursue literature, not drama, as a career. Helen suggested that Judy might learn about theater through college. Judy looked into the possibility of Yale Drama School and was told she stood a good chance of admission but was one year below the minimum entrance age. She had to decide how she would fill that intervening year.

Mary Shank was an old friend of the family who ran her own theatrical agency and who, with her husband, had just moved into the Seventy-fifth Street building. Helen sent Judy to Mary for advice. Mary knew Abe well, well enough to know that he was sensitive about his lack of training and formal education. Mary told Judy that there was ample time for theater down the road and that for now her youth might be a handicap. There had been talk of a scholarship from NYU, which meant college would cost her nothing and could do a lot to strengthen her for the eventual perils of show business. But Judy was impatient to be out and on her own. She wanted to contribute to the family's income. She couldn't go to college just to serve her mother's sense of decorum, or worse, her sense of dependence. Mary could see that the girl's mind was made up.

Judy knew where to find a sympathetic ear. She turned to Abe. The relationship had suffered in recent years, even if Abe was unaware of his daughter's enduring bitterness toward him. For all his obvious faults, he had taken too much meddling from the Gollombs to suggest Judy walk that same acquiescent path. Despite what he may have wanted for his daughter, he understood it was most important to support what she wanted for herself. Abe got in touch with Sylvia Regan, who had recently left the Theater Union to spearhead audience promotion for the Mercury Theater. Abe, the deal-maker, made one for Judy.

In January 1938 Judy graduated from Julia Richman and finished first in her class. The next day she took her first step into the theatrical world and for five dollars a week joined the Mercury as an assistant switchboard operator.

4

~~~~~~~~~~~~

"**W**ho the hell cut me off?"

Judy bit her lip, transfixed by the welter of blinking orange lights in front of her. John Houseman's baritone called again from the far office, "Who the hell cut me off?" No answer came. None was necessary. Judy frantically pulled plugs and jabbed them in random holes, hoping for the best. The board started humming at her, and Judy cried. It was a familiar scene.

Since coming to the Mercury Judy had brought fresh confusion to the already chaotic theatrical organization. Her plan was to use the job as an entrée to rehearsals, script reading, and, with luck, an introduction to Orson Welles. So far she only disrupted phone calls, weathered Houseman's colorful outbursts, and sobbed. In fact that is how she first came to the attention of Welles and Houseman—as the girl who sat at the switchboard and cried.

There were quieter moments at home on Seventy-fifth Street. Helen had resigned herself to the possibility that Judy might never attend college. Although Helen's job at the Henry Street Settlement ended as WPA funds began to dry up, she gave private lessons in people's homes. If they had no piano, she sketched a keyboard on the kitchen table, taught fingering, and left the rest to the imagination. The apartment on Seventy-fifth Street was stuffed with relatives or Helen's friends, and the West Side had no nightlife to offer a restless sixteen-year-old. After a day's trauma at the Mercury, Judy liked to get together with her girlfriends and wander the streets of Greenwich Village.

The East Village of Abe and Helen's youth had all but disappeared. Café Royale had fallen on hard times and would soon close. The Rand School was long gone, and what remained of the socialist movement seemed stodgy next to the fervent idealism of Communism that gained currency with the establishment of the WPA. The Village, especially the West Village, became an incubator for progressive political, literary, and artistic thought. It was reminiscent of the avant-garde lofts and salons Joe Gollomb had frequented during the mid- and late twenties. Among the many centers of this renewed bohemian life (foremost was Stewart's Cafeteria) was a basement dive on Seventh Avenue South. It was called the Village Vanguard and was the brainchild of Max Gordon, a Lithuanian by way of Oregon and Reed College who left Columbia Law School after six weeks to pursue his fascination with writing and Village life. In the five years since it had opened, the Vanguard acquired a modest reputation as a late-night hangout for poets and artists, drunks, insomniacs, and impostors.

The Vanguard had a stable of misplaced men of letters, including John Rose Gildea, Harry Kemp, Joe Gould, Jack Sellers, and the legendary Max Bodenheim. Eli Siegel acted as MC and received a modest wage. The others accepted food from Max and passed the hat. The Village held a powerful allure for artists and political activists and those to whom Max referred as Village Kids—rebellious and nonconformist students and other young people who disdained uptown café society for the gritty, lively atmosphere downtown. The Vanguard was popular with this segment, since it was decidedly bohemian, inexpensive, and, without a liquor license, subject to no age restrictions.

Judy was a Village Kid who was often seen in the vicinity of the Vanguard but had not ventured inside. She was in the neighborhood one night when rain began to fall. She stepped inside the nearest doorway, which happened to belong to the Vanguard. With nothing better to do than wait out the storm, she descended the dark stairs to the small bistro a full flight below street level. The ambience and commotion at once struck a responsive chord with her childhood visits to the Royal. Though only sixteen, Judy had a certain womanly build and composure. Still, she was clearly not the sort of patron the place normally attracted. Max spotted her immediately, and hoping to shield her from those poets who fancied themselves ladies' men, walked over and introduced himself. They talked over soft drinks and Judy told him that she was running the switchboard at the Mercury and waiting for her chance to slip into theater. Max asked if she had other friends in the theater. Judy widened her soft brown eyes and in all sincerity lied, "Yes." Though she had no way of knowing, Max was ready to get rid of the poets. He was tired of their antics and especially tired of a hand-to-mouth existence that was usually his hand to their mouths. Judy offered a suggestion. "Why don't you put a show in on weekends?"

"What kind of show?"

"Oh, songs and skits." That wasn't getting much response. "Social satire."

That got a nibble. Max had just been to see *Pins and Needles* on Broadway and thought he knew what she was talking about, not really suspecting that she had little idea what she was talking about. The conversation ended on a cordial note, with Max saying he would like to take a look at her group sometime. Judy thanked him and walked back up the stairs to the rain-slicked street. It was all she could do to hold back her excitement. She had her break. Now all she needed was an act.

Judy had a history of problems with her throat. She was hypersensitive to pain and every so often her voice became raspy and she would whisper until the soreness passed. The problem had returned the previous summer, and Helen, who was fast imparting her own hypochondria to her daughter, arranged a week's vacation for the two of them at Unity House, the ILGWU's adult summer camp in Pennsylvania. Taking its cue from its neighboring retreat, Tamiment, the camp had a series of makeshift theatrical productions for the entertainment and diversion of its guests. When Judy arrived, the players were about to tackle Gilbert and Sullivan's *The Pirates of Penzance*. She sat in on rehearsals and helped out with the props and sets. The musical director was a young man named Leonard Bernstein. The pirate king was played by Adolph Green.

Green had since formed a group called Six and Company. Like any of a hundred similar acts, they were spare-time performers with tired routines who begged work with ladies' clubs and toured the lesser Catskill resorts. What little income Adolph had came from jobs as a carpet measurer and as a runner on Wall Street. Judy got in touch with Adolph and told him of Max's offer. The following week, Six and Company braved the regulars at the Vanguard, and the reception was rough at best. The group promptly disbanded, but Max told Judy and Adolph to keep at it. Adolph remembered a young man he had met at the Ninety-second Street Y named Al Hammer, who had been half of a two-man comedy act called Hammer and Sickle. Al dropped the partner and made the rounds as a monologist on off hours from his job as a shipping clerk in the garment district. Al was joined by another of Adolph's acquaintances, a young woman with a degree in drama from NYU and a keen desire to become an actress. She had purposely stopped her studies two credits shy of a teaching certificate as an added incentive to her theatrical ambitions. But her work was confined to a handful of lines in a road company of *Having a Wonderful Time* and a stint in summer stock in East Hampton. She had nothing to lose, and so Betty Comden agreed to join Adolph, Judy, and Al. Betty in turn brought along a friend from NYU, John Frank, who played piano and lately guitar with a group called the Peasant

Singers, with which Betty had also performed and which specialized in Ukrainian folk songs.

The five of them gathered at the Vanguard one Sunday night and performed individually. There was no act, and no audience to speak of. The boozy clientele began to defect in the face of such amateur entertainment. Those who remained protested loudly and demanded to have their poets back. Max was patient. He told the kids to keep at it.

Up until then they had been using other people's material. When they learned that further use would require them to pay royalties, they became writers. They got together at Betty's parents' place on the West Side and roughed out several skits and songs. John Frank was a superb musician who contributed his own original melodies and transcribed those that the others hummed at him. Added to these tunes were clever lyrics with a literate satirical edge. By the end of the week they had a grab bag of bits and a loose sense of structure. The Sunday show was going to be an audition before an audience, after which Max would decide their fate.

It was a select audience—the group papered the house. There were relatives, spouses, fiancés, and an eager claque from the NYU Drama Department. Judy had the biggest contingent: Helen, Joe, Rachel, Harry and Maude, Sylvia Regan, and Abe, who sat separately with a few union buddies. She was young, terrified, and needed that security blanket of family. Some uninvited locals wandered in, looking to kill a little time. But Max had banished the poets for the evening, hoping to protect the frightened newcomers from catcalls and invective.

The opening number was shaky, but it did lay down the evening's theme of good-natured gripes about New York life. The momentum picked up through several blackout sketches and some amusing brainy songs. Despite rough edges, the material often transcended the performances, which, with the exception of Al, were energetic but rather unpolished. As the evening progressed, the players took encouragement from the audience and each other. Individually they had been colorless and unremarkable. Together they were engaging and distinctive.

The performance finished to hearty applause, which was as much as Max expected. What he hadn't expected was his own thorough enjoyment of the group. He was about to wave them over when a man rose at the rear of the room, applied thumb and forefinger to the sides of his nose, and howled, "Bah! Amateurs! Rats! You stink!" Bodenheim had slipped in while Max's back was turned. Max pacified him with a stale sandwich, rounded up the group, and handed them his verdict: "You're hired." The next order of business was a name for the act. Max suggested the name he had been using informally, Judy and the Kids. Judy objected, explaining that this was a collective venture and that nobody deserved top billing. They settled on the Village Vanguarders. That was soon shortened to the Vanguarders, and then discarded entirely. Within the month they were calling themselves the Revuers, a title for which Judy's Uncle Harry claimed credit.

It was a rags-to-rags story. The Revuers played weekends only, two shows a night, one at ten and a second at midnight. At the end of each evening, Max sat them down as he tallied the receipts from sandwiches, Cokes, and setups for patrons who brought their own booze. The portions generally came to five bucks per person per night. Naturally the take varied with the size and thirst of the audience. But while the act was building a certain following, crowds were not exactly beating a path to the Vanguard's door. The Revuers were a well-kept secret.

Creative conferences moved to Helen's flat, which offered space, encouragement, and above all a piano. The group convened there daily to go over new material. Somehow they had gotten the idea that they needed a new act every week, which required an enormous amount of work. No one bothered to tell them that nightclub acts usually stayed the same and let the customers change. It wasn't until a few more outspoken regulars started shouting requests that it occurred to the group to slow the output and polish the better old bits.

Helen loved having the kids around. She fed them and looked after them, and in the case of the ever-rumpled Adolph, did the laundry and ironing. Helen believed in the group's potential, and that went far to ease the disappointment she felt, but mostly kept from Judy, regarding the college issue. Anyone could be the mother of a college girl, but how many of her friends could claim a daughter who was a rising light in the entertainment world? Judy was just as accepting of Helen. She made no apologies to the others for her mother's odd ways. She had none of the self-consciousness or embarrassment teenagers sometimes feel for their parents. It was the best kind of reciprocal arrangement: the group needed a friendly place to work, and Helen needed to be needed. To them she was just a sweet, offbeat lady who told silly stories and laughed at their jokes, and happened to be Judy's mother. Helen did not attempt to tell them their business. Joe did.

Joe was as much a fixture on Seventy-fifth Street as ever. If he happened to be there when the group was having a writing session, he felt compelled to share his superior wisdom. Judy at times considered it an imposition, but the others didn't seem to mind. Adolph and Al had both attended De Witt Clinton, where Joe's fame lingered long after he left. They had read some of his books and had heard of certain show-business contacts. They could use all the help they could get, and besides, Joe might be full of himself, but he seemed harmless.

Abe actually had more of value to offer, but he was busy with his latest Broadway experiment. The *Africana* debacle had only sharpened his interest in show business. Abe's labor activism had been halfhearted at best. His brother, Joe Tuvim, now the manager of Local 142 of the ILGWU, was the family socialist. Abe saw himself as a small-time Sol Hurok, and toward that end joined Mary Shank's talent organization. Beginning in the mid-thirties, the Rockefellers had engineered a Good Neighbor Policy toward South America. Mary handled many of the resulting cultural-exchange programs. As it happened, Abe had retained a number of connections from his Mexican sojourn in

1917. What with the World's Fair coming to Queens, Abe and Mary figured that Broadway would be conducive to a show with a decidedly international flavor.

Abe arranged to have himself appointed U.S. Representative of Fine Arts by the Mexican government. A show was brought to New York as an adjunct to the Mexican exhibit at the World's Fair. In effect, the Mexican government was acting as a Broadway producer, the first time anything like that had ever happened. Abe and Mary predicted that the fair crowd would easily negotiate the short distance from Queens to Times Square and guarantee its success.

Mexicana opened at the Forty-sixth Street Theater in late May 1939, billing itself as "A Musical Extravaganza in 2 Acts and 27 Scenes." It was an invigorating evening of music and dance, and the critics liked it. But the World's Fair connection never materialized and Broadway patrons, most of whom associated Mexican culture with mariachi bands and the runs, stayed away. The show closed after two months and Abe the impresario had his second Broadway setback in as many tries.

Judy's contact with the fair consisted mainly of a song of protest she sang as part of the act. Dressed as the Statue of Liberty, she complained of the tourist attention shown the World's Fair at her expense. She finished on a somewhat catty note announcing that Liberty would still be here when Flushing "is a dump again," refering to the ironic fact that the fair was constructed on the site of the old Corona garbage dump in Queens. The lyrics were perhaps less notable than Judy's rendition, which she belted in a throaty, bluesy fashion á la Sophie Tucker. Regulars asked for the number constantly. Judy, whose own singing voice was untrained and ordinary, was already showing a fine flair for mimicry. Even more, the Revuers were gradually taking form as a quintessential Village act; cerebral, topical, incisive and appropriately, if self-consciously, alienated from mainstream culture. While some of the material lacked real bite, the group shared a kinship with artists and others who saw themselves as apart from and often superior to life in the rest of the city. They were becoming part of the local color, a troupe of neo-bohemian minstrels.

While Abe was having his troubles, the Revuers were having unimagined good fortune. A critic with the *Post* had gotten wind of the act and stopped by unannounced one night for the late show. The house was nearly empty and the group was wondering whether even to go on. They performed and the next day received an excellent review. Not to be outdone, the *Times* critic paid a visit and found the group much to his liking. Then came another stroke of luck. E. J. (Jack) Kahn had just joined the staff of *The New Yorker* and was assigned a department called "Tables for Two," which kept tabs on events of note at the city's nightclubs. A friend suggested Jack catch the act at the Vanguard. Jack lived on Fourth Street off Bowery and knew of the Vanguard, though in its former incarnation. He dropped in late one night and was thoroughly charmed by the routines. He gave the group a write-up which by *New Yorker* standards was positively effusive, but in his enthusiasm he forgot to list the individual players by name. He made up for that omission in a later piece and became one of the act's most loyal fans. He also became infatuated with Judy.

In the short time since the Revuers had formed, the act had experienced an accelerated evolution. Distinct stage personalities emerged, drawn largely from offstage traits. Adolph was blustery and unkempt, Betty was cool and sophisticated, Al was antic and deadpan, John was charming if often hidden behind the piano. Judy was innocent, enchanting and open, and deceptively naive, a sort of ingenue. But with Judy, there was an added transformation that was astonishing.

She had never been the sort to turn heads on the sidewalk. She was five-feet-seven and big-boned. She had broad shoulders and narrow hips. She was extremely self-conscious about her ankles, which she considered too thick, and her breasts, which she considered too small. She had a propensity for plumpness. Her face was round and smooth as a baby's bottom and, in repose, just as mysterious. With Judy it was necessary to look beyond the usual terms of beauty.

To start, she had the peculiar magnetism of an essentially shy person. Her doubts about her attractiveness made her more attractive. Like some chemical valence, her paradoxical sense of self-worth and incompleteness gave her a great combining power for others. In intimate surroundings, people were invariably drawn to her. The clue to her mystique was her face. It had character and womanly definition but in many ways was a child's face. Emotion played across the features with winsome ease. If Judy smiled, you smiled. If Judy laughed, you laughed. Her occasional crying fits were less contagious, probably because they had more to do with mood or frustration than deep pain. Judy kept her pain much better hidden than that.

People were drawn by Judy's smile but spellbound by her gaze. The soft brown eyes had a kind of soulful translucence. They were friendly and feeling and seemed to give off their own special light. Friends and strangers alike were strongly attracted by the glow. There was nothing unusual about her voice except when she sang. Then it sometimes had the thin lilt of a penny whistle. She was not especially light on her feet, but her movement had an awkward grace.

All these qualities followed Judy onstage. Her terrible stage fright only enhanced her appeal. Betty seemed self-contained. Adolph could just as easily play to an empty parking lot. But Judy seemed to need the audience. The one time she tried to overproject, she lost them. After that she kept it small. Audiences were entertained by all the players, but Judy they loved and were perfectly willing to meet more than halfway. That was the magic of her transformation: her natural charm gave over to natural charisma onstage. And ever so slowly, Judy began to believe in herself.

A fat man from Pittsburgh ambled backstage after a performance and stopped Al. "I wanna talk to the girl."

"Which one?"

"The pretty one."

That had come to mean Judy. She said hello, made small talk, and then as politely as possible brushed him off. The same thing happened with different men almost nightly. Judy resented those who approached her as just another showgirl, and she invariably rejected the advances. Above all she objected to the implied insult to Betty, who had been instrumental in the act's progress. Still, there was little Judy could do. She was the people's choice, the Revuers' centerpiece, and the others could take consolation in her ability to attract fans. Whether or not customers came to see Judy, they stayed to see the act.

Jack Kahn made his nightly tour of nightclubs and arrived at the Vanguard in time for the late show. Judy threw over a burly pharmacist named Murray and started dating the handsome, rugged-looking Kahn. Once or twice they double-dated with Betty and a lawyer friend of Jack's named Bob Wolfe. Some nights they would take in a movie or a show. More often they went off on their own to other after-hours spots, or simply to some all-night diner for a hamburger and talk.

Judy talked mostly about the act—how it was going, where they might find new material. It was clear to Jack, a Harvard graduate, that she was well-read and highly intelligent, but she didn't say much about books or politics or world affairs. For that matter, neither did he. They both made their living via nightclubs and entertainment. They were new to this world, it dazzled and intrigued them. Theirs was a fun, casual relationship which was never sexual, although that was more Judy's doing than Jack's. She was inexperienced with men and, what with Abe's past, neurotically fearful of physical intimacy, which seemed to carry the implied threat of rejection. Dates regularly ended at Helen's door with a hug, a smile, and a kiss.

The Revuers were still essentially beginners. They built their own set, which had a habit of coming apart in mid-performance. Their costumes were often the result of Helen's needlework. Their dressing room was the ladies' john. Their first routine of the night always included overcoats as a defense against the

Vanguard's reluctant heating system. Everything, right down to the audience, seemed impermanent, and so it came as a surprise to Betty and Adolph one night when they arrived to find the stairway jammed with people and a line strung around the corner. They ran across the street to a pay phone and called Max.

"What's going on?"

"Come to the back door, I'll tell you."

Word had gotten out about the hot new act at the Vanguard. The crowds were not only hip Villagers but people from uptown and, with greater frequency and to the unending delight of the players, theater people and literati, café-society sorts not so much slumming as sampling the Vanguard's discovery. Judy had seen to it that Houseman knew of the act. Jack Kahn collared ever friend with a spare evening. And even Uncle Joe had helped spread the news. But the key had been the good notices, especially the *Post*'s, and the rest was old-fashioned New York word of mouth.

Like any comedy act, the Revuers could get a dozen different responses from a dozen different audiences. They didn't have the tried-and-true one-liners of a stand-up comedian. They didn't have the metronomic timing of a vaudeville troupe. Even after they eased their compulsion about constantly providing new material, the insecurity remained. George S. Kaufman said satire was what closed Saturday night. The Revuers were defying the odds, but they knew they were only as good as their audience. They were unique, even chic, but they had to stay on their toes or risk sudden disfavor.

For Betty and Adolph it led to severe ups and downs. If Orson Welles and his friends came in and laughed at every last in-joke, they were euphoric. If the Electrolux salesman from Passaic happened by and requested "Melancholy Baby," they were despondent. Al was more durable—he had performed for garden clubs on Long Island and lived to tell about it. Judy was in a constant state of anxiety. She felt nauseated before every show and sometimes threw up. On occasion she threatened not to go on and would give in only after a pep talk and a couple of stiff drinks. The problem was self-image. Betty and Adolph wanted most to be performers, but audiences responded more to their writing than to them. Judy wanted to be a writer, but her most valuable contribution was as a performer. But if there was any residue of envy, it was never verbalized; frankly, they were just grateful to the working.

Judy continued to see Jack Kahn. Thursday nights they would go back to the flat that he shared with William Shawn, amateur pianist and heir-apparent to *New Yorker* founder and editor Harold Ross. Jack, who played the drums after a fashion, and Bill would have jam sessions with their mutual friend harmonica player Larry Adler. Other players came and went. Judy would often sing in a voice that was about as good as the accompaniment. The best times were spent cruising in Jack's Plymouth convertible. Judy was especially impressed with the car, since it was the first model to feature an automatic top. These were the things that counted in the summer of '39.

The Revuers' income grew with their popularity. Still, it was a pie sliced five ways, one of the disadvantages of a large act. Judy's share averaged twenty-five dollars a week. These were good times for Helen: she had a successful daughter, her own work, the daily company of the kids, and relative financial security. And yet Judy continued to worry about her. Always at the back of her mind was the fear that Helen might suffer another breakdown. When Judy was at work she called home frequently. She told Helen how the show went, whom she was seeing afterward, when she expected to get in. The phone was only the outward sign of the growing mutual dependency. The umbilical was there and would be there at least as long as mother, daughter, and grandmother were roommates.

Judy still managed to get away occasionally. Later that summer she and some girlfriends rented a cabin not far from Woodstock, New York, an artists' colony. The others would stay the weekend, but Judy arranged to catch the six P.M. bus back to New York in order to make the Friday show at the

Vanguard. She awoke from an afternoon nap to find some women visitors, friends of friends. She introduced herself and explained she was performing with a group in the Village and would have to be getting back soon. When she discovered that the others already had plans to go bar-hopping in Woodstock, work suddenly seemed less important. She did what any teenager might do in the face of missing a good time—she sat down and cried.

One of the visitors was a social worker for the New York Department of Welfare. Her name was Yetta Cohn, and she offered Judy a lift to the bus stop. They talked along the way and Judy dried her tears. By the time they reached the bus stop she felt much better. Judy thanked Yetta for the ride and invited her to stop by the Vanguard some night.

Three weeks later Yetta was returning to her apartment on Horatio Street after dinner with friends. It was around 11:30 when she remembered the invitation and decided to take in the show. Judy was getting ready for the midnight performance. She spotted Yetta and gave her a warm greeting. She brought over Betty and Aolph and introduced them. Yetta enjoyed the show, with its brand of gentle social satire, and thought the performers were fresh and bright, if somewhat untrained. She came back several times with friends and one night asked Judy to dinner the following Tuesday.

Judy told her, "Sorry, I can't make it."

"What about Wednesday?" Yetta asked.

No again. Judy then went into a lengthy explanation. "Monday I have dinner with my Uncle Joe. Tuesday I go to my Uncle Harry and Aunt Maude's. Wednesday I eat in with my mother, Helen, and Gramma. Thursday I go back to Uncle Joe's, and Friday the whole bunch comes to our place. Saturday I go out on a date, and Sunday I visit my father. Monday it starts all over again."

Yetta blinked. "Are you out of your mind?"

Judy shrugged.

Yetta gave it one more shot. "Will you come to dinner

Tuesday? I'd like you to meet some of my close friends."

Judy nodded and offered to bring along some favorite classical records.

Tuesday evening Yetta was sitting with a few friends over drinks. They heard footsteps on the stairs, a split-second pause, then a loud crash. Yetta ran to the door and found Judy flat on her face crying among a number of smashed records. But what really caught her eye was Judy's outfit—bobby socks, a pleated skirt, and saddle shoes.

"How old are you?" asked Yetta, who had seen her only in slacks or evening clothes.

"Eighteen and a half," Judy answered, dusting herself off.

Yetta and her friends were twenty-nine. "I think you'd better go home."

Judy started crying again, and Yetta finally relented. They picked up what was left of the records and went inside to dinner. Yetta's friends were enchanted with Judy. There was no pretense of age or sophistication. Judy was obviously bright and articulate, but more than that, she was friendly, she was herself.

The others went home after coffee, and Judy stayed to talk. She recounted the events that brought her to the Vanguard instead of college. While she did not regret the choice against continuing formal education, she did miss the carefree social life that students seemed to enjoy. As a kind of token compensation, she often dressed in the current college vogue; thus the bobby sox and saddle shoes.

Judy and Yetta became close friends. Yetta stopped by the Vanguard regularly and even witnessed the Seventy-fifth Street clan firsthand. After an evening in the lap of the Gollombs, Yetta lectured Judy: "This is no way for a young woman to live." She could see that the assorted family pressures might stunt her friend's emotional growth. An only child can become an odd fusion of child and adult, with none of the normal, healthy intermediate steps. Judy thought over the advice and a few days later decided that she and Yetta should get a place together. Yetta pointed out that her Horatio Street studio suited her perfectly. Judy pointed out the stable next door—the horses were hardly ideal neighbors, with their clomping and snorting, to say nothing of the smells that wafted in on summer nights. Besides, the lease was almost up. Judy began to hunt for apartments.

She dragged Yetta to a place she found on Fifty-eighth Street. It was on the top floor of a newly renovated brownstone and was brightly lit by twin skylights. There was a small open interior balcony that served as one bedroom. Below it was a second bedroom, a little kitchen, and the pièce de résistance—a tremendous high-ceilinged living room with ample space for a piano. The asking price was a steep fifty-seven dollars a month. Yetta said that the city was paying her only thirty seven dollars a week and that Judy's income was variable at best. Anyway, the apartment was impractical. The skylight would bring dawn with a vengeance, and rainstorms would pound a tattoo that would make the Horatio Street horses seem like a serenade in comparison. Judy counted off the many advantages and finished by running upstairs and flinging open one of the skylights. A pigeon flew in.

Against Yetta's better judgment, Helen's unspoken disapproval, and Uncle Joe's vehement objections, Judy moved to 226 West Fifty-eighth Street.

5

~~~~~~~~~~~~~~~~~~

Judy huddled with Max between shows. A man named John Roy had been in touch with her. Roy was once the prep-school teacher of Nelson Rockefeller and now the managing director of the Rainbow Room, a posh supper club on the top floor of the RCA Building in Rockefeller Center. Max knew of the place and he knew what was coming.

"He wants to put us the Rainbow Room," she said. "He'll pay us $250 a week for the group."

Except for an August excursion to the Westport Country Playhouse, where they shared the bill with a young hoofer named Gene Kelly, the Revuers and the Vanguard had been inseparable. They grew up together, and now, Max thought, they would have to grow apart.

"Take it," he said.

Judy gave him a hug. Later the Revuers gave him a silver cigarette case with the inscription "To Max from the Kids." Max started to line up assorted blues and folk acts along with comedy and jazz. The Revuers dusted off their best routines and purchased bargain formal wear.

Opening night Judy was running late. She and Yetta rushed down to Rockefeller Center and arrived at the Rainbow Room elevator with only minutes to spare. The elevator operator insisted they were underdressed and refused them admittance. Judy was frantic. "I'm part of the act!" There may have been a little menace in her voice. The elevator operator took them the sixty-five stories to the top. It seemed to take forever. The dressing rooms at the Rainbow Room were situated above a grand staircase. Yetta found an open seat at a table with Helen, Uncle Joe, Uncle Harry, Aunt Maude, and Gramma. Judy dashed up the stairs smack into an elaborately dressed dancer. She'd forgotten that the performers made their entrance by these same stairs and had collided with the opening act, Jack Cole's Balinese Dancers. Few in the audience noticed. In fact, as the evening wore on, few in the audience paid much attention to anything but the food, the wine, and the commanding view of New York.

The Revuers were on for about an hour. They did their "A" material—spoofs of Joan Crawford, Queen Victoria, Noël Coward, Oscar Wilde, Broadway, Hollywood, everything. Nothing worked, not even the durable World's Fair stuff. With no lift from the audience, their timing was shot to hell. They finished to a polite ripple of applause and were followed by Al Donahue's dance band, which the crowd seemed to like better. Best of all they liked Dr. Sydney Ross, who came on last and did card tricks. The group could tell this was going to be a long three weeks.

At the Rainbow Room, the Revuers went to school. Betty and Judy got tips on stage makeup from the Balinese dancers, better known as the Kraus sisters. They also whittled their performance down to a peppy twenty minutes, and were careful to select only those routines with broader satire for these audiences, which were predominantly out-of-towners. They survived the notices and audience apathy and decided they had perhaps overreached. The distance between the Vanguard's cellar and Rockefeller Center's top floor was something more than sixty-five stories. The two were worlds apart.

Some good came of the booking. The Revuers appeared on a local radio show sponsored by Consolidated Edison and received a good write-up in *Variety* for much of the same material that had buried them at the Rainbow Room. From there they went on to an engagement at Spivy's Roof, a posh café-society supper club on East Fifty-seventh. The program listed the Revuers by name and gave each of them a brief bio. Judy gave her age as eighteen and claimed to have begun as a sculptress and modern dancer before directing several stock companies and joining the Mercury Theater as a script reader. It was less significant that she stretched the truth than that she still had trouble seeing herself as merely a performer.

The act played well at Spivy's. These were mostly society people and show-business insiders, not high-rollers from the sticks. The Revuers could be as oblique and esoteric as they liked and not worry about losing their audience. The material stood up and supported the performance, which in many ways continued to lack polish and professionalism. The players had only one complaint. The stage was set up in such a way that they were forced to make their entrance from an outdoor balcony. It was late November and snowy, and they came on dusting flakes from their hair and clothes. Judy was especially concerned about her brand-new beaver coat, which was the product of weeks of consultation at Seventy-fifth Street. The prospect of ruining the coat was less worrisome than that of having to go shopping with Helen, Gramma, and Maude again.

Meanwhile, the Revuers came to the attention of Ruth Morris of the William Morris Agency. She was convinced they were ideally suited for an intimate legitimate revue and put the word out among theatrical producers. Ruth arranged an audition for Cheryl Crawford, co-founder of the Group Theater and soon to engineer the resounding success of *Porgy and Bess*. The group visited Cheryl's place on East Fifty-second, got acquainted, and ran through a few numbers. She found them clever and engaging, but didn't think the act was Broadway material. She told them thanks but no thanks. As they left, Judy handed her a song she had written.

It was six months between major bookings. The group played benefits and one-nighters, but whatever momentum they had built up at the Vanguard seemed to sputter after the Rainbow Room. Things were looking bleak. Judy waited out the lull at home on Fifty-eight Street. Yetta had since taken a job with the New York City Police Department for twice what she was making at the Department of Welfare. The roommates were making rent but couldn't afford such frills as a telephone. They relied on a hall phone, which rang night and day for Judy. There were agents with offers that never materialized. There were men asking for dates, which Judy generally declined. And there was Helen.

Yetta had insisted on one condition before moving in with Judy. Friends, colleagues, and lovers were welcome to have the run of the place. But Judy's family was not to visit without an invitation or first calling. Yetta was not about to be part of a home away from home for Joe, Harry, Maude, and Gramma, whom she very much disliked, or Helen, whom she basically liked. As a result, many of the family spats and incidentals that were discussed at Seventy-fifth Street now took place over the phone. If there was still that vestigial umbilical, it was a vast improvement over what had preceded it.

With the move to Fifty-eighth Street Judy hoped to establish her independence. At first it was more a case of shifting dependence. Judy did not make friends easily, and while the Revuers were becoming a second family, they could not begin to meet the many needs that surfaced in her break from the Gollombs. In effect Judy turned to Yetta as mother, sister, and friend, and found complete acceptance. It was not the controlling conditional affection of the family, nor the illusory affection of men who responded to a Judy that Judy still didn't quite believe in. It was a strong, mutually respectful, nurturing friendship that encouraged Judy's previously impeded growth as an adult.

There were soon the signs of change. She was happier, more relaxed. She could come and go at her leisure without the annoyance of constantly reporting her whereabouts. Judy enjoyed turning the apartment into a home, and if some of the accoutrements were less than elegant, she could not have been more pleased with the results. She made no apologies to guests for the sparse furniture or the miscellaneous tableware. This was the way she lived, and she had nothing to hide. Yetta marveled at the changes in Judy. In a relatively short time she had gone from something of a stalled late adolescent to a wise and responsible young woman. Yetta found herself learning from her roommate, and that pleased her no end. There was no superimposed professional bond; in fact, their work worlds could scarcely have been more different. They were two independent individuals who enjoyed many of the same things: bright lively people, good music, good food, funny conversation, Michigan rummy. They enjoyed each other, though they didn't always see that much of each other. Judy kept late hours and often returned home around seven A.M., just as Yetta was preparing to leave for the department. They would share a cup of coffee, swap gossip, and not cross paths again till that evening or sometimes the following morning. When time and finances permitted, they would dine out at one of the many small inexpensive French restaurants that lined West Fifty-seventh Street.

Dining in could be just as satisfying. Yetta's twin sister, Naomi, was married to a man who owned a catering establishment. He would send over gourmet fixings, which he modestly called "care packages." Yetta's mother would also drop by carrying shopping bags full of delicacies. Not to be outdone, Helen repeatedly arrived with enough fully cooked food to last for days. In fact, with time Helen had adjusted quite well to Judy's new living arrangement. She never came by uninvited or unannounced, and she gradually curtailed her phone calls, which in the beginning had been as many as a dozen a day. Helen had also managed somehow to see that the apartment was graced by a handsome grand piano. If she feared that Yetta had partly replaced her in Judy's life, she gave no hint of it to either of them. On the surface the distance seemed to benefit both mother and daughter. For the first time in years Judy and Helen were interacting through choice and genuine fondness instead of obligation and neurotic interdependency.

There was one setback. Abe met Yetta through Judy and asked her out for a date. Yetta assumed it was innocent enough and accepted once and then a second time. Word reached Helen, who was not at all happy with the news and let her daughter know in no uncertain terms. Before there could be a third date Judy asked Yetta, "Please don't see my father any more. My mother is very upset." Yetta gladly complied, but was again reminded of Helen's grip on Judy. During one free weekend, Judy went with some friends to Mt. Tremper, New York. Along the way they stopped at a diner (so she could call Helen) and stayed for lunch. Judy ordered a hamburger and after eating it and the one ordered by a friend, ordered another. The counter man asked, "Are you sure?" Judy said yes. He looked at her, then at her empty plate, and teased, "I'd rather bed than board you."

With the grand piano came the Revuers. The group met unfailingly each afternoon at Fifty-eighth Street. When they were working, they rehearsed; when they were between jobs, they wrote. At odd intervals Adolph was virtually a boarder. Chief among the intermittent house guests was Leonard Bernstein. These were Judy's salad days, and she savored them, even though the act entered something of a protracted dry spell.

The Revuers did what they could to keep up morale. The prospects were dwindling when they learned that NBC radio wanted them for a weekly network spot. The group was offered $250 a week for twenty five weeks. The pay could have been better, but the national exposure was more valuable than mere money. They could use some of the old bits, have steady work, and continue to scout other opportunities. They accepted the offer and had their debut that March at 9:30 P.M. on Tuesday: "Yes, here are the Revuers . . . five clever youngsters who write and perform their own material . . . original lyrics, original music."

Each show was devoted to a different theme for satirical dismantling. Other attractions included a roster of guest singers, one of whom was Dinah Shore. As usual, the reviews were mixed, calling the group promising yet uneven. The shows got better as they went on, and, as hoped for, the job was parlayed into other jobs.

One offer came from an outfit called Musicraft, which was producing a series of 78's entitled *Night Life in New York*. The Revuers recorded their old standby, "Joan Crawford Fan Club," which poked fun at the actress's many famous foibles. The bulk of the recording was given over to a breakneck mock Hollywood epic, "The Girl with Two Left Feet." Judy played the title role of Maryrose Rosemary, a squeaky-voiced ingenue with all the guile of a puppy. The piano accompaniment was handled by Adolph's friend and onetime roommate, Leonard Bernstein. The album was released, and except for select friends and relatives, forgotten. A booking at the Hall of Fashion at the World's Fair had much the same result.

The Revuers were doing better by Rockefeller Center these days. In October they appeared at Radio City Music Hall and did five shows a day sandwiched between the Rockettes and the feature film. The Music Hall was something of a vaudeville holdover, a poor man's Broadway. With its art-deco gingerbread, gilt-edged pipe organ, movable orchestra pit, and the largest indoor stage and movie screen in America, the Music Hall itself was half the show. The other half went to everything from animal acts to Christmas pageants, with the ever-present Rockettes kicking away like some crazed centipede. If ever there was a wrong audience for the Revuers, this was it.

The group approached the opening gingerly and professionally. They set aside the fast highbrow material and sought some common denominator. Each of them prepared a takeoff on a different type of song—pop, jazz, folk, opera. Wary of the Hall's echoey acoustics, they kept dialogue to a minimum and packed it all into a trim, well-paced act. To their amazement, the audiences liked them.

Playing to daily crowds of six thousand in a theater slightly smaller than an airplane hangar had many drawbacks. It also had its rewards. The Music Hall treated its performers well.

The Revuers had real dressing rooms instead of bathrooms, they made their entran from a stage wing and not some snow-covered fire escape, they even had a rehearsal room with a grand piano. Another fringe benefit was the regular screening of new movies. The management used its performers as a test audience for newly released motion pictures. Between the third and fourth shows, the cast would go back to a small screening room, have a look, then rate what they saw. Actually, there was a compelling incentive to be tough critics: the Revuers ran as long as the current feature.

Everything was going well for the group when one day Adolph failed to appear after the second show. Judy phoned all over town but couldn't find a trace of him. As their cue neared, Betty desperately portioned Adolph's bits among them. The Revuers went on, one shy.

Downtown at the Algonquin Hotel Jack Kahn and Philip Wrenn were having a few drinks. This was the anniversary of their employment by *The New Yorker*—same day, different year—and they celebrated annually with some sort of spree. They were mulling over options for this year when Jack saw Adolph with a boutonniere and a young woman he introduced as the former Elizabeth Breitel. They had just been married at City Hall. Jack insisted on an impromptu wedding reception, and one or two bottles of champagne later, Adolph appeared backstage at the Music Hall, woozy but happy. The others were not in an especially festive mood, having just filled in for him on no notice. Judy was furious. She tried to be considerate of others and expected as much in return. But she could not stay angry with Adolph. She felt a sisterly love for him, and made special allowances for his behavior. For Judy, Adolph was Adolph—a lovable shlemiel.

The Revuers were coming to the end of their contract at NBC radio, and the prospects were not good. Already some union men had been around to shake them down for money, threatening to get the show canceled if they refused. They paid, but needn't have bothered. NBC dropped them after thirty-two weeks. To make matters worse, a second engagement at the

Music Hall fizzled and the act was released after only a few performances. With their options fading, they turned to the one man they knew they could count on. By the first of the year the Revuers were back at the Vanguard.

Heywood Hale Broun was the son of writer Heywood Broun and feminist Ruth Hale, both of whom had died. Days he worked for a jazz-record label, which added little to his income. So he moonlighted for the newspaper *P.M.*, and in what time remained, made the rounds of jazz spots. Woodie had heard that his friend drummer Zutty Singleton was playing a gig at the Vanguard. He walked downstairs and to his horror saw five white comedians. He was about to turn and walk out when he noticed Judy. He stayed for the show and then had Max introduce him to the group. Woodie was pleased at the warm reception they gave him. He came back every night after that, and like Jack Kahn before him, soon knew every routine by heart.

Woodie had a car, a steady job, and an expense account through *P.M.*, and so he soon had the company of the Revuers. The midnight show finished at two and the lot of them would take off for Reuben's to unwind over coffee and pastrami. It was always Betty who eventually said, "We have to rehearse tomorrow. Let's go home." Woodie would pick up the tab and then give Judy a lift home.

One night after work they all went to a hamburger joint called the White Cow. Somehow they started fantasizing about what they would do when they made it big. Woodie didn't pay much attention until Judy's turn came and she spoke of directing, and writing, and happiness. He'd heard her talk plenty about the first two—she always had some play or story she wanted to get to, if only she had the time. But happiness? It hadn't really occurred to him that she was unhappy. She had her moods and an infrequent show of temper. That was understandable, given her youth and the strain of performing. Otherwise she had looks, brains, friends, suitors, enough money to get her through the next utility bill, and more success than a nineteen-year-old had a right to expect. Before he could give it much thought, Betty called curfew as usual, Woodie got the check as usual, but something about the ride home with Judy was unusual. By the time they had said good night he realized that he was beginning to understand Judy. He was beginning to fall in love with her.

Adolph wasn't pleased when he saw that Woodie was seriously interested in Judy. He returned Judy's sisterly love with a kind of clumsy big-brother cautiousness. Woodie could see that he was upset and finally took him aside one night. "Look, Adolph, I don't want to marry her, I just want to go to bed with her." It might have been more truthful if he had said he wanted to go to bed with her first, then they could talk about marriage. In any event, the discussion eased the tensions. Adolph had observed Judy with many men over the past couple years. He was not privy to the particulars of her private life, but he did know that she had not gone to bed with a man yet. Adolph and Woodie were soon on good terms again.

If Woodie failed to get anywhere with Judy, it was not for want of trying. He waited for her each night after work, and they would go for a bite, a drink, a drive. For a time it was a cozy, casual relationship. But then Woodie witnessed a gradual change. The more they saw of each other, the more she seemed to test him. One night he was a bit late getting to the Vanguard and found her sitting at a table with some people. He waited a minute or two, then said, "I'll take you home."

"I'm busy right now," she said, hardly acknowledging him.

"Hey, I'm not a cabdriver," he said. "I'm going now, Miss Tuvim," and he turned and left.

The next morning the phone rang at Woodie's apartment. It was Adolph. "What did you do?"

"What do you mean, what did I do?"

"All I know is Judy's mad as hell at you."

That did it. Woodie went back to the Vanguard that night and pulled her aside. Before he could get a word out, she fumed, "I'm furious."

"Furious about what?"

"You didn't wait last night."

"What was I supposed to do?" he asked. "Stand next to the coatroom? Either you come with me at that point or you ask me to join your group or you say I'll see you tomorrow. There's a limit."

"I thought you would wait," she persisted.

"That's what you always think."

From there the argument degenerated, and he left. The next day he cooled down and gave her a call of truce, but she refused to talk to him. That went on for three days. On the fourth day Judy not only talked to him but acted as if nothing had ever happened.

It was then that Woodie remembered something a psychiatrist friend once told about the symbolism behind the pawnbrokers sign. There are three balls, and these are the three interrelated objects of the dependent. First is the actual specific need or dependency. Second is the resentment of the person on whom you are dependent. Third is the omnipotence of total dependence: like the baby in the crib, I am king, I will have my needs met. Woodie realized that to whatever degree Judy depended on him, he had damn well better come through. And yet she was always a little bit angry with him because of his loyalty. And then from time to time she would be crushingly rude to him; that, he felt, was the demonstration of omnipotence.

With men, at least, Judy was still sitting the fence between adolescence and womanhood. One moment she might seem calmly in command and the next do something childish. You never knew which to expect. This duality dated back to Helen's breakdown, when adulthood was virtually thrust upon Judy. She never fully experienced the frivolous, indulgent side of childhood, and so vestiges of those impulses seemed to follow her into maturity. That was part of the ongoing attachment to Helen; whatever else went on between them, this was still Judy's mother. It was a way of preserving an interrupted youth.

Woodie's love for Judy was tempered by his growing understanding of her, but it was not diminished. He resigned himself to the limitations she placed on their time together, and hoped for more. That August, five months before the United States entered the war, Woodie opened his mail to find a 1-A draft card. He went down to the club that night and told Judy. She was extremely upset, which surprised and touched Woodie. This was an added dimension of Judy's psyche with which he had not reckoned—a profound, almost tortured sense of caring. If her dependency made her powerful, her sensitivity made her vulnerable. She swung between the two extremes with those who meant the most to her. Her defense against those she simply could not trust was to demote them in her mind to some lesser status. To these people, she was friendly and considerate but never truly open.

As the war approached, Adolph, John, and Al were exempt from service and so the act was able to continue. The Revuers were still having their ups and downs. The summer of 1941 consisted mainly of downs. The group hired a booking agent who put them on the road and ran them through every supper club and roadhouse east of St. Louis. Some of the engagements were better than others, but none was anything to write home about, though Judy found lots of reasons to phone Helen. Their experiences on the road reminded them they were primarily a New York act. Their experiences in New York reminded them they were primarily a Village act. It was a logic of decreasing possibilities, and by the end of 1941 the string seemed almost played out.

As had happened so often in the past, salvation was only a phone call away. Irving Caesar was a veteran Broadway lyricist, composer, and playwright who had gotten his start in *Pins and Needles* of 1922 and went on to such hits as *No, No, Nanette* and *George White's Scandals* of 1931. His impressive list of songs included "Swanee," "My Mammy," "Tea for Two," and "I Want to Be Happy," to name only a few. Caesar decided to add producing to his many titles and came up with a property which he called *My Dear Public*. It was a revue disguised as a book show. The meager plot concerned the efforts of an actress manqué to have her wealthy husband back a musical which is to star her as a sultry harem queen. It was a minor twist on the stock backstage sugar-daddy theme that was as familiar to twenties musicals as star-crossed lovers and taps. Caesar didn't mind cliché. All he wanted was a loose format for specialty acts. The plot—which consisted mainly of auditions and rehearsals for the fictional play—gave him that if little else.

Caesar beat the bushes for appropriate acts. There was no problem finding old-timers—casting offices were always beset by ex-vaudevillians between trips to the Catskills. New acts were much harder to come by, which is how the Revuers happened to come to his attention. On January 12, 1942, they signed for four hundred a week. The script cast them as separate characters who came together as a hip Village comedy act. This was the level of imagination and subtletly at which the play operated. But that didn't trouble the group at first. They at last had a legitimate vehicle, and even if it seemed shaky, countless performers had gotten big breaks in bad Broadway shows.

After some whirlwind rehearsals, *My Dear Public* had its first out-of-town tryout in New Haven. It was far worse than imagined. Part revue, part book musical, the production combined the worst elements of both. There was no story or characters to speak of, just enough to rob the numbers of the sort of disjointed exuberance a revue demands. Oscar Hammerstein was brought in to try to salvage the show, but the very concept was faulty and there was nothing much he could do. The company went on to Boston and prayed for a miracle.

Yetta had persuaded Judy to take a more practical apartment on the floor below their first place on Fifty-eighth Street. Along with the more conventional quarters came the convenience of their own telephone. Yetta was reading late one night when the phone rang. It was Judy and she was distraught. "Yetta you have to come up right away."

"I've got to work tomorrow."

"You've got to come."

"Why? What's wrong?"

"I've been raped!"

"What?"

Judy tried to explain about one of the actors in the company but was too upset to make sense. Yetta did her best to calm Judy and promised to take the first possible train. The next morning she called her boss at the police department and arranged time off from work, then packed a bag and by noon that day was at Judy's hotel in Boston. Judy was still shaken. Yetta asked her to describe what happened.

The show wasn't going all that well, and anyway, Boston's pretty dull after New York. One of the actors, Johnny Buckmaster, asked her out for a date. Why not? He was good-looking, very British, the son of the famous actress Gladys Cooper.

"We went out, had a couple of drinks. Came back. He invited me up to his room. Had a couple more drinks, then he attacked me. He raped me."

Yetta sat there shaking her head. "Stupid girl. Why did you go to his room?"

"I don't know, it just happened," she answered. "But you don't understand. I liked it!"

So that was it. No doubt Buckmaster had pushed himself on Judy. He was known to be aggressive and erratic. But it seems he had gotten a fair amount of encouragement along the way. It was as if Judy's fear of men was so great that her first sexual encounter had to be passive and almost violent. Helen had been a victim of sorts, and now so was Judy. This was not rape, it was something more and something less. By calling it rape Judy could divest herself of any responsibility.

Judy begged Yetta to stay, and Yetta managed to get the rest of the week off. That Sunday the company left by train for the Philadelphia opening. Yetta was going as far as New York, and Judy insisted they sit together for that stretch of the ride. Every time Buckmaster passed in the aisle, Judy turned her head away. The schoolgirl behavior made it apparent that far from abhorring the man, Judy actually liked him. Yetta said nothing about it, but she was disappointed in her friend. Jack Kahn, she could see. Woodie Broun, she could see. They were cultured, appealing men with their own style and outlook. Buckmaster seemed shallow and strange at the same time, hardly the man she'd have expected Judy to take as a first lover, even if the circumstances were rather unsavory.

Whatever Yetta thought of the man, she knew Judy was acting ridiculous. "For God's sake, Judy. You're being silly. You've got to work with this man," but she stopped. Judy was too agitated to listen, her mind seemed overloaded, aware that she had crossed the line into womanly sexuality with all the dangers that implied for her.

Yetta got off in New York. *My Dear Public* went on to Philadelphia and closed.

The Revuers were shortly back on the local nightclub circuit. The experiments and folly of the recent past gave them a heightened sense of who they were and where they belonged as performers. No more movie houses, supper-club penthouses, or country clubs. And definitely no more Podunk dime-and-dance dives. They played the elite club circuit, Ruban Bleu, Café Society Uptown and Downtown, and Max Gordon's thriving new partnership venture, the Blue Angel. There were off nights and flat audiences, to be sure, but the Revuers were a more seasoned act, more professional. They were flexible and confident, they knew how to reach an audience. When the material didn't click, they no longer became frantic and depressed. They did each show and looked forward to the next. They acquired a small but dedicated following.

Toward the end of the year they agreed to take the act on the road for a prestigious engagement at Chicago's Blackstone Hotel. They canceled two days after opening. It seems John Frank had developed a drinking problem. Until recently it had been manageable and the group covered for him. By the time they reached Chicago it was clear he was in need of professional care. They returned to New York without him and two weeks later drew up a severance agreement through their attorney, Jacob Kupferman. John was generously guaranteed an ongoing financial interest in the group. They parted with regret but without bitterness.

Other changes were taking shape. Betty married a man named Steve Kyle, whom she had dated for years. With the exception of Judy, the Revuers were all married, and perhaps that began to alter their outlook on things. Despite their current success, there was a growing uneasiness among them. They were no longer the wunderkinder of the Vanguard days. Aside from Judy, they were in their mid- and late twenties and faced the likelihood of families. They had not succeeded in radio or on Broadway. The pay and acclaim of nightclubs was passable, but they were ambitious and wanted more. They started to think about motion pictures.

One Sunday Judy mentioned this to Abe, and before she knew it, he had talked to a few people and finagled an audition with the president of Columbia Pictures, the fearsome Harry Cohn. Cohn lived on the West Coast but maintained a New York apartment in the East Fifties. Accompanied by Abe, the Revuers met there one evening. They were ushered into an office where the gruff, stubby Cohn sat drowsily at a large desk. Introductions were made around the room when Cohn's wife, Joan, came in.

"Oh, Harry," she said, "you saw these kids at the Music Hall."

"I didn't see them kids at the Music Hall," he complained.

"You were there."

"I fell asleep."

On that propitious note he told them to get on with the audition. The group started their Joan Crawford Fan Club number, which was as Hollywood as they had. Cohn's eyelids drooped. They sang louder and he interrupted them. "Wait a minute. If I were you . . ." and he proceeded to rewrite the number for them. Harry Cohn was many things—a writer he was not. The audition fell apart and the group was about to pack up when he reached into his coat pocket and came out with a small rectangular metallic object. He told them proudly, "This is a German spy camera." Cohn took Judy aside, snapped a few pictures, said good night, and let them find their way to the door. Apparently Hollywood would have to wait.

Since the closing of *My Dear Public* Judy had gotten over her aversion to Johnny Buckmaster. In fact she decided she liked

him. They saw each other once or twice, then he showed no
further interest. She was mourning her unrequited affection
when Woodie hit town on a three-day pass. He gave her a call
and asked if she wanted to go out that night. She said sure. He
asked what she wanted to do. She laughed and said she'd like to
see *Oklahoma!*

Oklahoma! had opened just three weeks earlier and set
Broadway on its ear. It took pull just to get seats a month in
advance. Woodie decided to give it a shot and went to see a
ticket broker who used to handle his father's account. The man
said he'd like to help out but there were simply no tickets on
such short notice. He suggested Woodie try the theater, ask for
a Mr. Smith and say he was being shipped overseas the next
morning, could he have two house seats? Woodie got within a
block of the St. James Theater and was turned back by crowds
and mounted police. He went back to the broker to thank him
for his effort.

"You'll never believe what happened," the man said. "It's a
benefit tonight. Some guy who didn't want to go to the benefit
came in and sold me the tickets. They're yours." And for old
times' sake, he sold them to Woodie at a discount.

Woodie arrived at Judy's door in his sergeant's uniform. She
asked him where they were going. He told her *Oklahoma!* She
couldn't believe it. The evening was magic. They loved the
show and went out drinking and dancing afterward. As he
brought her home he thought to himself: If she doesn't take me
to bed tonight, she never will. They got to Fifty-eighth Street,
went upstairs, and Judy kissed him good night at the door.
What Woodie didn't know at the time was that she was still
trying to sort out the experience with Buckmaster. She felt her
old fear had been confirmed: intimacy had led to rejection. It
was much more important to Judy that she keep Woodie as a
friend than risk losing him as a lover.

Nicholas Ray lived in the Village on Sixth Avenue. He was
born in Wisconsin and studied architecture with Frank Lloyd
Wright. He came to New York in the mid-thirties to pursue his

interests in American pop and folk music and became involved with the Theater of Action and the Living Newspaper, where he met Elia Kazan and John Houseman. Nick knocked around working at CBS radio, then with Gadge (as Kazan was known to friends), and finally with Houseman, who had formed the Phoenix Theater Company after the Mercury had dissolved. In 1941 Houseman was made vice-president of David O. Selznick Productions, but left shortly after the Japanese attack on Pearl Harbor. Houseman was appointed chief of the foreign service of the Office of War Information radio division. He then hired Nick to oversee programming for shortwave transmissions of American folk music, which the Axis countries had long since banned.

Through his many jobs, Nick remained an aficionado of the Village Vanguard. He had witnessed the birth of the Revuers, and when they departed for classier climes, he was instrumental in bringing about Max's folk phase with the likes of Josh White, Leadbelly, Pete Seeger, and Woody Guthrie.

Nick met Judy during the early days at the Vanguard and they became friends. Before long Nick numbered himself among Judy's growing list of admirers. Judy did not at first return the affection. She liked Nick and saw in him a kind of versatile brilliance. She also saw a certain self-destructive streak in his hard drinking and intemperate life-style. Despite the strange episode with Buckmaster, Judy was a good Jewish girl in many ways. She liked to go slow with men, as Broun and Kahn would readily attest. And while she was not in the habit of clearing dates with her mother, Helen's opinion did count for something, and her opinion of Nick was low. It wasn't that he was likely to corrupt Judy—she was an indifferent drinker, discreet, and sexually still something of a prude. She just didn't know if they were right for each other. The choice was made for Judy when Nick decided to leave New York. Houseman's duties with the OWI had brought him to Hollywood, where he stayed on to accept a job as producer with Paramount and later RKO. Nick's other mentor, Gadge, was heading west to direct films, and he invited Nick along as an assistant. There was a distinct drift west.

The William Morris Agency had been handling bookings for the Revuers off and on for the past year. It was a patient, fatherly association, and the agency had helped them out periodically with loans to get them through jobless times. As the Revuers' audience gradually narrowed to a faithful New York cult, there was little more the agency could do for them, and they parted company. But before they could find another representative, one found them—Kurt Frings, one of Hollywood's biggest agents. A film version of the popular radio show *Duffy's Tavern* was in the works, and Frings could get the four of them a spot. He sweetened the offer with a booking at the fashionable Hollywood nightspot Trocadero.

Adolph and Al were all for it. New York had them labeled and slotted as a sophisticated cabaret act. They were working and making decent money, but it seemed a dead end. Hollywood might mean new life for the act. Judy and Betty were less enthusiastic. Past attempts at broadening the material had backfired, and movie comedy was nothing if not broad. Furthermore, with the exception of the Marx Brothers, the Ritz Brothers, and Burns and Allen, movies had never been particularly kind to acts. The Trocadero was appealing, but there was no reason to assume their material would play better there than Cincinnati.

Adolph and Al prevailed. Within days the Revuers were on the Super Chief for Los Angeles. They arrived and called Frings the minute they stepped off the train. "We're here!"

Frings told them the picture had been canceled.

6

~~~~~~~~~~~~~~~~~~~~~~

The Revuers moved into a small dump over a real-estate office on La Brea near Wilshire and considered their predicament. With the help of Frings they had squeezed the producers of *Duffy's Tavern* for one thousand dollars. That covered travel costs and bought some time. They could play the run at the Trocadero, catch the next train east, and forget they'd ever heard of Hollywood. Or they could look for another engagement, and stick around in hopes of turning up another film deal. There was a third possibility which they had so far avoided discussing—disbanding.

The Revuers never had a master plan. They came together by chance and stayed together by perseverance and the grace of a loyal following. The personnel had remained the same over four years, less John Frank. Through all the vicissitudes they functioned as a unit of distinct individuals. If defection or dissolution was ever in the air, it was not mentioned openly. At least not until Hollywood. The *Duffy's Tavern* debacle opened their eyes to the realities of continuing as a group: it's easier to sell one item than a matched set. At one time or another each Revuer was confronted with the hypothetical question: What would you do if you were offered a job alone? The biggest concern was over Al. He had an unorthodox comic style that might translate well to movies. Plus he had a wife and a child and he was less mobile than the others. When it came Al's turn to answer the standard question, he told them he didn't know what he would do, but he had a pretty good idea.

The response at the Trocadero was excellent. According to recent Hollywood custom, the audience was filled with agents and producers who afterward sent business cards backstage on which they had scribbled a given performer's name. The cards came from every major agency and studio in town, and every one was for Judy. The offers were for standard contracts beginning at $150 a week with provisions for increases over a possible seven-year studio indenture. Many contract players had risen to the heights of feature and even starring roles, but for each one of them, hundreds more languished on the back lot until the studio orphaned them. The offers could be a genuine opportunity. Judy knew they could just as easily be a ticket to oblivion. However uncertain the future of the act was at the moment, it was safer and more secure than an entry-level spot in the Hollywood factory. Anyway, she was already homesick and couldn't imagine going it alone. Judy turned down the offers as fast as they came.

There is an unwritten code in show business: that which is easily gotten is probably not worth getting. Had Judy jumped at the first bait dangled before her, she might well have sealed her fate with the anonymity of a contract player. By refusing, she became more desirable. Studio people who knew no more about her than her Revuers numbers and her reluctance suddenly *had* to sign her. The offers increased, and the others braced themselves for the inevitable crisis.

Yetta came to Los Angeles for a vacation and immediately saw the gathering storm. She got together with Judy, who ambivalently reported her newest proposition. "Twentieth Century-Fox offered me four hundred dollars a week. What do you think?"

"I think it's fantastic," Yetta answered.

Judy was not so sure. The money was unimportant except as an objective measure of how seriously the studio seemed to take her. More important was the group and what they might think of her leaving. She would have been much more comfortable were the tables turned. She could have been understanding or forgiving or mad as hell, and in a strange way that would have affirmed the rejection she was coming to expect out of life. She didn't care for the idea of doing the rejecting.

Yetta laid out the hard facts. "Face it, Judy, the act isn't going anywhere. It's too late. The group's used up all its resources. You have to make a break. You can't afford to turn down four hundred dollars a week." Little as Yetta was acquainted with Hollywood, she was a shrewd woman and understood the mentality at work. You can hold back and increase your market value. You can also overplay your cards and turn up empty-handed. Such maneuvering was the last thing on Judy's mind, but the realities remained. She might put off the studios till they lost interest entirely. Then, what if the act still broke up? She'd be barefoot in Babylon. Judy insisted she would make no move without the consent of the others.

"So have a meeting," Yetta advised.

Of all the stock movie plots the Revuers had lampooned over the years, none could have topped this for cliché and melodrama. The group met at the La Brea apartment with its tacky bamboo furniture and cardboard armoire, and Judy disclosed the Fox offer. She asked them what she should do. Al was resentful, certain she had been sought sheerly for her looks and that he would ultimately be sought for his talent. He told her to go, he could make it on his own.

Betty and Adolph were not angry or vindictive but sad. The act had been a source of income, true; more than that, it had been a second family. There were rivalries and feuds, forbearance and friendship, which was nothing more or less than an average family experienced. Like Judy, Betty and Adolph had grown up with the act; they viewed the prospect of a breakup as something more than the termination of a professional arrangement. It was heartbreaking.

Betty and Adolph spoke up. It would be absurd to keep the act artificially alive. Judy should take the job with Fox. The rest of them would find work as a unit or separately. It had been unrealistic to assume the Revuers could stay together indefinitely. Sooner or later one of them would have been lured away. It just happened to have been Judy. She hadn't been underhanded. She hadn't solicited the offers behind their backs. The studios came to her and she put them off as long as she could. This was fate, and it would be foolish to pretend otherwise.

If they thought that was the end of it, they underestimated Judy's loyalty. She was convinced that all the act needed was a chance. Once the studio put them in a movie, they would be so good that there would be no further talk of disbanding. Judy entered contract talks with Fox and said she would sign provided her partners were also signed. This was a breach of Hollywood etiquette. Legend had it that the small-town cheerleader or the leggy chorine was so grateful for a shot at the big time that she demanded nothing and asked only to please, up to and including sexual favors. And here was this upstart from New York who seemed indifferent at best, bargainng on behalf of friends. Loyalty, altruism, disregard for money—she spoke a strange language. It only confirmed her difference, and that difference was what the studio wanted; that was the root of the mysterious thing movie people spoke of in hallowed tones as "star quality."

Fox made a counteroffer. They were about to go into production on a musical entitled *Greenwich Village*. If Judy would sign the standard long-term contract, the studio would take the others on short-term contracts with an option for extension. It was less than ideal but better than nothing. Judy gave them the seven years they wanted, starting at $400 a week. The others were given a six-week guarantee, also at $400 a week each. Judy felt she had managed the best she could under the circumstances. She was confident the group would be a hit and the rest would be gravy. In the triumph of the moment, it never occurred to her that this might be the studio's opening gambit in a divide-and-conquer strategy.

Sylvia Regan left the Mercury Theater about the same time Judy had. While the Revuers were in their first cycle of success, Sylvia tried her hand as a playwright and wrote *Morning Star*, which enjoyed a strong Broadway run and led to several touring companies. The wartime draft was beginning to deplete the ranks of movie-script writers, and in early 1941 Sylvia heard from a Theater Union friend who had since gone Hollywood. *Morning Star* had secured her reputation as a writer and within weeks her agent negotiated a deal. Sylvia went west with her husband, Abraham Ellstein, and started work at Twentieth Century-Fox.

Sylvia and Abe Tuvim had lost touch in recent years. What little she heard of Judy's fortunes she heard by the grapevine. She was understandably stunned when she went to the studio commissary one afternoon and bumped into the Revuers. She learned they had already begun work on their film and that everything was going better than imagined. They were given two musical numbers and assigned their own choreographer and musical arranger. They were also being used as extras, which Judy found less than thrilling, having once been pushed to the floor by an elderly woman determined to have her face on screen. Small complaints aside, they were enjoying the experience and they were getting to meet the movie's stars, Don Ameche, William Bendix, and Carmen Miranda. There was no doubt that Fox was giving them every chance to make it. Sylvia congratulated them and wished them well.

They worked on *Greenwich Village* for eight weeks, then crossed their fingers and waited to hear from the studio. Judy had her first real chance to look around town. It didn't take her long to realize there was no town. There were long lonely boulevards lined with palms like scrawny old men. There were buildings but they were too short and the colors were all wrong—pink, blue, beige. How could you trust buildings with colors like those? In New York you had gray and brown and black; those were colors for buildings. Even the vegetation here was suspect, the yucca plants seemed too green. Back home an orange was something you bought from a vendor on Times Square. Here you picked it off your neighbor's tree. And what about Los Angeles nightlife? As far as Angelenos knew, there was no night, only perpetual afternoon. Judy missed New York, her friends, her nighttime circuit, her mother. But little as she liked Hollywood, she loved movies.

Sylvia was sitting in her office one morning when she got a call from the front gate: "Miss Betty Comden and Mr. Adolph Green are here and they would like to see you." Sylvia said send them in. For the dejected sight that greeted her, they might have come to report that Yamamoto had just come ashore at Redondo Beach. "Sit down," she told them. "What's wrong?"

"We've been cut from the movie," Betty replied, almost too upset to speak.

They had just viewed an advance print of *Greenwich Village*. Each time the story built to their musical number, it jumped to the next scene. It was fairly thorough surgery; all that was left of them was the extras stuff. Betty had one line of dialogue as a hat-check girl. Al thought that perhaps they had been too funny and that William Bendix had them excised to reduce the competition for laughs. Betty and Adolph disagreed. They believed that the whole thing had been a ploy to get Judy, that the studio never had any intention of using their footage. Sylvia didn't think the conspiracy theory washed. Not only had the studio gone to considerable expense, but it had sent a number of in-house producers and directors to the set to have a closer look at the act. There was no point trying to unriddle what had happened. Motion-picture studios did not exist to be understood. Betty and Adolph could theorize until they were blue in the face, that wouldn't undo the damage. Judy was in, they were out.

Adolph mentioned the possibility of an offer from Monogram, one of the poverty-row outfits. Sylvia looked at him and Betty and knew what she would have to tell them. In a short time she had come to know the facts of life for actors in Hollywood. "Look, you might get little comedic parts in films. You can never be stars. You're not handsome enough to play leads. You can hang on, and maybe nothing will ever happen to you here. Why don't you go back to New York and write a big musical? You're so talented. You write words, you write music, you're witty, and you'll be great." Sylvia knew that Betty and Adolph had done the bulk of the writing for the act. She had no way of knowing that their real passion was performing. If a writer is rejected, it hurts, but in the end it's words on paper. If a performer is rejected, it's flesh and blood. There are always more words and paper. An actor has only one face. Sylvia's counsel seemed to fall on deaf ears. Betty and Adolph left as shell-shocked as they arrived.

One month later Sylvia and her husband left their place on Rodeo and Olympia to walk the block and a half to the Brown Derby. She spotted Adolph looking very lost and forlorn.

"What are you doing here?" she asked.

"Betty went back to New York," he said, "and I can't decide what to do."

Sylvia bought him dinner and repeated her advice. That was the last she saw of Adolph. She continued to bump into Judy periodically on the lot or at local parties, but they only exchanged pleasantries. Judy did not come to her for conversation or companionship. For the first time she was trying to stand on her own.

Adolph eventually joined Betty back east. They saved what they could from the Revuers material and got a booking at the Blue Angel. They phoned Al begging him to join them. Al had a wife, a child, and a house. He wasn't willing to uproot himself just to get back on the old nightclub grind. He may also have had doubts about how well the act would work without Judy, but above all, he was not interested in resurrecting a group that in his mind had run its course. Al was starting to get some bit parts in pictures and was optimistic about further offers. Betty and Adolph pleaded, but without results. The final parting was not amicable.

With the departure of Adolph and the estrangement of Al, Judy was more alone than she bargained for. She kept the place on La Brea and spent some time with writer Julius Epstein, who with his twin brother, Philip, was one of the top writers in town, having just completed *Casablanca*. Julius gave Judy an insider's tour of Hollywood, taking her to Warner Brothers, where she was greeted politely by Peter Lorre and not so politely by Humphrey Bogart. He also showed her that the best milkshake in town was to be found at the Universal commissary. He escorted her to elite cocktail parties and introduced her to luminaries. Judy was drawn to his gentle manner, his wry wit, his contempt for Hollywood mores, and his weakness for practical jokes. But they were never more than good friends and he could not look after her indefinitely. Judy was lonely and craved steady companionship. She phoned Yetta and asked her to move west to become her business manager.

Yetta had gotten a small taste of the movie business when she was out visiting before. Julius took the two of them to dinner one evening. There was a steady stream of industry people who came to the table, fawned over Julius, barely acknowledged Judy, and totally ignored Yetta. The next morning Judy signed with Fox and Julius insisted the three of them have dinner that night to celebrate. Again came the people, only this time they fawned over both Julius and Judy, and totally ignored Yetta.

Yetta had a good job on the force and the respect of her peers. Delighted as she was with Judy's success, she had never wanted to share the glory vicariously. She didn't need to. Yetta had her own friends, her own life. Helen, Harry, Maude, and even Joe were frustrated, lonely people who played out many hopes, dreams and fantasies through Judy (with Gramma, they had attended every opening the Revuers had in New York). Judy's patience with them and her tendency to humor them only encouraged the interference. None of them ever cashed in on her fame. The increased sense of importance and purpose they got from her was of greater value than money.

Yetta was more complete in herself. Her friendship with Judy preceded the public recognition and continued apart from it, which was something Judy treasured. Judy didn't shop friends by the label. Friendship wasn't a fashion she changed with the season. New York was diversity. At Fifty-eighth Street you might find anyone from a struggling composer to a young writer to a precinct captain to an offbeat mother who misused words and taught piano. Hollywood was not so egalitarian. You had to be seen with the right people in the right places. Visibility was everything, and if you were not in the business, you were not just an outsider, you were nobody. Yetta knew Judy's idea was less a business proposition than a cry of loneliness. But she could not disrupt her life just to pamper her friend. Judy had made a decision to make movies. She was twenty-two, self-supporting, and she would have to stand by that decision. There remained the question of finances. Yetta had witnessed firsthand Judy's loose ways with money. She suggested Judy send back $125 each week from her paycheck, which she would deposit in a savings account as a favor. In effect Judy had a business manager. She still wanted company.

Helen spoke fluent Jewish Mother. If you asked how she was feeling and she said fine, that meant not so good. If you asked whether she needed money and she said no, that meant she was broke. If you asked whether she wanted to come out and live with you in Hollywood and she said eh, that meant she thought you'd never ask. Back east Helen frequently communicated with Judy by rumor. Then Maude or Joe or one of Helen's friends would call and say what was going on. With Judy out west, the rumor hotline broke down. Long distance phonecalls were costly and imperfect. Letters took forever. When Judy finally learned that Helen was going around grumbling about being abandoned and not even receiving a heartfelt invitation to come out, she was incensed. She had enough to worry about without having to decipher Helen's messages and play diplomat. She phoned and insisted she come out. Helen agreed. As it was, Judy spoke fluent Jewish Daughter, otherwise known as reflexive guilt. After the independence of Fifty-eighth Street and the move west, it was an enormous step backward.

With Helen safely en route, Judy proceeded to get involved with Nick Ray. It was as if she were ashamed of her continuing dependence on her mother and would make a show of free will by seeing the one suitor Helen least liked. On the surface Judy was simply resuming an interest that had been interrupted a year ago with Nick's departure for Hollywood. They always had plenty of interests in common—theater, music, writing, directing. Added to that was another bond: they were young, gifted, and sorely out of their element in Hollywood. They also shared the friendship of John Houseman.

Houseman was a friend of actress Doris Dudley, who had a beach house in Santa Monica. Judy, Nick, and Houseman drove out there one afternoon. Judy had a few drinks, Nick had a few more. Both were depressed: Hollywood was squandering their talent. Life was awful, they agreed, and it looked worse with each drink. Somebody suggested a dip in the ocean. Judy and Nick waded out into the waves, when with inebriated wisdom they decided that life was no longer worth living. They swam straight out into Santa Monica Bay. The swells grew, the currents stiffened, and they changed their minds. The only problem was, they were a good distance from shore. Groggy and exhausted, they eventually struggled back to the beach. Houseman helped them to the house and provided them with coffee and dry clothes. Once the fright of the halfhearted suicide attempt receded, they had a good laugh. For such talented misunderstood people their stunt was like an overwrought scene out of *A Star Is Born*.

Helen arrived in Los Angeles and moved in with Judy over

the real-estate office. It was the first time they'd lived together in over four years, and the reunion was rocky. Judy was waiting for something to break at Fox and Helen was feeling the strain of her first real separation from friends and family. The tension eased once Helen was reunited with a cousin, Mary, who had come west years ago. The adjustment went speedily from there. Helen liked the weather, the glamour, and most of all she liked having Judy to herself again. She was so content that she was not even tempted to return east when she learned that Rachel had died. In truth, she almost seemed relieved at the news. For her part, Judy did what she could to make her mother feel welcome. She took her to dinners, to parties, and occasionally even on dates. People never objected to Helen's presence as something odd or unnatural. Helen was Helen, no matter the company, fracturing the language and exuding her enjoyment of people without regard for title or status. Judy did not treat her like some unwieldy social baggage. She was not in the practice of apologizing for intimates. Helen was just a peculiar person-ality who happened to be Judy's mother. There was at once something tender and pathetic about that.

Since signing with Fox, the only thing that had changed for Judy was her name. The publicity people maintained that Tuvim was too difficult to pronounce. Judy thought this was nonsense. She had never found that to be a problem in the past. The publicity people noted that in the past she had been a member of a group and was lucky if the public remembered her first name, let alone her last. All the while, Judy suspected that the real objection was that Tuvim was Hebrew, and much as she hated to admit it, that was a serious consideration. The movie-going public was hardly prepared to accept a starlet of even nominal Jewish extraction. Industry veterans posed the standard example: How far would Theda Bara have gotten as Theodosia Goodman?

There was an added side to Hollywood's habit of renaming its minions. Although there was the infrequent instance of a performer coming from theater reputation and name intact, moguls emphasized the discovery side of the business. A Louis Mayer couldn't write, direct, or act, but he could discover, claiming a kind of mystic vision of star material. A calculated Hollywood mythology grew up around this way of thinking. Whereas theater actresses ascended slowly through hard work, study, and mastery of their craft, movie actresses were found like coins on the sidewalk. The more outlandish the setting for discovery—the counter at Schwab's, a picture in a magazine, an act at the Trocadero—the better to reaffirm the myth. Renaming was part of this ritual of alchemy. Darryl F. Zanuck, head of Fox, was a leading practitioner of renaming, and he was making no exceptions.

Judy was not so easily outmaneuvered. She granted "Tuvim" might not be the most memorable name for a starlet, but wanted no part of the stagy aliases offered by the publicity people. "Tuvim" comes from "tovim" which is Hebrew for "good." "Yom tovim" means "holiday," and so Judy came up with "Holliday," adding the second "l" to avoid confusion with singer Billie Holiday. The experience taught her that even within the studio factory, there were small ways of keeping your identity.

In Hollywood it was one thing to be employed, and quite another to be working. Judy drew a weekly check but got no film assignments. She figured the only way to stir any interest was to make herself as fetching as possible. For a young woman who had a low opinion of her looks and a high opinion of food, this took some doing. She was not athletic and so dieted without benefit of exercise. Her apartment opened up onto a tar-covered roof area, where she went daily for sunbathing. She had her hair cut to frame and flatter her face, with a sultry spill of curls over the forehead.

Within months her weight was less than it had been since high school and her skin had taken on an exotic tint. She bought a new outfit and arranged a photo session at the Powers and Conover model agency. She arrived, fixed herself up, and the photographer said great. Five minutes later the photographer looked up and said "What happened?" Her clothes looked rumpled, her hair looked confused, and what little self-confidence she projected went off when the lights went on. Other starlets could be molded—they were all size five, a little bit blond, a little bit naive. They conformed to clothes, to lighting, to coiffure. Their glossies were virtually interchangeable, they were chameleons. Judy's face had character. No matter what was done cosmetically, she was Judy. Her glamour had a half-life of five minutes.

Finally she received a call from casting about a film version of the Dorothy Fields/Cole Porter musical *Something for the Boys*. Judy came in and had a look at the script. They showed her her part, and seconds later she looked up in disbelief. "It's two lines."

"But it's Technicolor," they reassured. "How many girls get the chance to be seen in full color? Think how beautiful you'll look."

For once, Judy was susceptible to flattery. At least she'd be able to show off her trim figure and tan. That fond hope lasted until she reported to wardrobe and came out wearing overalls, a bandanna that fully covered her hair, and a pair of goggles that made her look like an insect. With an outfit like that they could have saved the trouble and used a bit actor in drag. The producers explained that the movie was intended as a morale-builder for servicemen. By that they meant shapely women were supposed to cram every spare inch of film. Judy thought they were trying to build something more than morale.

After limited negotiations Judy won a small concession and would be permitted to lift her goggles before reciting her lines. She came to the set a few days later wearing her Rosie the Riveter uniform and spoke her first uncut lines for film posterity: "I knew a girl once who had carborundum in her teeth, and she turned into a radio receiving set." At least it had certain plot value. Carmen Miranda was that radio set in a story which didn't bear repeating and which also starred Phil Silvers, Vivian Blaine, and Perry Como.

Whether by dint of this compliance or a wish to extract some return on a $400-a-week investment, Fox came to Judy about another role that required several lines and no overalls. Moss Hart had written a play about the gallant young men of the U.S. Army Air Force and the sacrifices demanded of them and their long-suffering young wives. *Winged Victory* had a successful run on Broadway and was now being made as a movie under the direction of George Cukor. Judy came in to read for the part and Cukor was somewhat put off by her dime-store glamour getup. But that only heightened his reaction to the reading that followed. She was untrained and inexperienced, he could see that immediately. Yet she brought a sensitivity and originality to the character that none of the other actresses under consideration had found. When she was through, he asked if she could do the same thing before cameras. Judy said sure and was given her first real role.

The story focused on several cadets who face the rigors of flight school in preparation for the perils of actual combat. Edmond O'Brien was Irving Miller, affectionately known as "Brooklyn," the spark plug and father figure for the current crop of cadets. Judy played Ruthie, his New York Jewish wife. So much for studio efforts to anglicize their protégé.

Winged Victory was a service picture whose entire male cast consisted of enlisted actors. The Air Force lent full cooperation through technical assistance and flight photography. The women had a secondary status and didn't even appear until the film was over an hour old. Judy's sequence begins at graduation ceremonies, continues through a weekend furlough, and ends with the pilots' departure for the Pacific. Ruthie and Irving have a young son, and so Judy was made up to look older than her real twenty-two years. She was very convincing as the wife and mother. She wore tailored conservative clothes that emphasized her hard-won figure. Her pear-shaped face with its shy smile, gentle dimples, and kind eyes was very photogenic. She handled her lines with a soft sexiness and self-assurance and seemed very much the sort of woman Irving Miller would have chosen. She even held up under such dialogue as "You're quite a goil, Ruthie."

Winged Victory was completed that September and released two months later. The movie was well received, even though it concentrated more on the human side of events rather than the blood-and-guts combat footage audiences were coming to expect. People brought their own personal experiences to the story, and that helped bridge various theatrical excesses. The reviews made little or no mention of Judy, but she stood up well in her first feature role and was improved for her work with Cukor, one of the top directors in the business. Still a single truth stuck in her mind: she had done nothing a hundred other movie actresses couldn't have done just as well.

Yetta and Judy kept in touch by phone. Yetta called whenever the checks stopped coming. Judy called whenever she felt like it, without regard for the three-hour time difference. Yetta's phone rang one morning at three o'clock. She answered ready to hear some tale about studio politics or how Helen put sugar in the stew again.

"Hello, is this Yetta Cohn? I'm sorry to bother you at this hour, this is Nick Ray."

She vaguely remembered a Nick whom Judy had known in New York. She'd never met the man.

"Look, I know you're Judy's best friend," he continued. "I thought you could help me. Judy's broken off with me."

Yetta didn't even know they'd been seeing each other. She could tell he was very upset and probably a bit drunk. She did what she could to comfort him, adding, "I'm terribly sorry, but there's nothing I can do."

They talked for a few minutes longer, he apologized again and said good-bye. Later, when Yetta mentioned the call, Judy confirmed that she had been seeing him, that it hadn't worked out, and that there was nothing more to say about it. Helen had no influence over the split. Whatever reason Judy had for leaving Nick, she kept to herself.

In late autumn 1944 Yetta decided to check in on Judy and came out with her good friend Ruth Brooke. Judy met them at the station in a dilapidated old limousine she had purchased for $700, with an enclosed chauffeur's compartment and a speaking tube to the rear. Judy was a terrible driver but Los Angeles is a driving town and she insisted on taking them for a tour of the Hollywood Hills. Between the oversized car and the narrow winding roads it was like a lethal roller-coaster ride. Judy thought it was hilarious until she lost control on a sharp curve and the car skidded onto the lawn of Pickfair, the fabled estate of Mary Pickford and Douglas Fairbanks. Judy had the car towed back to the road and by popular demand kept to the lowlands.

There was an Alice-in-Wonderland quality about Judy in Hollywood. None of her past experience applied here. There was no scale, no aesthetic balance, no sense of locale. Judy seldom went to the symphony or ballet back in New York. She liked theater and nightclubs, both of which were in short supply here. Appearances had never impressed her, and here appearances were everything. She was a nighttime urban person in a daylight decentralized town. So much of what she witnessed here seemed unreal if not downright surreal. But there was an underside to it all that was painfully real. Judy recounted:

"Remember the red suit?" Judy and Yetta wore the same size clothes. A block from their old place on Fifty-eighth Street was a swanky dress shop known as Wilma's. The prices were astronomical, far more than the two of them could afford. One of the salesgirls there, Lee Williamson, was a girlfriend of Abe Tuvim. Lee was very fond of Judy, and whenever a sale was approaching, she would call and give her first crack at the reduced merchandise. Wilma catered to a select clientele, many of whom happened to be kept women, so the clothes tended to be flashy and pricey. Judy and Yetta shopped according to their more conservative tastes and budget. Their prize purchase was a dressy tailored red suit with a white satin blouse. When Judy left for the coast, Yetta insisted she take the outfit.

Judy with her father, Abe. *(Author's collection)*

On vacation in France. From left, Judy's mother, Helen; her grandmother Rachel Gollomb; her uncle Joe Gollomb; and Judy. *(Author's collection)*

Judy *(far right)* after winning the junior high school division in a citywide essay contest. *(Author's collection)*

NEW YORK

Winners of State Chamber Essay Competition

Herald Tribune photo—Frank

Ruth Narins, New Utrecht High School, Brooklyn; Charlotte M. Crawford, Cathedral High School, and Judith Tuvin, Junior High School 125, Queens, who captured honors in their respective divisions

The original Revuers, as seen in 1942. From top, Adolph Green, Betty Comden, John Frank, Judy, and Al Hammer. *(UPI)* Below, the Revuers in a scene from the film *Greenwich Village*. From left, Adolph, Betty, Al, and Judy. *(Courtesy Lee Israel)*

Judy Holliday, movie starlet. *(Author's collection)*

Judy with Paul Douglas in the famous gin game scene from the Broadway play *Born Yesterday*. *(Wide World Photos)*

At home in the hi-fi room on Waverly Place. *(Nina Leen*, Life *magazine,* © *Time Inc.)*

Clarence Kold looks on as Katharine Hepburn cross-examines Judy in a scene from *Adam's Rib*. *(Author's collection)*

Judy, as Billie Dawn, eavesdropping on Broderick Crawford in the film version of *Born Yesterday*. *(Author's collection)*

Above left, with William Holden in *Born Yesterday*. *(Author's collection);*
Right, Judy tearfully accepts an Oscar for "Best Actress" for her role as
Billie Dawn in *Born Yesterday*. *(Wide World Photos)*

Judy with a disappointed Gloria Swanson, who lost her bid for an
Oscar, and José Ferrer, who won "Best Actor." *(UPI)*

Gloria Swanson congratulates Judy as José Ferrer looks on. *(UPI)*

A congratulatory kiss from husband David Oppenheim. *(UPI)*

Judy continued, "One afternoon my agent Kurt Frings called. He said Darryl Zanuck wanted to see me. He was very excited. 'This could be your big chance. Get dressed, I'll pick you up.' I put on my best outfit, the red suit from Wilma's."

A short while later Frings pulled up outside Judy's apartment, driving the inevitable status symbol of the successful Hollywood agent—a baby-blue Cadillac convertible with the top down. Some other actress could take a drive in the open air and come out looking radiantly windswept. Judy would probably come out looking like Harpo Marx. She got into the car, and Frings looked her over. "The outfit is all wrong, but we'll fix it when we get to the studio."

They drove to Fox, through the front gate, and straight to the wardrobe department. Frings was shown a number of dresses; then he picked one and handed it to Judy. She went to a nearby dressing room and reappeared a few minutes later in a striking pleated dress with a plunging neckline. Plump, Judy had no bust to speak of. Slender, there was almost nothing at all.

Frings studied her and shook his head—still not quite right. He consulted with the wardrobe lady and returned with a pair of falsies. Judy took them, made the necessary adjustments, and voilà—cleavage. Frings grinned. "There!"

He took Judy to the main office building and escorted her past four secretaries before coming at last to Zanuck's personal secretary, who told them they would have to wait and asked them to be seated. Thirty minutes later a buzzer sounded on the secretary's desk and she announced, "Mr. Zanuck will see you now." The two stood and stepped toward the office. The secretary then instructed, "Not you, Mr. Frings, just Miss Holliday."

"Then I knew I was in trouble," Judy recounted. "I went in through these great big doors and into an office that seemed to be bigger than Grand Central. Way down at one end was Zanuck sitting in an electric wheelchair and dressed completely in a polo outfit, including a mallet. Suddenly he rolled down the room in his wheelchair, swinging the mallet. I made the mistake of standing in front of a couch. The chair stopped and he jumped at me. I lost my balance and fell on the couch. He landed on my lap and said loudly, 'I must have you! I must have you!'

"I stood up and he fell on the floor. I pleaded, 'But, Mr. Zanuck, you can have any beautiful girl in the studio. Why pick me?'

"Again he pushed me, again I landed on the couch with him on my lap, pawing at me and saying, 'You belong to me. You belong to me.'

"That did it. I struggled to my feet, he fell on the floor. I pulled out the falsies and told him, 'These belong to you, Mr. Zanuck, but I don't.'"

Yetta and Ruth could see the absurdity of it all, but they were not laughing. "Then what?" they asked.

"I walked out," Judy answered. She might also have added that she walked out on her future at Fox. Darryl F. Zanuck did not take sexual rejection lightly.

Prior to Yetta and Ruth's arrival Judy had received an invitation to an afternoon tennis and cocktail party at Charlie Chaplin's estate. Though Chaplin had curtailed his acting since the advent of talking pictures, he was still a power in the industry and invitations to his home were highly regarded. Judy planned to spend the early afternoon in Beverly Hills with Yetta and Ruth and then have them drop her off at the party. They had some drinks and a long laugh-filled lunch at Trader Vic's. Slightly tight, the three of them went over to Rodeo Drive and window-shopped. They came to Adrian's, an exclusive boutique run by the fabled designer. There was one concave display window in which a lone spotlight shone dramatically on a single elegant pair of shoes that surely cost a fortune. Judy and Ruth simultaneously looked down at their feet; both were wearing simple Mexican sandals. Without saying a word to each other, they removed the sandals and propped them on the exterior ledge just beneath the Adrians, so that they seemed to be part of the display. The three women laughed and walked back to the car.

The Chaplin mansion stood at the far end of a long circular driveway. The place was already alive with guests when Yetta drove up. Judy stepped shoelessly from the car and waved good-bye. By the time Yetta and Ruth navigated the remaining half-circle back to the entrance, Judy was there and flagged them down.

"I decided I'd have more fun with you than at this silly party," she told them. They cruised back to Adrian's, snatched their shoes from the ledge, and took off for a night on the town.

In a community as inbred and status-conscious as Hollywood, parties were serious business. You courted producers and directors. You sniped at rival actresses. You chatted up the gossip columnists. Party lists were published like box scores: you saw how you were doing in the standings, whether you were first string, second string, or on your way to the minor leagues. Judy had no gift for this sort of society; what's more, no interest. It was like a desert lake—a mile wide and an inch deep.

A few days later Judy and Helen and Helen's cousin Mary went down to the train station to see off Yetta and Ruth. Christmas was approaching. Judy looked around at the gaunt palm trees and the pavement shimmering with heat, and thought of the Rockefeller Center tree and the shop windows along Fifth Avenue and the many people she missed. Yetta and Ruth stepped onto the train platform and Judy burst into tears. The conductor called passengers aboard. Helen turned to Judy and commanded, "Go on. Go back with them for a week, I'll be all right."

Judy was dumbfounded. She hugged Helen, and without so much as a toothbrush, took off for New York.

Two weeks later Judy was reluctantly back in Hollywood waiting for the studio's next move. She didn't have to wait long. A call came for her at the apartment, and the conversation lasted only a moment or two. Judy approached Helen and with more relief than grief said, "They didn't pick up my option." Within days they were on a train east. Judy had Christmas in New York after all.

Not long after Judy's abrupt departure, Sylvia Regan was driving her regular route to Fox. She pulled wide to avoid a man on a bicycle, when she noticed the man was Bobby Lewis, whom she'd known from the old days of the Group Theater. She stopped, said hello, and offered him a lift. He thanked her and tossed his bike in the back.

"Bobby, what are you doing here?"

"Oh, I was signed by MGM."

Sylvia thought of her own periodic doldrums at Fox. "Are they giving you anything to do?"

"You know what it's like in these Hollywood studios," Bobby reflected. "They hire you for your talent, but if they catch you using it, they fire you."

Sylvia sighed and thought of Judy.

7

~~~~~~~~~~~~~

The lobby of the Adelphi Theater was packed with first-nighters. With all the fidgety tuxedos it looked like a penguin convention. The occasion was the opening of *On the Town*, and judging by the level of anticipation after just the first-act curtain, the show was well on its way to becoming a hit.

Less than a year ago Adolph had straggled back from the West Coast and joined Betty in an abbreviated version of the Revuers for an engagement at the Blue Angel. As far as they could tell, Judy and Al were on the road to success in pictures and they were on the road to perpetual nightclub limbo. Leonard Bernstein dropped by one night between shows. Lennie was riding the crest of popularity gained through his scoring of Jerome Robbins' ballet *Fancy Free*. He had with him two young men, Paul Feigay and Oliver Smith, who were eager to co-produce a musical comedy based on the ballet. Would Betty and Adolph be interested in supplying the book and lyrics? He didn't have to ask twice.

The threesome went to work at once. Betty and Adolph

talked through the material, with Betty taking notes in longhand as she had with the Revuers. Sometimes the lyrics preceded the music, other times the reverse. In short order Betty and Adolph completed the story of three sailors on shore leave in New York City. There were no fewer than three romantic subplots, the central one having to do with an elusive Miss Turnstiles whose picture is spotted at the outset on a subway billboard. Jerry Robbins reworked portions of *Fancy Free* and added new choreography. Lennie exercised his fondness for popular music which he intermingled with symphonic passages unprecedented in Broadway musical comedy. Betty and Adolph the writers remained faithful to Betty and Adolph the performers and installed a pair of plum character parts for themselves.

The producers went about capitalizing the show and got a commitment from RKO in return for first refusal on film rights. That agreement went by the boards when MGM purchased the film rights outright for $100,000 in cash up front, with an additional substantial investment in the stage production itself. It was the first time a deal of this sort had taken place, and this was before the show had even gone into rehearsal. The early tryouts confirmed expectations. Although the rest of the score was excellent, the undisputed standout was the rousing opening anthem, "New York, New York." The show worked beautifully, with an unusual balance of song, story, and dance.

Judy was fresh from her break with Fox when she attended the December 28 opening with Yetta and Ruth. At the first intermission she went to the lobby for a breath of air. Ruth could see she was upset. "What's wrong, Judy?"

Judy answered, "This is a great show. They've got it made." Then she observed, "They're going to make it, and I'm not." There was no anger or jealousy in her voice. There was no self-recrimination about leaving the act. She was simply making a statement of fact. Only a year ago Judy had been in, Betty and Adolph out. Now all that had changed. *On the Town* would be a many-sided triumph for them: in one stroke they had a theatrical hit, principal acting roles in that hit, and a built-in link to the same Hollywood that so recently had treated them so roughly. This was Judy's measure of her own career progress, and as far as she could tell, she'd come full circle to nowhere.

The last two acts of the musical were as good as the first, and the curtain came down to a standing ovation. Judy made her way through the giddy commotion backstage. Her eyes widened, her smile flashed, and she congratulated Betty, Adolph, and Lennie. She then left them to their well-deserved celebration. She felt genuinely happy for them, and genuinely sorry for herself.

To make matters worse, Judy could not move back in with Yetta. Without funds for a place of her own, Judy rejoined her mother on Seventy-fifth Street. Helen could not have been better. She was understanding, nurturant, with unflinching faith in her daughter. She gave Judy all the privacy she wanted, and even kept the family at arm's length. But the very apartment was a token of Judy's failure. She felt like she was back at the Mercury switchboard again.

Fortunately for Judy and Helen, Yetta's prudence with the Fox paycheck had left them a slight financial cushion. Just how slight was clear when Judy went on a shopping trip with Helen, paid a substantial sum for a mink coat and had to borrow cab fare back uptown. Judy went home, snuggled in her fur, ate what she pleased, and caught a cold.

A few days later Judy met Adolph for lunch. When they were through, Adolph announced he had to see Herman Shumlin about something. Judy tried to excuse herself, but Adolph persuaded her to come along. "It won't take a minute." Shumlin was a leading director whose credits numbered three Lillian Hellman plays. Two years earlier he had braved Hollywood to direct the film of Hellman's *Watch on the Rhine*. At present he was casting a play by Luther Davis adapted from Frederic Wakeman's novel *Shore Leave*. All parts had been filled except that of Alice, a good-hearted tramp. Adolph knew this but said nothing to Judy. He told her that he wanted to invite Shumlin to see *On the Town*.

Shumlin took one look at Judy and offered her the role. Judy was flattered, but instead of jumping at the chance, asked for time to think it over. She told Shumlin she'd get back to him, and left with Adolph, who took her aside the second they were out of the office. "What, are you crazy? Take it."

"I've never been onstage before as a character. Sure, I've done skits and the movie, but that was different. I don't know if I can sustain a character."

Judy went off to talk it over with a friend. Later that day she went back to Shumlin's office and signed for the play.

Kiss Them for Me told of three veteran Navy pilots on four-day leave in San Francisco. The play had its lighter moments, but it was hardly a nonmusical version of the resolutely upbeat *On the Town*. Freddie Wakeman had served as a combat pilot in the Pacific and had considerable insight into the conflicting emotions of fighting men on leave. The pilots fall prey to a war profiteer and navy red tape as their plans for a good time are soon thwarted. By close they are fully disenchanted with civilian life and eager to get back to the lethal logic of combat.

The cast was strong, and it included Richard Widmark and Jayne Cotter (later Meadows), each in their fourth Broadway appearance. Of the principal players, Judy was the only one without prior experience in legitimate theater, and it showed. She was determined to create Alice through detail and not broad comic strokes. In her fear of overprojecting, Judy undercompensated and throughout rehearsals was barely audible. The cast was encouraging and Shumlin explained to her that subtlety was fine but futile if the audience had to resort to lip-reading.

The production moved to Philadelphia for tryouts and Judy readied herself for the amenities of real theater. She and Jayne were taken backstage and shown first the bathroom, which looked like it belonged in a downtown bus terminal, and then down a long hall to the dressing room they would share, which if anything was a variation on the bathroom. The paint was peeling, the light was bad, and the sink had fallen from its wall brackets and wobbled on pipes like stilts. Judy's initiation into legitimate theater was complete when the house janitor showed up the next day and accused the girls of breaking the sink by sitting in it and relieving themselves. The more Judy and Jayne denied it, the more positive he was. And Judy had thought the dressing room at the Vanguard was bad.

The Philadelphia opening was spotty. The first two acts played well, but the third act descended into melodrama and finally gung-ho bravado and the audience didn't buy it. Judy was the one consistently bright spot. She began to come up in voice and performance without succumbing to caricature. The tart with a heart of gold was a theatrical staple, but Judy brought something distinct and fresh to the character. Alice was sweet and likable and almost childlike in her eagerness to please. Judy gave her a high, small, nasal voice that sounded as if it were pushed through cellophane; it had a peculiar cadence and lyricism somewhere between a giggle and a whimper, which was thoroughly endearing. Two friends had come from New York to see the opening, and when it was over they told Judy, "You stole the show." Judy was more concerned that there would be a show to steal.

Kiss Them for Me opened in New York at the Belasco Theater on March 21, 1945, to mixed reviews. The critics noted that the play fell victim to its shaky third act, and while they differed in their opinions of the performances, they agreed to a man that Judy's Alice was a triumph. The notices were not enough to close the show, and producers John Moses and Mark Hanna tried to build an audience, using Judy as a drawing card. A publicist concocted one stunt which brought Judy to Roseland with a reporter and photographer from *P.M.* newspaper. Wearing her purple broad-shouldered scoop-necked costume, she joined Seymour Peck and Wilbert Blanche at the Fifty-second Street dance hall, which was a favorite with servicemen on furlough. Judy spoke about her days with the Revuers and her Hollywood folly. At Peck's request she discussed Alice and told how by avoiding obvious laughs she was getting more and better laughs. Judy pushed her voice up an octave and recited a line from the play: "Even when I carry *Fortune* magazine, people still act like I'm from the wrong part of town." It was not an obvious gag line, yet Peck laughed as audiences had every night. He asked her more about her approach to acting, and a peculiar thing happened: she demurred. "Actors are always talking about their parts. You know the old gag—about the actor who meets an old friend. The actor talks and talks and talks. Finally he says to his friend, 'Now let's talk about you. What did you think of my last play?'" Another young actress might have milked the interview for all it was worth. This young actress was different.

By now they had attracted a crowd, and Judy accepted a sailor's invitation to dance. She granted one more dance to another sailor, and then said she had to get to the Belasco for that evening's performance. The dozen or so servicemen groaned, and Judy invited them to come see the show. She made her way out of Roseland and down Broadway in her snug purple dress with a uniformed retinue.

That was as far as Judy played the publicity game. She avoided the flashy nightspots where performers on the make worked the columnists for plugs in the papers. Instead she kept to out-of-the-way places. If local gossips wanted to see her, they could buy a ticket at the Belasco. Judy had an added incentive for a low profile. She was having an affair with a married man.

Freddie Wakeman had closely followed the progress of his adapted novel. He was tall, good-looking, with a quick mind and a sometimes brash charm. He had a wife and two children. Through the early phases of the rehearsal and run Judy and Freddie had no more than a nodding acquaintance. When the show fell on hard times, the cast got together and decided that in order to keep the show open and find an audience, they were willing to accept share cuts, provided the author would agree to a proportionately lower share. Judy was elected spokesman. She saw Freddie, won the concession, and soon was seeing quite a bit of him.

Hotel rooms were scarce in wartime New York. The city overflowed with servicemen out for a good time in a hurry. As with ground and air transportation, many hotels gave priority to men in uniform. Judy and Freddie often met at Seventy-fifth Street for meals, but for anything more than dining, the place was not so roomy and Helen was not so broad-minded. They were forced to take what few vacancies they could locate, and that brought them to some Manhattan fleabags the likes of which Judy had never seen.

Judy introduced Freddie to Ruth Brooke over dinner one evening. It started out pleasantly enough. He had a certain style and wit, and Ruth could see where Judy might well be attracted to that. He was also arrogant and flip, which were traits Judy ordinarily detested. Over coffee Ruth put a cigarette to her lips and Freddie struck a match, which he held table-high. Ruth waited several seconds before he brought the match to the cigarette.

"You're a lady," he told her.

"What do you mean?"

"If you weren't, you would have lowered your cigarette to the match instead of waiting for me to raise it to you."

Ruth thought: "You, you son of a bitch, are no gentleman." She wanted to take Judy aside and say: What the hell are you doing with him? This guy's a real shit. But there was no point. For whatever time Judy was involved with a man, she was totally involved. She supported his work, she tolerated his faults. It might have been dependence or devotion or both. Certainly it was the antithesis of the passivity that helped doom Helen's marriage to Abe.

Freddie had begun a second novel, an insider's look at the ruthlessness and venality of the advertising business, in which he had worked for years. Judy indulged her fascination with writing, if only vicariously, and that had a lot to do with her continuing the affair. Whether or not she made any meaningful contribution to the book is unclear and unlikely, but she did come up with its title, *The Hucksters*. The novel created a stir on publication amid rumors that it was a roman à clef, and quickly became a best-seller. *The Hucksters* was dedicated to "J.H.," whom Freddie claimed was theatrical producer Jed Harris. Sometime later Judy confided to intimates that she was J.H.

Kiss Them for Me closed after 111 performances. As with Hollywood, Judy's Broadway experience deposited her not far from where she began. She did receive considerable press attention, but she was wiser for her years as a Revuer and understood that old newspaper clippings were meant for scrapbooks or the bottoms of bird cages. The experience had an unexpected bonus, though, when Judy was given that season's Clarence Derwent Award for the best supporting performance by a nonfeatured player. The distinction helped less than the $500 cash gift it carried.

Judy and Helen had all but gone through the Fox savings and the reduced Broadway paychecks. Harry did what he could, but bills went unpaid. Judy was unemployed several months when she auditioned for and was offered Betty Field's role in a touring company of *Dream Girl*. Judy turned it down, although the decision was more reasoned and less high-handed than people assumed. A tour paid decent wages and kept you onstage before an audience. But it required prolonged absence from New York and could become a kind of working exile. Judy had resolved to make it in New York or not at all. She sequestered herself in Helen's apartment and did crossword puzzles to stave off mental stagnation and ate to stave off depression. The puzzles worked, but the more she ate, the fatter she got and the more depressed she grew.

There were two Max Gordons of note in town. One was a nightclub impresario, the other was a ranking Broadway producer. There was one Garson Kanin, a former musician and actor who became the protégé of George Abbott and then Samuel Goldwyn, with a handful of directing credits in theater and in movies. Midsummer of 1945 Garson and his wife, Ruth Gordon, joined Max Gordon, the producer, for dinner at the Colony in Manhattan. Ruth and Max were not related, although he had just produced a play which she had written and performed. Toward the end of the evening, Gar, as he was known, handed Max a thick manila envelope and said, "Here is a play I have written. Tell me as soon as possible what you think of it."

The next morning Max turned to page one of *Born Yesterday* and did not stop turning pages until he was done. He made a luncheon appointment with Gar, bought the option for $1,000, haggled percentages, and granted the author's demand to direct. The deal marked time while Gar directed a play starring Spencer Tracy. Then for better and worse, things began to pop.

Born Yesterday told of a crude, menacing, self-made junkyard magnate named Harry Brock. Brock comes to Washington, D.C., to buy influence on Capitol Hill and brings along his mistress, Billie Dawn. Billie is a hard-boiled ex-chorus girl whose knowledge consists mainly of a few suggestive dance steps, some chirpy melodies, and a vast store of carnal knowledge. Brock hires a journalist with *New Republic* to do what he can to make Billie presentable in polite society. The plot hinges on Billie's rebirth culminating with her disgust for Brock and his vulgar underhanded ways.

Gar had written the play with Jean Arthur in mind. Jean, who was best known for a series of thirties-vintage Frank Capra film fables in which she played variations on an independent but vulnerable career woman, didn't think much of the play. This did not concern Max, who found her manner somewhere between aloof and timid, neither of which were conducive to theater. Gar was unyielding. He talked Jean into signing for $2,500 a week plus a percentage of the gross, and then assured Max he had made the right move.

A month later Gar was in Max's office pleading, "What am I going to do?" Jean demanded line changes before the show ever went into rehearsal. By the time they were in rehearsal, her dissatisfaction extended to entire scenes, to say nothing of the show's healthy sprinkling of gentle gutter language. A star is customarily granted changes within reason. But Gar saw Jean undermining his original conception of Billie, and that scrambled the whole play. Max angrily recounted his early doubts over casting and informed Gar that it was too late to recast the lead. New Haven was two weeks away and he'd have to manage somehow.

The New Haven opening went better than anyone expected. The tranquillity was short-lived. Jean complained of a bad throat, and her performance steadily paled through the Boston opening. She missed several shows. Mary Laslo, who had a minor role as a manicurist and doubled as the understudy, went on gamely but was ill-prepared for the burden. At each performance a number of theatergoers left before the opening curtain and asked for refunds. Max could have cut his losses and closed—it would not have been the first time a production fizzled on the road. But the tryouts so far showed the problem was the star, not the play. It was equally clear that Mary Laslo could not carry the show if Jean suddenly left for good. Max was walking a high wire without a net.

Gar brought in three separate name actresses to see the show and was handed three separate refusals. The primary deterrent was Paul Douglas as Harry Brock. The more Jean resisted the play, the more he chewed the scenery, until Douglas, then best known as a radio announcer, was commanding all the better notices. No established actress seemed willing to fight those odds. Meanwhile, through a mixture of flattery and threat, Jean performed a few more times in Boston, but was lackluster and repeatedly went up on her lines. That weekend the production was due to move on to Philadelphia for its final tryout. Gar and Max arranged to stop over in New York for the sole purpose of finding a suitable backup for their skittish star.

John Houseman had returned east to direct a musical called *Lute Song*. The show was on the tryout circuit one step ahead of *Born Yesterday*, whose troubles were an open secret in the business. Houseman's show, on the other hand, looked to be in good shape, so he arranged a week away and left matters in the capable hands of his assistant director, Nick Ray. Houseman owned a country house in New City, a small town on the

Hudson not far from New York. Judy had been a frequent guest there in the past, and Houseman invited her to come up for the week. Judy arrived, moped, did crossword puzzles, wrote poetry, and ate.

On Thursday the phone rang at the Seventy-fifth Street apartment. Helen answered and was greeted by a man's voice.

"Hello, this is Max Gordon."

"Oh, Max, I'm so glad you called. I don't know what to do with Judy. She's depressed. She's fat as a pig. She does nothing but eat. She's in real trouble. Max, you've got to help me. I don't know what to—"

"Just a minute, can you tell me how to get in touch with—"

"Max, I'm telling you this girl's in terrible trouble. We're in bad shape. We can't pay the bills. She doesn't look for work. All she does is eat."

"Please, I want to get in touch with Judy Holliday. I want to talk to her about a job."

Something clicked in Helen's mind. Why would Max mention Judy's last name? "Is this the Village Vanguard Max Gordon?"

"No, madam! This is the Broadway producer Max Gordon!"

Max had produced plays by Edward and Jerome Chodorov, two brothers with a sister named Belle. Belle Chodorov was a theatrical agent, and it was she who had mentioned Judy to Max. At the same time, Gar had gotten a tip about Judy from the show's designer, Mainbocher. Neither Max nor Gar had seen Judy in *Kiss Them for Me*, but her name was the first thing they'd agreed upon in weeks. On Friday morning Judy came to Max's office. He looked at her, talked with her, but did not give her a script to read. He asked her to step out of the office for a minute and called Gar. "Listen, I've got Judy here, she's absolutely right. I'm sending her over to your hotel right away." Judy went with Belle, and Gar seconded Max's opinion. Nothing more was said.

Max and Gar arrived in Philadelphia on Sunday and were hustled over to the Warwick Hotel, where a Dr. Barborka told them that Jean Arthur was suffering from nervous exhaustion and could not continue. This time there was no flattery, no threat. It was obvious that Jean had been wrong from the start and that Gar's misjudgment had been as much to blame as her own reluctance. Judy was called and told to be in Philadelphia the next day. She got in touch with Freddie Wakeman and asked him to take her down. She then called Woodie Broun. "I guess you heard the news about *Born Yesterday?*"

Yes, he'd heard.

"Well, don't get your hopes up. I hear they've got June Havoc all lined up and they're just bringing me there to help keep her salary down."

Just the same, Woodie wished her luck.

8

~~~~~~~~~~~~~~~~~

J udy arrived at the Warwick Hotel late Monday afternoon. Gar showed her a room, handed her a script, and said, "Read." Two hours later she met with Gar and Max and in the course of discussing the character, recited two long monologues from memory on the lone reading. Gar looked at Max; they knew they had their Billie. "When do we open?" Judy asked.

"Whenever you're ready," Gar said obligingly.

The words were no sooner out than Max corrected, "Saturday night." Judy and Gar were stunned. Max repeated, "Saturday night."

The first priority was to learn the lines. Under normal circumstances a director will keep his cast on book up to two weeks. The assumption runs that it is important to first gain a grasp of character and that a forced, if accurate, recitation can become mechanical and block true character development. Judy was afforded no such luxury. Fortunately she was not a method actor who needed the painstakingly slow and subjective approach of motivation. Judy figured as long as the audience believed her character, what she believed was secondary. She was more technical and cerebral than most actors. For comedy and crisis casting, that was ideal.

Judy had something else working in her favor. John Houseman and Nick Ray were in Philadelphia with *Lute Song* and by chance were also staying at the Warwick. The affair with Nick had resolved itself into a firm, loving friendship. Judy would rehearse days at the Locust Theater, then return to her hotel room, slide into bed, and work late into the night, with Houseman and Nick cuing lines and offering pointers. In effect she had not one but three directors. She rarely ate, and for the odd hour or two that the coffee and Dexedrine wore off, she slept. Max had been concerned about Judy's weight. By the time she reported to Mainbocher for a fitting, the alterations were far less than imagined; she'd already shed ten pounds. The transformation continued when Paul Schmidt arrived from Elizabeth Arden and styled Judy's short hair into a tight nest of light red curls with blond highlights.

Despite the remarkable progress, Judy questioned the wisdom of a Saturday opening. Max had already put back the New York opening one week, and that was as far as he intended to go. He took Judy aside during a rehearsal break. "If you go outside the theater and look, you'll see a long line of people. You know what they're doing? Getting their money back, that's what. There's only one night we can open this show to a full house, and that's Saturday night. We have to open to a full house."

For some reason Judy's crises read like bad Hollywood melodrama. She hadn't really needed Max's the-show-must-go-on oratory, but it made him feel better. As a matter of fact, Houseman and Nick realized that Judy responded to the mounting strain with astonishing calm and concentration. Overnight she seemed to come to life and looked more radiant than either could recall.

Since childhood Judy had grown to expect crisis. In a strange way, that made life safer and more predictable. Relationships continued to be a source of risk and confusion, but she could handle events. Some called her a fatalist, but scratch a fatalist and you'll usually find a nervous optimist. One thing was certain: for a woman with many insecurities, she possessed undeniable nerve. She had a way of escaping inner doubts with a kind of practical mastery. As a Revuer, offstage fear had always converted to onstage grace and excellence; the moment she could stop worrying about herself and start worrying about an audience, she was fine. This deep-seated wish to please was a large source of her performing ease. The fact that she'd been better able to please audiences than herself was something she would eventually have to face. For now, the pressure of *Born Yesterday* was the kind of crisis she loved, a problem for which she ultimately could provide the solution.

Judy could not have been less like the character she was playing. Billie Dawn was uneducated, street-wise, by turns sassy and sullen. She had the cheap theatricality of a dancer who mugged from the chorus line and saved her best dramatic moments for rich thugs like Harry Brock. She was a veteran showgirl with showy tastes and an offhand sexuality. Her wants never went beyond furs, jewels, and a good time. Harry was her meal ticket, and so long as he supplied the creature comforts, she supplied the rest. She hadn't cracked a book since grammar school, and as far as she could tell, magazines and newspapers were for masochists who liked eyestrain.

As with Alice in *Kiss Them for Me*, Judy avoided caricature. She gave Billie a naive charm and child's ingenuousness that contrasted with the outward brassiness. Her attention to detail led to a rare blend of simplicity and density, a sort of unformed integrity which lent credibility to the show's more transparent plot turns. As Jean Arthur had played it, Billie's intellectual, cultural, and ethical awakening seemed sudden and artificial. With Judy it seemed natural and real. Ironically, if Judy had any vague model for Billie, it might have been her own mother. Helen had a similar naiveté, a good-natured daffiness, an openness to people and a willingness to laugh at herself. The high nasal voice was Judy's invention, as was almost everything else about the character. But if friends ever wanted an eloquent defense of Helen, they had to look no further than Billie.

As late as the Saturday matinee, Judy appeared firmly in control. She was happy and confident and surprisingly relaxed for someone who just days before had no more immediate challenge than the morning crossword. The show opened officially that night, January 12, to a full house that included two of the production's better-known backers, George Kaufman and Moss Hart. Gar and Max watched spellbound as Judy delivered what to their minds was a perfect performance. The Philadelphia critics thought as much, with one or two complaints about an overly contrived plot.

The rest of the Philadelphia run was a piece of cake. Max had his customers back and Gar got no backsliding from his four-day wonder. The only discernible problem was with Paul Douglas. Although the reviews were uniformly positive for the entire cast, Judy had clearly stolen Douglas' thunder. She hadn't tried to upstage him; if anything, she underplayed the part. But Douglas, also in his first major role, had expanded into the vacuum left in Jean Arthur's sketchy work and he was now losing ground to a full-blooded Billie. Had it stopped at a bruised ego, Judy might have been more sympathetic. At one point toward the end of Act II, Harry has an argument with Billie and ends by hitting her across the face. Gar staged the encounter with Douglas' back to the audience, partially obscuring Judy so that the stage slap would look more realistic. After the reviews came out, Douglas made it more realistic yet and one time gave Judy an actual cuffing. Judy later told Woodie, and raged, "I hate Paul Douglas." Woodie's answer was uncharacteristically blasé: "Everybody hates Paul Douglas."

The production moved to New York, and Judy moved back in with Helen. The advance word from Philadelphia was superb, but that could cut both ways. Philadelphia critics went expecting a show that was in trouble and were pleasantly surprised. New York critics would go expecting a show that was a hit and could just as easily come away disappointed.

Born Yesterday opened at the Lyceum on February 5, 1946. Judy was in total command of her gifts as an actress. Her Act I gin game with Douglas was a masterpiece of timing and pantomime. More memorable than that was her Act II curtain line, when, after the violent argument with Harry, Billie moves to exit, turns back, and asks gently, "Would you do me a favor, Harry?" "What?" Then, answering her own question with exquisitely false aplomb, "Drop dead?"

The play finished to a sustained ovation, and backstage was bedlam. Judy's relatives and their assorted hangers-on were all in attendance and descended on her dressing room en masse. She couldn't see her friends for the family. Eventually Woodie Broun, joined by a reporter friend, whisked Judy and Yetta away. For some reason there was no cast party, so on Woodie's recommendation, they went to the Stork Club to celebrate in a manner worthy of a newborn Broadway star. At length the maître d' condescended to acknowledge them. As a working newspaperman Woodie considered himself a man about town and took charge of the situation. "I'd like a table for three."

"I'm sorry, we have nothing," the maître d' answered, huffy and disdainful.

Woodie grew angry and started to say, "This is Judy Holliday!" but caught himself, realizing that word traveled fast in New York, but not that fast. He had hoped to impress Judy, and was failing miserably. Judy saw his embarrassment and said, "Forget it."

They went across the street to a chic if lesser watering hole, the Barbary Club, and were seated immediately. They no sooner ordered drinks than Judy asked for the phone.

"Who are you calling?" Yetta asked.

"Mother."

Yetta sighed. Judy got through to Helen and of all things wanted to know where a Cousin Millie had been that night. Cousin Millie was a sixty-year-old eccentric who may or may not have been a distant relative of Helen's; nobody seemed to remember. Cousin Millie was a frequent dinner guest at Seventy-fifth Street and a favorite of Judy's. While waiting in line at the Stork Club, it had occurred to Judy that Cousin Millie was absent backstage, and she wanted to know why. The response was lengthy even for Helen. When Judy finally got off the phone, Woodie and Yetta asked if anything was wrong.

It seems Cousin Millie had recently taken work soliciting donations by phone for an organization. As far as she knew, she was doing some sort of service to humanity. The Manhattan district attorney thought otherwise and just that morning had raided the premises. The organization was in fact involved in an elaborate bit of flimflam and the office workers were arrested as accessories and taken to the Fourteenth Precinct on Thirtieth Street. Yetta could see that Judy was upset by the news. "Look, I'm on the police force. Why don't we go down and see Cousin Millie. Maybe I can do something for her." They hurried through their drinks and sandwiches. The reporter friend excused himself, Woodie picked up the tab, and they piled into a cab for Thirtieth Street.

The desk lieutenant at the Fourteenth looked up and saw three people in evening clothes. Yetta identified herself and asked about Cousin Millie. They were shown to the cell, where Cousin Millie sat on a jailhouse cot and wept. Judy did what she could to comfort her, but Yetta was unable to obtain a release. Yetta told Cousin Millie that a lawyer would be waiting there first thing in the morning and that the lieutenant would keep an eye on her that night. Judy kissed Cousin Millie good-bye.

The visit had taken a few hours and the city editions were already on the street. The threesome stopped at a newsstand and tore through the reviews. As in Philadelphia, there was minor quibbling about dramaturgy, but the critics were unanimous in their praise for Judy. She was the find of the season. After the night's episodes at the Stork Club and the Fourteenth Precinct, Judy, feeling more lost than found, said good night to Yetta and had Woodie take her home to Seventy-fifth Street.

It was a joyless end to what should have been a joyous evening. Judy's behavior was almost superstitious, as if she had to seek out a minor mishap to assure that the major happiness was real and reliable. She was genuinely concerned about Cousin Millie but she also happened to be the most convenient crisis. It could just as easily have been Harry home with an abscess. Judy had her first glimpse of success and spooked. Success was nice, but you had to earn your luck.

Lute Song opened one block from and one night after *Born Yesterday*. The musical starred Mary Martin, and the notices were generally good, but the show was considered esoteric and the prospects for commercial success were not good. Neither show had had a peaceful time out of town, and Judy and John Houseman agreed it was a blessing they both made it to New York at all. They met for lunch that Saturday to celebrate. So much had happened so quickly for Judy, and yet Houseman was struck by how little she had changed. She was excited, of course, though not at all immodest or self-impressed. She was happy to be working, thankful for the recognition, and extremely grateful to Houseman and Nick Ray for their help in Philadelphia.

They finished lunch and Houseman walked Judy to her matinee. He remembered that the Saturday New York *Sun* ran a large theater section and stopped along the way to pick up a copy. He turned to the theatrical page and there was a big ad with pictures of Judy and Paul Douglas alongside each other. Houseman showed the paper to Judy. "Isn't that wonderful?"

Judy looked it over, then wisecracked in her best Billie Dawn voice, "Yeah, if I'd rehearsed more than forty-eight hours I wouldn't be sharing billing with that son of a bitch."

Born Yesterday was playing to packed houses and Judy was making $500 a week. She had no concept of money and so never stopped to think that there might be some disparity in those figures, at least not until her agent, Dick Dorso, pointed it out. When contracts came up for renegotiation, Dorso wanted her weekly salary doubled to $1,000. Max tried to hold the line at $750, but Dorso would not budge. The impasse came to the attention of George Kaufman, who could be as tight-fisted as he was talented. Kaufman berated Dorso and Judy, and also fired off an angry letter to Max, virtually calling him gutless. When the smoke cleared, still no agreement had been reached. Max decided to dump the problem in his playwright's lap and instructed Judy to take up the matter of pay with Gar. Before Judy could consider her next move she got a call from Gar. "I understand you're unhappy."

Judy was caught off-guard. "Well I wouldn't say—"

"I'll pick you up after the theater and we'll talk about your problem."

That night after the show a chauffeur-driven limousine waited for Judy outside the stage door. Inside were Gar and Ruth, whose pet name was Bug. Judy got in, and Gar ordered the driver to the Stork Club, scene of Judy's opening-night brush-off. As the car made its way across town, Gar mused, "I love money. Money means I can have a limousine take me to the Stork Club. It means I can buy Bug here anything she wants. Jesus, money is wonderful."

Judy took this as an auspicious beginning. They arrived at the club and were ushered without delay to an elite inner room. Gar summoned the sommelier, ordered champagne, and turned to Judy. "Now, then, what seems to be the problem?"

"Well," Judy confided, "it's a question of money."

"Money?" Gar recoiled. "What's money?"

Ever the good student, Judy quoted from the limousine lecture: "Money means you can have a chauffeured limousine. Money means you can buy Bug anything she wants." Judy became flustered, unable to continue. She grabbed her handbag and ran crying from the place. She would not compromise her dignity and pride for the sake of dollars. At no price would she endure rudeness.

Max considered possible replacements, but it was a waste of time. Much as he hated to admit it, Judy was the play. The mishandling and mistreatment only stiffened Dorso's resolve. He turned down offers of $750 and $900. Finally Max's general manager, Ben Boyar, steered a middle course that allowed all involved to save face. If Judy would accept $900, they would throw in a car as a bonus. A truce was called, and Judy signed a run-of-the-play contract. A few days later she went out to pick up her bonus and discovered that Ben Boyar had gotten her a secondhand car.

Judy held very high standards. In part this was a logical extension of her own high integrity. It was also a psychological safeguard she had developed in childhood: friendship made you vulnerable, and if a friend betrayed a trust, he was no longer a friend. That reduced the risk of hurt, along with the number of close friends. As a corollary, Judy acquired a certain professional withdrawal. Outwardly she would remain cordial and open to superficial interaction while inwardly she would draw strict emotional boundaries. She continued to respect and accept Max and Gar professionally; personally she kept her distance.

For the first time Judy had her career in order. *Born Yesterday* settled in for a long run, she knew what she was doing today, tomorrow, a year from now. That left her to face her personal life. What few relationships she'd had were fleeting and unfulfilling, escapes from discontentment with life. Life was good in 1946 and Judy was eager to share it with one man. She talked increasingly to family and friends about marriage. When the *Daily Mirror*'s Sidney Fields dropped by Seventy-fifth Street to interview her about the play, she talked about little else. She told him she was dabbling in painting and sculpture, refinishing furniture, and was even trying her hand at a novel. But she was lonely, and what she really wanted was a man.

Fields asked her what she had in mind.

"Nothing much. He has to be smarter than I am. Much smarter. I like writers. I don't like actors. They're impossible. They're vain exhibitionists, and they all live in a big vacuum. You need them on the stage. Do you have to have them in your life?"

Fields was concerned that the article might read like a classified ad. Did she really want him to write what she said?

"Put it down. Say I want to get married. I'm as eligible as hell. Gee, it's almost as hard as finding an apartment."

9

〜〜〜〜〜〜〜〜〜〜

Woodie Broun suspected something was up when Judy broke their date at the last minute. The opening-night folly had been bad enough, a quick sandwich and a courtesy call to the Fourteenth Precinct. That was all unforeseen, but this was clearly Judy's fault. Woodie called and said, "I'll pick you up after the show."

"I forgot," Judy told him. "I made another date. You don't mind."

"I do mind," Woodie snapped back, and hung up.

Judy went out instead with a young classical musician named David Oppenheim. They had met a few years before when David was still a struggling clarinetist at the Eastman School of Music in Rochester. David was in town visiting his friend Leonard Bernstein, who took him to see the Revuers at Café Society Downtown. David was introduced to Judy and made up his mind to see her again. He called a few days later at two in the morning and asked if she wanted to go for a walk. Judy said no thanks.

David went off to war and while serving in Germany he came

across Judy's picture in *Life* magazine for her work in *Kiss Them for Me*. He clipped the picture and told buddies this was his girlfriend. David returned to New York during the summer of 1945, resumed playing the clarinet, and renewed his friendship with Lennie, who helped get him a job performing with the New York City Symphony at City Center. A year passed before David got back in touch with Judy. By then she had opened in *Born Yesterday* and was advertising her availability. David looked her up under the pretext of signing some civil-rights petition. This time Judy was more receptive and they started seeing each other.

David was six-feet-two with thick dark hair and a winsome schoolboy grin. He was well-fed and looked younger than his twenty-six years. Judy's close friends claimed they saw a vague resemblance to her father. The two men were alike in coloring and size, but David had a certain softness, whereas Abe was gentle in a bearlike way, and David's sexiness was more understated than Abe's.

Actually David was very much like Judy in the scope and curve of his thinking and in a disarming charm that could give way suddenly to dark, distant moods. Like Judy he tended to be a loner, with many casual but few close friends. Helen, who had frowned on Nick and Freddie, heartily approved of David. He was educated, handsome, talented, and Jewish. Uncle Joe was not so sure, although it had less to do with David personally than with the threat he might pose to Joe's patriarchal posturing. But the family endorsements were incidental. Judy loved David and meant to marry him as soon as she could get him to propose.

It was a relatively brief but at times bumpy courtship. There were some heated quarrels after which David would disappear. This was special torment for Judy, who kept close tabs on her loved ones. But for every fight there were many more good times, dinners out or evenings in with plenty of bright talk and laughter. Even Uncle Joe had to admit they were an impressive pair. There was a strong attraction between Judy and David, and when they were right together, their incandescence could light a room. Marriage moved from possibility to probability to certainty. David proposed and a date was set.

Sure as she was about David, Judy was concerned that the marriage get off on the right foot. She was sufficiently publicity-wise to know that the press was an imperfect mirror with a potentially painful impact on life. A year and more onstage with Paul Douglas taught her that. Judy was a naturally private person and wanted to preserve the privacy of her wedding. Beyond that she was afraid that the press might turn it into an item of theatrical gossip, and the last thing she wanted was to read about Broadway star Judy Holliday marrying some anony-mous clarinetist. David deserved better than that. As a precau-tion, the ceremony would not be held in a public facility where a nosy employee was sure to leak word to Winchell or Killgallen. And since Judy was working, there was no time to retreat to some discreet place out of town. The options rapidly narrowed to one location—Seventy-fifth Street.

It was an odd array of people that crammed into Helen's apartment on January 4, 1948. There were David's mother and brother, Adolph, and Betty and Steve. Harry and Maude fussed and meddled. Abe and Helen seemed perfectly at ease with each other. Joe made a pretense of reconciliation with Abe and Yetta, both of whom he had hounded with poison-pen letters in the past. The rabbi, a cousin of Yetta's, was also the official chaplain for Actor's Equity. At the last minute Yetta learned he planned to use the event for some personal publicity. With some strong language she told him that the wedding was to remain secret, and he agreed.

Toward late afternoon David arrived from a day-long record-ing session. There was a brief ceremony after which the guests were served champagne and cold cuts. The affair was catered by Fine and Shapiro Delicatessen. It was a Sunday, so Judy had no performance that night and none the next. The newlyweds left by late evening and grabbed a cab for a quiet honeymoon at the Plaza. They had already leased a flat on Waverly Place in the Village, and so by day's end Judy had the two things that had eluded her—a husband and an apartment. She also had a mother to whom she was still very much attached. After a romantic stay at the Plaza, Judy and David spent their second evening of wedlock over dinner at Helen's.

Yetta instinctively cringed when Judy mentioned that dinner. From her days on Fifty-eighth Street Yetta knew that without stiff ground rules the family would be forever underfoot. There would always be the phone calls and the regular visits uptown; that much was inevitable. But unless David firmly established the autonomy of the marriage, he was asking for trouble. At face value the dinner at Helen's seemed innocent enough. In Yetta's mind it was a test, a sign that the family was not losing an only child, it was gaining an address in the Village.

The apartment at 158 Waverly Place was a seven-room floor-through in a small red-brick building. Judy turned the chore of decorating into a challenge for her new hobby of resurrecting old furniture. She scoured local junk shops and on off days she and David drove the secondhand car out to country secondhand stores. Before long the place looked like a home for wayward furniture. Some pieces were antiques, many were just old things. And there was one brand-new grand piano which Judy bought for David.

Waverly Place became a gathering spot much the way Fifty-eighth Street had been. David was playing first clarinet with the City Center Opera and his workday finished around the same time as Judy's. He would drive over to the Henry Miller Theater, where the play had since moved, pick up Judy, and arrive at home in time to greet the small crowd that collected there regularly at midnight. There were theater people, musicians, and usually a Gollomb or two, eating, drinking, performing, talking, and playing games. New faces like Carson McCullers, Jane Bowles, John LaTouche, and Arthur Laurents passed among such regulars as Adolph, Betty and Steve, Lennie, and a composer acquaintance of David's who became very close with Judy, Alec Wilder. There were rarely announced parties, and the visitors were usually manageable in number. But the door was never locked and the place was seldom empty. The gatherings generally broke up somewhere between three and four in the morning. It was an artist crowd, and mornings were for sleeping, afternoons and evenings were for working. By midnight the cycle began again. These were good times.

That spring David was walking in the vicinity of Carnegie Hall when he ran into a couple he had known at the Eastman School. Jim Buffington played French horn; his wife, Ruth, played violin. Both were extremely talented musicians, but were new to town and were barely scratching out a living. They had a small place in the Bronx and were playing jobs and waiting for their union cards to come through. They asked about David, and he told them he was with the City Opera and living in the Village with his wife of several months, Judy Holliday. Ruth and Buff had not been in the city long, but they knew that Judy was the star of a current Broadway hit. It seemed their friend had done very well for himself. David ran off for an appointment, but not before inviting the Buffingtons to drop by Waverly Place as soon as they got the time.

Time was one thing they had plenty of, and a few days later they joined the midnight crowd. It was clearly fast company full of movers and shakers, and they felt somewhat ill-at-ease. When David introduced them to Judy, they found an instant ally. Judy tended to stay on the fringes rather than compete for attention with the assorted showmen and extraverts. Buff and Ruth had the sensibilities of musicians, which Judy liked, without a trace of the vanity and self-promotion she so disliked. The three of them talked for some time.

During a second visit, Buff sat down at the piano and started noodling around with an old tune or two. Judy wandered over and sang along, and the bond was forged. Judy seemed to know every show tune ever written, and what few melodies Buff didn't know, he faked. The Buffingtons were asked back often, until an invitation was no longer necessary. When Adolph and Betty weren't running through old party routines, Judy would join Buff at the piano, where, fortified by a couple of cocktails, she sang. She didn't have a very strong voice, but her knowledge of lyrics was encyclopedic, and besides, she was singing for her own pleasure and amusement. It was the perfect way to unwind after a long night onstage. Buff was a large quiet man with gentle eyes and a smoky voice like a horn. Ruth was a lovely woman with a kind smile and an unspoiled vitality and sensibleness much like Judy's. These were friends of David's that Judy truly liked. More important, she felt they liked her for herself and not some invented name on a Times Square marquee. For Judy the Buffingtons were an island of sanity in a sea of ego. She was at least as flattered by their genuine affection as they were by hers.

Not all of Judy's friendships fared as well at Waverly Place. There evolved an unspoken friction between David and Yetta. It may have been due to David's possessiveness or a disregard for someone who worked outside the show-business community. More likely it had to do with Judy's style of relationships. She was completely caught up in David's life—his work, his wants, his hopes. It was not only flattering, it gave him the upper hand in the marriage. Judy's relationship with her mother was a hopeless snarl of interdependency, but while Helen could be a terrible nuisance, she posed no immediate threat to David.

Yetta, on the other hand, was unique in Judy's experience—a long-standing friend who had always treated her as an equal. That friendship weathered the radical ups and downs of Judy's early career. In a real sense Judy had grown up in Yetta's company, with all the acceptance and faith that entailed. Yetta was not intimidated by Judy's moods. She was the one person who was willing to confront her during periods of depression or withdrawal. And though there were many feuds and silences, Judy respected and trusted Yetta, and the bond not only survived but thrived. Their friendship existed wholly apart from Judy's marriage, and that form of intense independence proved unsettling for David, though Yetta urged the marriage.

Unlike Helen, Yetta was careful to respect the privacy of Judy's marriage. She refused to visit without first being invited, and though the invitations were constant, they were viewed with mixed feelings. During an early visit, David was very

friendly to Yetta's friend Ruth Brooke. Toward Yetta he was
aloof and remote, almost brooding. There were drinks, then
dinner, then skirmishes. Yetta made some casual remark which
David promptly put down. She pretended that it hadn't
happened, but after coffee made some excuse and left. Once
outside, she protested to Ruth, "How dare he do that to me. I
don't need that. I'm not going back there again." She got home,
walked in the door, and the phone rang. It was David with an
apology. It was obvious he'd been scolded and put up to the call.
Yetta tried not to take the incident personally. She knew
David's moods could be mercurial and she had seen him turn his
sarcasm on others as well. "It's all right, David. It doesn't
matter." Tensions would ease through subsequent visits, and
then, without warning, it would happen again, the distance and
the put-downs, the apologies. The scene was replayed several
times and might have eroded a flimsier friendship. In this case it
actually strengthened the friendship by forcing it from under
David's disapproving eye. It was not clear whether this affected
the marriage.

In her way Judy could be just as inhospitable as David,
especially where her father was concerned. The years had not
eased her resentment toward Abe. It didn't matter to her that he
had established professional security as the executive director of
the American Zionist Council, or that he was making a genuine
effort to mend fences with his family. So much of Judy's
personality was rooted in her reaction to Abe's leave-taking
twenty years before, it was as if she could not truly accept him
without somehow rejecting a part of herself. Her present
success and happiness did not relieve her anger. She had been
unable to share her problems with him in the past and was
unwilling to share her contentment with him now. Judy's
intricate closeness to Helen magnified the distance from Abe.
The Gollombs had the run of Waverly Place, but Abe's
unannounced visits were treated coolly and formally.

Family and friends were invited to the Village for Judy's first
Christmas dinner. In the midst of afternoon cocktails Abe

showed up uninvited. He was escorted to the living room and handed a drink, and then another. At length one of the guests glanced at her watch and wondered about dinner. She walked to the kitchen and saw everything simmering, including Judy.

"It's four o'clock. What are you waiting for?"

"I'm not serving dinner until he leaves," Judy said.

"It's Christmas," the guest pointed out. "He obviously has no place to go."

Judy was unmoved. "I can't help that. He wasn't invited, and I'm not serving dinner until he leaves."

There was nothing more to be said. Abe was slow on the uptake, but he eventually realized he was unwelcome and invented some reason to go. He was no sooner out the door than dinner was on the table and the incident seemed forgotten by all. Still, Judy had acted rudely and unreasonably. Abe certainly could have shown greater sensitivity, but that was no excuse to deny him the courtesy Judy might have extended a complete stranger. What good could this small-minded rejection of Abe do Judy's lingering feeling of childhood rejection? If Judy was considerate and giving to others, she still had a strong need to be cared for and intuitively understood by the men in her life. Here was the boundary between the child and the adult in her. Abe had failed her, and she could not yet bring herself to forgive him. Judy was counting on David to meet her emotional needs.

It was a sumptuous meal. When they could eat no more, they returned to the living room and opened presents. David's gift to Judy was heavy and rectangular. She eagerly tore at the wrapping, and there was an unabridged dictionary. Judy smiled and kissed David, but there was an ache in her eyes. She believed in her brains but doubted her femininity. This only confirmed those doubts.

On January 4 Judy and David celebrated their first anniversary. He gave her a beautiful antique diamond ring which didn't help much with her word puzzles but did her heart untold good. A month and a day later Judy celebrated the third anniversary of *Born Yesterday* and looked ahead to a fourth year with serious reservations. She was no fonder of Paul Douglas, although she had never reported the problem to David for fear of a possible altercation—a clarinetist can ill-afford a hit to the mouth. The show won her a good measure of fame and financial security, but it also threatened to fix her in the public mind as the dim-witted dye-job, Billie Dawn. Judy was careful to indicate to interviewers her I.Q. and highbrow reading tastes. But people believe what they see over what they read, and onstage they saw a totally believable dumb blonde. Her run-of-the-play contract perpetuated the very image she was eager to shake. Through David she deepend her interest in music, and through Judy he pursued his interest in theater, serving at one point as the musical contractor for an Arthur Laurents play, *The Bird Cage*. Together they wrote songs. These were mostly diversions and did not soften what had become Judy's professional nemesis. Her loyalty to *Born Yesterday* brought her no closer to the planned movie version of the play.

Garson Kanin had worked for Harry Cohn, which was something like mortal combat. Cohn enjoyed a good fight, and Gar gave it to him, though both men were often the worse for the effort. A few years earlier they'd had a falling-out over a script Cohn commissioned from the Kanins and then rejected, and which was later sold to Universal as *A Double Life*, where it eventually became an Oscar-winning vehicle for Ronald Colman. When Gar put *Born Yesterday* on the block for Hollywood he gave strict instructions to his agent, Abe Lastfogel, that it was for sale to anybody but Cohn. Lastfogel asked if he was open to negotiation, and Gar answered no, "Not for a million bucks." Two months later Cohn purchased the film rights for a record one million dollars. It was a bold move which many at Columbia considered foolhardy. The movie business was faltering before the advent of television, and the outlook for recoupment in a dwindling market was something less than optimistic. But Cohn prided himself on his gambler's instincts, and besides, was thoroughly tantalized by the character Harry Brock. It would be some time before Gar confessed that Harry Cohn had in fact been the rough model for Brock.

Meanwhile the writer and the mogul were back to their old tricks. They agreed that George Cukor should direct, and that was the last thing they agreed on. Gar wanted Paul Douglas to repeat his role, but Cohn wanted Broderick Crawford, whom he had under contract and who had just received an Academy Award for *All the Kings Men*. Cohn pointed out that the stage role had been offered in the first place to Crawford. Gar gave in on that and went to bat for Judy as Billie Dawn. Cohn's gruff reply was, "That fat Jewish broad?" He was not about to gamble a million dollars on an unknown, even if she was the backbone of the Broadway production. Cohn mentioned several contract players—Rita Hayworth, Lucille Ball, Alice Faye, Barbara Stanwyck. Gar just shook his head.

Judy did not know the particulars of the negotiations, but she did know virtually every actress in the business was being mentioned and she hadn't even been offered a screen test. To make matters worse, she had spied Rita Hayworth in the audience one night taking notes. Little over a year earlier, Hal Wallis had pleaded with Judy to star in *My Friend Irma*. Judy refused and asked, "What about Marie Wilson? She created it on the radio." Wallis took the advice and cast the original. Marie Wilson then turned around and launched a minor publicity campaign in an attempt to win Billie Dawn, not for Judy, but for herself. It was hard enough finding people to live up to Judy's standards in private life; in show business it was hopeless. The list of possible Billies ballooned—Gloria Grahame, Barbara Hale, Evelyn Keyes, Jan Sterling. A movie would be the perfect ending to Judy's long association with the role. She had poured so much of herself into the part, it was like having a piece of her soul up for public auction, and she was powerless to prevent it.

Judy was wrong to think she was without allies in the business. While Harry Cohn was sweating out his million-dollar baby, Garson Kanin and Ruth Gordon were putting the finishing touches to a screenplay written for Spencer Tracy and Katharine Hepburn at the request of Louis B. Mayer at MGM. The story was about a husband and wife who are lawyers and who take separate sides in an assault case with distinct feminist overtones. During a get-together with Spencer and Kate, Gar lamented Cohn's mishandling of *Born Yesterday* and particularly his refusal to test Judy. Somebody suggested that they expand a minor role in the MGM picture, cast Judy, and let that be her screen test for the intractable Cohn. The conspiracy was hatched, and Judy was approached, but unconvinced. She granted it was a nifty role, but as Doris Attinger, the woman who wounds her philandering husband, she would be drab and dowdy. An unflattering character, even one that fit the broad stereotype of dumb blond, might reinforce Cohn's hunch that Judy lacked the raw glamour needed to put Billie across on screen.

Judy was still weighing the offer when she answered the door at her apartment one afternoon and was greeted by Spencer and Kate. They came in and chatted about how much they enjoyed Judy's work onstage and how terribly misguided Cohn was about her. Kate especially felt that the MGM picture was the best way to grab Cohn's attention. Judy had long been a Tracy and Hepburn fan; she looked to Kate as a model of integrity in a gritty industry. When she stepped outside of the moment and realized that these two people had actually come to her, she was not simply flattered, she was floored. Judy thanked them for their kind words and counsel and said they could count her in.

In June 1949 Judy started work on *Adam's Rib*. She had put on some weight, and when Gar first saw her on the set, he let her know, singing "Judy's Busting Out All Over." She ate nothing, drank V-8 juice, and in three days dropped several pounds. Judy was a bit stiff with fright in the beginning, but Kate soon put her at ease with the help of director George Cukor, who had believed in Judy as far back as *Winged Victory* and was now a faithful party to the "outwit Cohn" conspiracy.

The New York exteriors were shot at Lexington Avenue and

Fifty-second Street. Doris Attinger was shadowing her way-ward husband and nervously munching candy bars. It was the kind of pantomime at which Judy was most expert, but the first day before cameras was rough. Kate visited the set from her nearby Turtle Bay apartment to lend moral support. Judy apologized to Cukor and the crew for her initial ineptitude, shook off her nervousness, and the next day performed the sequence flawlessly. When the location shooting was over, Judy arranged leave from the stage and headed west with the company for studio scenes.

Judy registered brilliantly as Doris Attinger. She timed the Kanins' shorthand dialogue to the last ellipsis. Her soft voice rose and fell with the flat intonations of lower-middle-class New York. Her statements read like questions and her sweet impassive expression lagged a good second or two behind her words. Kate was determined that audiences get a good look at Judy. In their two major scenes together Kate saw that the angles favored Judy and at one point played with her back selflessly to the camera. When somebody later suggested some cutaways to Kate during Judy's scenes, she commanded in her chilly Bryn Mawr tone, "No. This is the way it's supposed to be."

She was right, of course. For those instants that their faces were together on camera, a fascinating visual geometry took place. Kate was all angles and hollows; her sharp nose, classic cheekbones, and sure gaze were precise and mobile. Like a mime in white-face, Judy's features seemed immobile until a thought or emotion formed slowly like an object rising through water. It was a fascinating study in contrast, not too different from the unusual visual rapport Kate shared with Spencer.

Judy completed her portion and was about to return east and resume her stage work as Billie Dawn when word filtered down from Columbia that she was to report for a screen test before leaving town. She was given a script that bore only a passing resemblance to the dialogue she had internalized for over three years. Evidently Gar and Cohn's running one-upmanship extended to the writing as well. In light of the lucrative purchase price for the rights, Cohn wanted Gar to adapt the play gratis as a "labor of love." Gar said no, and Cohn hired Philip and Julius Epstein for twice Gar's regular fee. Had the dialogue been identical or completely changed, Judy might have given a confident reading. But the intermingled lines of old and new threw off her timing and confused her conception of the character. A full day before cameras left her exhausted and glum, despite a sympathetic director and crew that had come in on Father's Day. Afterward she seemed disenchanted with the part in particular and dumb-blond characters in general. She talked about the possibility of a straight dramatic role for the coming Broadway season. "At least it will raise my mental status."

Judy's pessimism aside, Kate was more convinced than ever about who had to play Billie on film. She actively stumped for Judy, and according to some, intimated to Cohn through channels that if he ever hoped to employ Hepburn he'd better give full consideration to Holliday.

Adam's Rib was released one day after Christmas, and the critics warmed to the screen reunion of Tracy and Hepburn. The reviews were equally pleased with the supporting cast of Tom Ewell, David Wayne, and Judy's standby from *Born Yesterday*, Jean Hagen. Special note was made of Judy's performance, and the industry whispered she had stolen the picture. Kate couldn't have been happier about the rumors if she'd started them herself. In fact, she had.

On New Year's Eve 1949 *Born Yesterday* played its 1,642nd and last performance, one month shy of its fourth birthday and eighth on the list of longest-running Broadway shows. Less than two weeks later, on January 11, it was announced that Harry Cohn in his infinite wisdom had chosen Judy to play Billie Dawn onscreen.

10

Judy was shown into Harry Cohn's office. She wasn't sure whether he recalled their hapless meeting several years ago, so she offered her hand. The squat, dour man ignored the gesture and instead circled her like a butcher appraising a side of beef. At length he said, just loud enough for her to hear, "Well, I've worked with fat asses before."

Nobody had to tell Judy that she'd gained a few pounds, just as nobody had to tell her that Cohn was intentionally provoking her. Cohn thrived on conflict, and when none was to be found, he instigated it. But Judy was a veteran of the Zanuck casting-couch wars and once more came to work on her own terms. When Cohn attempted to sign her to a standard seven-year contract, she refused. David's work was back east, and she hated Hollywood. Judy held out for one picture a year for seven years and a free hand to work in theater, radio, and television. Although Cohn was loath to admit it, he admired those few who stood up to him. Even more he admired Judy's talent, the quality of her mind, and her integrity. She was not a shallow glamour girl who relied on good looks and handy editing. She was an actress, in fact the only actress who could vindicate Cohn's million-dollar gamble. He needed her. They needed each other.

Judy took a place at the El Royale Apartments on North Rossmore, then reported to the studio's chief costume designer, Jean Louis, who took one look at her and thought to himself: My God, what will she look like? For an actress due to play the sexiest character to come along in years, she seemed to have all the allure of a den mother. There was a good reason for her listlessness. Shortly after Judy arrived in Hollywood, Uncle Joe died suddenly of a heart attack. Joe had long since been relegated to family figurehead, and he and Judy had been distant for years. Judy was saddened but more concerned about the effect Joe's passing might have on Helen. Luckily Judy had brought Helen along, and the excitement of Hollywood took much of the sting from the death. Helen was no longer caught up in Joe's life; she was not Joe Gollomb's sister, she was Judy Holliday's mother, and that identity alone strengthened her. How Judy would hold up in the coming weeks remained to be seen.

Judy delivered herself to Jean Louis's designing genius, and even he was amazed at the changes wrought. There were thirteen costumes in all that charted the character's growth from tacky to tasteful. The early tight-fitting outfits had been a particular worry, given Judy's weight and apparent lack of glamour. But as George Cukor was the first to say, Judy saved her acting for the audience, and he'd take someone who could act beautiful over a model any day. The moment she put on the costumes, she became Billie Dawn. With her newly lightened hair and a loose-hipped walk she'd picked up from the rumba line at the Copacabana, she was the classic chippie made good.

Cukor prepared the movie as a play. The Epsteins had graciously bowed out and turned the script back over to Garson Kanin, who, with Cukor, opened up the action somewhat and laundered it of any unseemly political or sexual references. The cast, with Broderick Crawford as Harry Brock and William

Holden as the journalist Paul Verrall, rehearsed for two weeks and then gave six performances for Columbia employees. By the time it was over, the cast gained confidence and Judy lost fifteen pounds.

Judy was still a little uncertain when they first went before the cameras. Throughout the Broadway run and the studio run-throughs she had adjusted her reading to the audience reaction. There was no audible reaction on the set, and she found that disconcerting. There was also a silent barrier between the movie people and the stage people, each thinking they knew better how to play scenes. These minor obstacles soon vanished under Cukor's quietly masterful direction. The cast and crew warmed, as well, to Judy's friendliness and conspicuous absence of star temperament.

In mid-June the production shifted to Washington, D.C., for location work. Judy was afraid of flying, so while the rest of the cast came by air, she took to the rails. Cohn did not want his leading lady to travel alone, and he ordered Broderick Crawford to join her. The last thing Crawford wanted was to squander four days in a cramped train, but Cohn was adamant. It was a relatively minor chapter in what had become the longest and loudest running verbal brawl on the lot. Judy and Crawford passed the long hours talking and playing gin rummy for money. Crawford arrived in Washington immeasurably fonder of his leading lady and six hundred dollars poorer.

Cukor shot exteriors all over town. The itinerary read like a high-school field trip: Supreme Court, Washington Monument, National Archives, Treasury Department, National Gallery, Library of Congress, Jefferson Memorial. It took two weeks to get what he wanted, and then they all returned to Los Angeles to finish up the interiors.

Judy arrived at the studio to find a message from David saying he had closed the deal on a country home they had found together. It was a modest 18th-century farmhouse surrounded by woods, an hour drive from New York, not far from West Point. It would require some work, but Judy could not wait to get back and have at the place.

Born Yesterday concluded principal photography on August 12. Judy lingered long enough for a few obligatory newspaper and magazine interviews, then hurried home to David. It was a happy reunion. David had assumed his new position as head of the classical division for Columbia Records. His schedule as an A-and-R man (artists and repertory) drastically cut into the time he could spend performing on the clarinet, but this was of small concern to him. Although David was among the leading clarinetists in the country, he often dreaded concerts and was uneasy with the relative anonymity of classical musicians. Even violinists who had the benefit of a broad range of solo work seldom ascended to widespread national prominence. Musicians didn't make much money and enjoyed little recognition outside of a limited cultural sphere. David was ambitious by nature and more so for Judy's pending national exposure. He wanted more than the clarinet could bring him. The A-and-R job was a sure sign of upward mobility; it not only gave him authority but also gave him authority over other musicians. One other benefit was that the couple acquired an enormous and varied record collection. There was rarely a time when music was not playing at their home. Judy broadened her knowledge of classical pieces and acquired a taste for jazz, though she did not care at all for folk music.

The house in Washingtonville was a godsend. The basic structure was sound but the interior was badly in need of repair. For Judy it was like a mammoth piece of furniture to be refinished. She and David made what improvements they could by hand and left the exterior work to local contractors. There were setbacks—a carpenter who mistakenly tore down the wrong porch, an old barn foundation converted to a swimming pool that leaked. But gradually the house took shape; David uncovered the hand-hewn beams and cleaned up the large stone fireplace. Judy ransacked area secondhand shops for furniture which gave the house a lived-in, rustic feel. The Buffingtons, Alec Wilder, Adolph, and others came up often, and though these were many of the same people who frequented Waverly Place, the mood was palpably different. The country was not for fast talk and parlor theatrics. It was for reading and games and conversation and, above all, eating. There were wonderful times when the house fairly radiated good cheer and warmth. It relaxed the fevered metrics of city life. That was what Judy liked most about Washingtonville. She was never one to go tramping through the woods, she didn't know one bird from another, she didn't rise at five and make whole-wheat bread. This was her safe haven, a place to do nothing, a place to be nobody.

That June had been an eventful month in ways small and large. Judy turned twenty-eight and began her first starring role in movies. North Korean tanks crossed the thirty-eighth parallel into South Korea and precipitated the Korean War. Six Senate Republicans denounced junior Senator McCarthy for irresponsible charges about Communist infiltration of the State Department. And the editors of the weekly anti-Communist newsletter *Counterattack* published a slender hardback volume with the names of 151 individuals in the entertainment field with alleged links to the Communist party or front organizations—it was called *Red Channels*. Just what impact these seemingly disconnected events would have on Judy's life was impossible to predict.

Judy's name was among those cited in *Red Channels*. The book was sold for a dollar to subscribers to *Counterattack* and at first was dismissed as novelty literature for a fanatical fringe. The editors as much as admitted that many of the listings were undocumented and arbitrary. They cast a wide net, and though Judy turned up in the catch, she certainly had interesting company—Arthur Miller, Pete Seeger, Leonard Bernstein, even Dorothy Parker. The editors set forth three objectives: to expose Communist infiltration of the media, to show how actors and artists by choice or chance lent their names to Communist-tinged organizations, and finally to serve as a deterrent to further liaisons, however naive or accidental. Their primary targets were the radio and television industries, and so Judy, whose work at the time was exclusively in theater and movies, seemed initially unaffected.

But the sudden interplay of events that summer gave *Red Channels* an unforeseen veneer of legitimacy. McCarthy, Korea, and the jailing of two members of the Hollywood Ten, who had refused to cooperate with the House Un-American Activities Committee probe into subversion in motion pictures, signaled a darkening mood in the country. With the Russian detonation of an atomic bomb, the consolidation of Mao's takeover of China, the Hiss and Rosenberg cases, real concerns and fears were spilling over into national hysteria.

In addition to those in and out of government with a genuine uneasiness about the Communist threat, there evolved a class of career anti-Communists—businessmen and demagogues who sowed and harvested public paranoia. For them, the entertainment field was an eminently fertile ground. Movies had always been highly susceptible to public disfavor, and radio and television were essentially advertising media open to pressure from all quarters. *Red Channels* helped focus random fears. It quickly became an index, a directory, a kind of blacklist Yellow Pages for redhunters. The Cold War mentality shifted the burden of proof from the accuser to the accused. A cynical joke was making the rounds about the man who comes home one day and tells his wife he's been accused of being a rabbit. She tells him that's ridiculous, of course he's not a rabbit. He replies, "Yes, but how do I prove it?" Judy had no way of knowing that summer, but she was being investigated by the FBI.

In a letter dated June 14, 1950, the Bureau instructed its Los Angeles office to determine whether Judy was a member of the Communist party and, if necessary, assign her a Security Index Card. At the same time, the New York office was told to make available any pertinent information in its files. The apparent seed of the investigation was a confidential report prepared by the American Legion "in response to many requests for the records of various unsuitable individuals appearing on radio and television shows." In a prose style that equaled its inexact content, the report claimed "Judy Holliday has been a great solace to the Moscow-tied lads and lassies who look for big names as sucker bait for their front operations." There was a list of eight front organizations with which she was supposedly affiliated, concluding with a statement that was as condescending as it was misogynistic:

We won't assume that Judy Holliday pretends to know a lot about Spain, peace, Africa, the Russian theater, or intellectualism, but she has demonstrated her willingness to sign statements, lead picket lines, etc., for organizations cited as subversive by competent government agencies.

On August 15 an informant's report was filed with the Los Angeles office. The report purported to present details of Judy's front activities between 1947 and 1950. In fact it was a minor expansion on the citings contained in *Red Channels*. The Bureau may not have gotten its money's worth, but this was more than a case of bureaucratic double work. The citings in *Red Channels* were largely unsubstantiated, offhand, and the product of a private business concern. By being repeated in an FBI file, conjecture took on the weight and luster of fact. A second informant's report filed one month later detailed Judy's efforts on behalf of the Hollywood Ten. The report relied on newspaper clippings and held nothing of substance, and though it implied a degree of guilt by association, it concluded: "This investigation of the subject did not reveal positive evidence of membership in the Communist party, and, therefore, no recommendation for a Security Index Card is being made at this time."

Judy knew the rumors and rumblings of increased FBI activities. She did not, at this point, even suspect she was one of its many targets. To begin with, many of the listings under her name in *Red Channels* were unfounded. Others were simply the outgrowth of isolated small cash contributions. Still others were organizations whose goals and ideals she supported independent of reputed links. As she saw it, a shared conviction or attitude was undiminished for its association with the extreme right or left. She was a political independent who endorsed specific candidates or issues, not parties or party lines. Of course professional anti-Communists were making no such distinctions at the time. For them an individual could no more be a little bit left than be a little bit pregnant. Judy's best defense was her comparative obscurity. Aside from two shows on Broadway—which was New York provincial and beyond the pale of redhunters—and a few minor roles in movies, Judy Holliday was still an official unknown. A hunter is only as good as his catch, and Judy was small game. That was about to change.

Born Yesterday was not long in the can before Columbia realized it had a potential big winner. Everything about the film shone—the writing, the direction, the acting—and Judy was the stunning centerpiece. There is no surer draw for a film than an Academy Award, and Harry Cohn was sure that *Born Yesterday* would receive several nominations. It was rushed for a year-end release in order to qualify for the 1950 Oscars, which would not be named until April of the following year. In an attempt to build momentum for the public distribution of the film, advance screenings were arranged for selected critics.

William H. Mooring reviewed films for the *Tidings*, a Los Angeles-based diocesan newspaper. Fully three weeks before the official release Mooring published a piece on *Born Yesterday* that was not so much a critique as a condemnation. He began by noting Garson Kanin's support of Progressive Party presidential candidate Henry Wallace in 1948 and his active defense of the Hollywood Ten. Then he lowered the boom:

> It is the most diabolically clever political satire I have encountered in almost thirty years of steady film reviewing. Never have human symbols been more subtly molded to carry destructive comment through disarming comedy.

He went on to accuse the character played by Bill Holden of "making argument for all the world as if he'd freshly graduated 'summa cum laude' from the University of Karl Marx." For a film that was heavily seasoned with patriotic rhetoric and practically top-heavy with hallowed American documents and monuments, Mooring's review seemed misled bordering on paranoiac. Just the same, it was syndicated in twenty-two other diocesan papers, the Brooklyn *Tablet* and the New York *Catholic News* among them.

The response of the motion-picture community was uncommonly swift and direct. An editorial in the *Motion Picture Herald* criticized Mooring for "contributing aid and comfort to the enemy by false accusation." A spokesman for the conservative Motion Picture Association of America followed with a telegram to the diocesan papers saying: "I feel very deeply and sincerely that the picture gives warmth and positive support to the democratic ideals, principles, and institutions of America." Even Louella Parsons, gossip columnist for the archconservative Hearst papers, wrote, "If there are any pink ideas infiltered into *Born Yesterday,* they are way over my head." The controversy centered around Garson Kanin and the film text, leaving Judy untouched. By the time of the film's general release on December 26, most of the political shouting seemed to have died down. Then there were only shouts of praise.

Reviewers were falling over themselves trying to find enough superlatives to describe Judy's performance. In essence they said that Judy had given life and humanity to what might easily have been a cardboard cutout character. Billie Dawn was not simply a tasteless dumb blonde, but an uneducated woman who was the willing victim of certain cultural stereotypes. Because Billie was believable if stylized, her growth was believable and so too the story. The reviewers did not go so far as to say Judy single-handedly carried the movie, just that without her it would have been different and less. The particulars varied from review to review, but the clear consensus was that a new movie star had arrived on the scene. After a dozen years in clubs and onstage, Judy was discovered.

Judy never sought stardom. The whole idea struck her as silly and unreal. She wasn't the least interested in fulfilling fans' expectations for offscreen glamour. Acting was something she did and did well, and she was grateful for the critical and popular acclaim. She did not subscribe to the notion of stardom as a kind of natural nobility obliged to live out a storybook existence for the common folk. She preferred quiet evenings with friends to flossy parties with celebrities. She preferred slacks to gowns, Washingtonville to the Hollywood Hills. Judy was not falsely modest. She knew that she had done very good work on the film. Nor was she dishonest. She knew that a measure of fame came with the territory. But she was quick to indicate that the experience had not changed her. She still found Hollywood life largely dull, petty, and superficial, and said as much to the press. If Judy was interested in attracting an Oscar nomination, this was hardly the way to go about it.

Judy did not turn her back altogether on the advantages of success. She was open to talk about her own television show and made the first of several appearances on Tallulah Bankhead's popular radio program, *The Big Show*. Judy was nervous about the live performance and asked David to come with her to the studio. Shortly before airtime they were introduced to the star. Tallulah, well known for her freewheeling life-style, greeted the handsome young couple and looked from Judy to David and back again, then said, "I don't know which one of you to attack!" Judy laughed obligingly but saw to it that David accompanied her there from that time on. The show went well, with Judy playing a version of Billie Dawn. Most of the dialogue was scripted, but what Judy added by way of timing and incidental improvisation won over the audience, not to mention Tallulah's head writer, Goodman Ace.

In mid-February the Oscar nominees were announced and Judy was among them. It was a fast field, with Bette Davis for *All About Eve* and Gloria Swanson for *Sunset Boulevard* in the lead, and Judy, Anne Baxter, and Eleanor Parker bringing up the rear. Judy could be as competitive about her work as she was unassuming about herself. She wanted very much to win the Oscar, but she knew the competition was extremely stiff.

What slender hopes Judy held for winning faded when the controversy resurfaced about *Born Yesterday*. At the same time, she learned the liability of fame. In December Garson Kanin had been singled out by Mooring. The Catholic War Veterans who picketed *Born Yesterday* at New York and New Jersey theaters in March added Judy's name to their placards and leaflets. Judy was now big game and it was open season on even mildly left-leaning celebrities. The growing number of anti-Communist newsletters stepped up their attacks on her, and the source of data was invariably *Red Channels*. The book was now known as the Madison Avenue Bible, and nearly every advertising executive kept a copy in his top desk drawer.

Ad agencies were radio and television's lifeline to commercial sponsors. Anti-Communist pressure groups reached through the agencies to the sponsors about the casting and content of programming. Sponsors in turn pressured the agencies who packaged those programs. It wasn't long before the agencies learned a conditioned response: in order to avoid alienating pressure groups who alienated advertisers, ad executives consulted *Red Channels* before casting or packaging shows. Certainly some agencies and sponsors were more thin-skinned than others. A few even resisted pressure. But the net result was that *Red Channels* became a de facto blacklist. Those cited had to clear themselves, which was still a somewhat mysterious process, or risk unemployment. Judy's invitations for radio guest appearances tapered off. Network talks about the television show stalled.

Oscar night was exactly the sort of event Judy abhorred. The ceremony was held in Hollywood at the Pantages Theater. But several nominees were in New York, so a second gathering of some three hundred convened at a Spanish restaurant, La Zambra. There was a live network radio hookup and the plan was for New York recipients to say a few words before letting a Hollywood stand-in pick up the trophy. José Ferrer (up for best actor) and Gloria Swanson were currently costarring in a Broadway revival of Ben Hecht's *Twentieth Century*. That gave reporters an added angle and seemed to worsen the frenzied cheapness.

Judy wore a simple black outfit and sat with David at an out-of-the-way table toward the rear. She had bought Ruth Buffington a gift for luck and then placed six separate five-dollar bets against herself. Cameras flashed and strobed and made the place look like some overdressed carnival midway. With all the tensions and rivalries and strained smiles, it was an orgy of insincerity. The others didn't want you to fail, they just didn't want you to succeed at their expense.

As the evening's roll call narrowed down to the best-actor and best-actress categories, Ferrer, Swanson, and Judy were asked to move to a prearranged table. The press closed in for the kill, and Judy's pulse jumped. Ferrer was announced for best actor, and the reception was strong and honest. He too had been under fire from anti-Communist groups and had been subpoenaed to appear before HUAC the following month. Ferrer stepped to the microphone and said, "This means more to me than an honor to an actor. I consider it a vote of confidence and an act of faith, and, believe me, I'll not let you down." Helen Hayes accepted his Oscar in Hollywood and he returned to the table, where a reporter asked if his message had been political. Ferrer bellowed, "You're goddamned right," and mentioned charges that had been untrue and irrelevant besides.

As the nominees were recited for best actress, Swanson leaned over to Judy and whispered, "One of us is about to be very happy." Judy smiled nervously. A moment later Judy was named the winner and the light bulbs popped and the reporters shouted questions as she tried to make her way to the microphone. Before she could open her mouth, the radio hookup blared Ethel Barrymore from Hollywood as she accepted the Oscar for Judy. Half-crying, half-laughing, Judy came back to the table dazed. Swanson called, "Judy darling," and again whispered something. This time there was no smile; Judy's jaw droppped, her eyes burned.

Judy found George Cukor, who escorted her through the rain across the street to a Chinese diner where Judy called Helen, but mentioned nothing about Swanson's remark. She crossed back to La Zambra, stood for photographers, shyly thanked a throng of well-wishers, grabbed David, and slipped out at the first opportunity.

The first thing Judy did when she got home to Waverly Place was call Yetta. It was one-thirty, and Yetta was wide-awake. "Judy, we were all listening on the radio. I'm so happy for you."

Judy thanked her, but Yetta detected a note of disappointment.

"Was it because you didn't get to make a speech?"

Partly. As had Ferrer, Judy considered her award a gesture of support from Hollywood and wanted to express her gratitude. Yetta could tell there was something more. Judy mentioned Swanson. "After I came back from the microphone, Gloria Swanson waved me over."

"No kidding," Yetta said excitedly. "What did she say?"

"She snapped at me, 'Why couldn't you have waited till next year?'"

Yetta told Judy not to let that spoil the night for her. She congratulated her again, hung up the phone, and murmured to herself, "Why is it every time something marvelous happens to Judy, something bad happens too?"

David and Judy caught a few hours' sleep, loaded up the secondhand car, and drove up to Washingtonville. She was eager to sidestep reporters, who were sure to descend on Waverly Place. More than that, she wanted to protect David from the rude neglect of the press. The attention meant too little to her to risk David getting the Mr. Holliday treatment. Once in Washingtonville, they set about stripping some old pieces of wood and midway lost interest. That had become the norm up there—slap on a few strokes of paint, sand a few planks of floor, then call in the professionals and fix dinner. For country folk they could be very Greenwich Village.

By the time Judy returned to Waverly Place, much of the Oscar din had died down. That was to be expected. Less expected was the relatively tepid response within the industry. In hard practical terms, an Academy Award increases the market value of the winner. There are offers for guest appearances, mention of new starring vehicles, and often renegotiation of existing contracts. Judy was reaping few of those rewards. There were plans for an appearance on the Bob Hope show, but the sponsor, Liggett and Myers, pulled the plug even after the contracts had been signed. They didn't want their product, Chesterfield cigarettes, linked in any way to a woman who had donated money to the Peace Crusade program. Around the same time, there was renewed interest at NBC about a regular show starring Judy. But the advertising agency in charge of the NBC account placed a call to the New York office of the FBI asking about Judy's rumored Communist sympathies. The office responded that although an earlier investigation showed that she had never been a party member, she did seem to have a history of front affiliations. Their primary source again was *Red Channels*. NBC dropped plans for the show, which would have made Judy wealthy.

She was not doing much better by movies. Her original contract with Columbia called for a picture a year for seven years, with an initial fee of $30,000 and regular yearly increments of $10,000. These were extremely low figures by Hollywood standards, although there were provisions for renegotiation. But Columbia declined to review contract terms despite the Oscar. They did intend, however, to make more pictures with her. When, they wouldn't say. Judy was starting to feel the insidious undertow of the coming inquisition.

The theater was still a refuge. While Columbia's bid to acquire *Gentlemen Prefer Blondes* for Judy fell through, City Center cast her in a revival of *Dream Girl*. She had read for the lead five years earlier but then decided against taking the show on the road. It was a fortunate decision that helped set up the unlikely sequence leading to *Born Yesterday*. The current production of *Dream Girl* was part of a limited comedy repertory at City Center, but it was a first-rate New York production and a victory for Judy. The Elmer Rice play told of Georgina Allerton, an inveterate daydreamer whose excursions into fantasy embraced everything from social satire to burlesque. It was a fitting vehicle for Judy, who could show off the full range of her prodigious comedic gifts. Under Morton Da Costa's direction, Judy's portrayal of Georgina was original, owing nothing to Billie Dawn. The fact that many critics favorably compared the two said more of their own predisposition than of the actual performance. Judy had raised Billie Dawn to the level of a popular classic, a prototype. That is the highest achievement of an actress, but it is also the standard by which she is measured in the future. Judy wanted a role fully removed from Billie. If *Dream Girl* was just a half-step, it was a half-step in the right direction. In any case, the New York critics continued their love affair with Judy.

Success did not go to her head. As an actress she became more gracious and generous. After one particular performance of *Dream Girl* a friend visited Judy backstage and complained that a young actor was stealing the show. Judy said without the least trace of self-sacrifice, "I was letting him today. I think he's a very fine actor and I invited some people over from Columbia to have a look at him. I wanted him to look good."

Judy's compassion was not always so high-minded. That same spring she was driving near home when her cocker spaniel, Muffin, vaulted out a window and vanished. For days Judy drove through the neighborhood calling, "Muffin? Muffin!" When those searches turned up empty, she went public. Judy had never sought out the press for her own sake, but Muffin was another story. She had items planted in several local papers and was so innocent of her own fame that she had her name and number run as well. The calls were unceasing. Everyone had a dog answering Muffin's description. Of course the bulk of these were simply ploys to meet a famous actress, but Judy thought nothing of it and pursued each lead as if it were the last. One call brought her and Ruth Buffington out to a devastated slum in Brooklyn. As they drove among the ruined and rickety tenements, Ruth wanted to turn back, but Judy pressed on. They found the address, climbed several flights of unlit stairs, and knocked at the door. No one answered but a small dog yapped inside. After several minutes of conversation with the dog, Judy was satisfied this was not Muffin and, much to Ruth's relief, agreed to go.

Muffin never was found, but was replaced after a fashion by a dog named Poppy. Poppy was a rare breed with an even rarer resistance to training. The dog flunked out of two obedience schools and was being given its third and final chance. On graduation day Ruth got a call from Judy. "Well, Ruthie. I picked up Poppy from school, took him home to Washington-ville. What do you think? He goes straight upstairs and shits on the rug. Want a dog?" Ruth said she could imagine better references for a pet and politely declined. Judy could be persuasive. In just over a year Poppy would be soiling the Buffingtons' rug.

Judy could go through the motions of normal day-to-day living, but she could not banish the specter of the blacklist. Though apologists insisted the blacklist was a figment of guilt-ridden pinko imaginations, the facts remained. Judy had lost work in radio and television. Her movie career seemed momentarily stunted. And there was no guarantee that theater could hold out indefinitely against the political tide.

Most alarming had been the pickets. In theory Judy supported their right to protest. In practice she feared the intensity of their anger and resented the wanton inaccuracy of their propaganda; she knew the two could prove an explosive mixture. Later, when Judy played *Dream Girl* in summer stock, she went by train with Helen to a small town in Rhode Island. As they approached the platform, she looked out the window and saw a crush of uniforms. Her face flushed, her jaw set, she did not want to leave the train. It was not until Helen assured her this was not the CWV but a high-school marching band come to greet her that Judy finally relented. Judy may have remembered the advice of a friend: "Just because you're paranoid doesn't mean people aren't out to get you."

The method of accusing had progressed faster than that of clearing, which was still an imperfect science. It wasn't until professional anti-Communists realized that accusing and clearing were part of the same process that a system evolved. It was like sin and absolution under threat of damnation. There was even a choice of father confessors: American Business Consultants (the clearing Tweedledum to *Counterattack*'s Tweedledee); a handful of political columnists with access to HUAC; or HUAC itself. But as the renewed purge of Hollywood showed, none of these held the certainty of redemption, merely the possibility.

Harry Cohn's politics was Harry Cohn. He cherished individuality and toughness. Though he never made public his views on the substance of the redhunt, he instinctively disliked its methods. It was like two bullies accidentally showing up on the same street corner at the same time. For Cohn, bullying was mostly sport. For HUAC it was deadly serious. Columbia's record against the redhunters was mixed but better than most. There was no single policy. Some actors and writers were backed; some were fired. As Judy's situation worsened, there was no clear precedent for how Cohn might react.

The first thing Columbia did was to put Judy in touch with George Sokolsky, a Hearst columnist and one of the leading exposers and pardoners of heretics. Sokolsky instructed her to write a statement saying she was anti-Communist. Judy told him it was not his place to ask for statements from any citizen, since he was not an official government agency. The protests and pickets increased immediately. Judy returned to Sokolsky with a statement saying she was strongly anti-Communist and anti-Fascist. He told her that wouldn't do. Judy refused to delete the anti-Fascist remark, left at an impasse, and again the pressure increased. When Judy returned to Sokolsky, he advised that a simple statement was no longer sufficient atonement. Presumably the sin had grown proportionately with her fame. On this count the redhunters were oddly Marxist: they demanded from each according to his ability. Judy's market value was rising, and with it the price of exoneration. Sokolsky showed her a long typed list of names. "Identify four of them as Communist-party members," he explained, "and the pressure on you will end." Judy could have easily identified four times that number, were she the sort to inform. But of all the human vices, none was more vile to her than betrayal—it was the antithesis of the loyalty she so prized. Judy could not inform and keep her self-respect. She would not name names.

It wasn't clear whether Harry Cohn admired Judy's defiance or wanted to protect an investment. Probably some of both. What was clear was that he meant to go the distance with her on this. In a stroke that was vintage Cohn, he hired Kenneth Bierly, late of *Counterattack* and *Red Channels*, to conduct an independent investigation of Judy's activities. While Cohn pledged he would stand by the findings, Bierly's fee (rumored to be well above what Judy was then making per picture) and his desire to stay on the Columbia payroll were ample incentive for the findings to meet the boss's approval.

Meanwhile the Columbia legal staff arranged a conversation between Judy and Attorney General Tom Clark. The expressed purpose was to clear the air. The probable purpose was to pry the case loose from the FBI's hardening grip. The conversation took place on the first weekend of June. That Monday the attorney general's office requested information on Judy. The Bureau's L. B. Nichols merely offered that her name had been connected with numerous front organizations. The attorney general requested fuller details, and the Bureau responded with a fifteen-page memorandum instead of the actual file. The Justice Department was plainly involved in its own internal politics. In the course of these exchanges the attorney general inquired after the reputation of the Catholic War Veterans. Nichols replied, "To my knowledge it is a very high-class group and patriotically American." Nichols was then informed "that no further information was needed on this." This was the atmosphere of good-ole-boy authentication in which *Red Channels* grew from laundry list to scripture.

Columbia seemed to sense that a scheme of divide and conquer could just as easily leave them between a rock and a hard place. They could not afford to alienate the FBI. On July 12 L. B. Nichols received a sworn statement by Judy along with an annotated list of alleged front activities. The cover letter was on Columbia stationery and asked that both documents be shown to Director Hoover. Judy was determined to make a statement, not a recantation. She said she deplored Communism along with all forms of totalitarianism. This broke with the Cold War policy of opposing Communism at all costs, including supporting fascist regimes. She also spoke out against the repression and discrimination which seemed to surround the redhunt. "I am against censorship. I am against persecution of minority races and religions. I am against curtailment of civil liberties." She said her association with organizations came of idealism and good faith and that she never knowingly lent her name to Communist propaganda.

Judy then went through the list of her so-called front activities and in detail explained how some citings had been misconstrued, misinformed, and in many instances totally inaccurate. Her name had been used repeatedly without her approval. Where she was a willing sponsor it was due to the professed ideals of the group and not any adherence to party line. Finally she showed that the majority of *Daily Worker*-derived references to her attendance at political rallies and protests did not hold up to the simplest scrutiny. For supposed experts on Communism, the editors of *Red Channels* didn't allow for the *Daily Worker*'s habit of padding certain reports with random celebrity names. Judy had to soft-pedal her criticism of *Red Channels*, however, because of Bierly's association with the publication. To question his reliability then would be to question his reliability now as an investigator. Harry Cohn was not paying these prices to have his man discredited. And so *Red Channels*, the cornerstone of this Byzantine structure, remained to be exposed.

Bierly submitted the findings of his investigations that same summer. He told Columbia there was no evidence that Judy had ever belonged to the Communist party. He also dispelled rumors that Yetta Cohn had been a party member and had conducted meetings in the Fifty-eighth Street apartment. He pointed out that Yetta was a respected veteran of the New York

Police Department and that her friendship with Judy was not "in any way subversive or unpatriotic." Bierly assessed Judy's past activities with his own eight-point guide to political sympathies. He concluded that she was innocent of intentional wrongdoing, but that she should be more careful about those organizations she helped out in the future. He also relayed an inside tip that consoled both Judy and Harry Cohn: she would not be called by HUAC.

The *Red Channels* stigma seemed removed at last. Bierly giveth, Bierly also taketh away. Harry Cohn looked ahead to the next vehicle for his hottest star in years. Judy just looked relieved. She had withheld one crucial bit of information throughout the investigation. In an attempt to give her mother something to do, Judy let Helen act as her personal secretary. Helen answered letters, including the many left wing requests. The fact was, most of the documented donations to "front" organizations had been made, not by Judy, but in Judy's name by Helen. There was one other factor. In tune with the idealism of the WPA during the late thirties, it was likely Helen had briefly been a member of the Communist Party. Judy was terrified her mother would be called by HUAC and would suffer another breakdown.

By September Judy was in New York for location shooting for the latest Holliday-Gordon-Kanin-Cukor collaboration, *The Marrying Kind*. It was an intriguing fable of middle-class married life which resorted to none of the high style or froth of *Adam's Rib*. The script integrated humor, fantasy, and pathos, which was no small task. And if the narrative method of conflicting flashback—*Rashomon*—was contrived, little else was. The story held out no false hope, right up to its muted ending.

This was a transitional film for many. Ruth Gordon and Garson Kanin were swapping their facile patrician romanticism for a measure of popular realism. This was also a departure for Cukor along similar lines. For Harry Cohn this was a perfect vehicle for his proud find, Aldo Ray. Judy, who was less than thrilled with Ray, was more than thrilled with this opportunity to put Billie Dawn behind her for good. Her character, Florence Keefer, had none of Billie's traits or idiosyncrasies—the Kanins saw to that. For the first time Judy could build a role from scratch for film. This could mean the difference between a career as an actress in varied parts and a career of typecasting in versions of Billie. The film was finished in mid-November. Judy eagerly awaited its scheduled release in March 1952.

She was greeted instead by news of another sort. The redhunting frenzy in Washington had steadily worsened since summer. As more congressional committees entered the anti-Communist sweepstakes, the pressure increased to find name people to interrogate. McCarthy had already graphically proved that the bigger the name, the bigger the headline. It didn't take a deep thinker to realize that the biggest and most vulnerable names were to be found in show business. An entertainer has no constituency, no term of office. He is entirely at the mercy of public opinion. Committees that had no apparent mandate to investigate celebrities found one.

The Senate Internal Security Subcommittee was a prime example. It had been formed to oversee the Internal Security Act, otherwise known by its chairman's name, the McCarran Act, which required the registration of Communists and provided for the emergency detention of subversives. The Committee generally confined itself to global polemics, such as who lost China and why? But it did permit itself minor diversions, such as its upcoming hearing on Subversive Infiltration of Radio, Television, and the Entertainment Industry. For this spring sideshow the Committee subpoenaed four people: singer Burl Ives, comic Sam Levenson, actor Philip Loeb, and Judy Holliday.

11

~~~~~~~~~~~~~~~~~~~~~~~~~~

*P*eople were talking. People of character and standing, people with the clout to make a stand, people who swore to the last they would not give the Committee the time of day went in and spilled their guts. There were as many motives as there were witnesses—fear, self-interest, disaffection with the Communist party, cowardice, patriotism, disloyalty to friends, disloyalty to self. There were those who stood up. Many were blacklisted or jailed, a few were deported, a few killed themselves. It was a deadly business.

Judy was not brave, not in the classic romantic sense. She disliked conflict, she avoided confrontation. But she was highly principled. She possessed a strong inner sense of right and wrong which many close to her thought commendable but unrealistic. Judy's girl-scout morality was nearing the acid test: the boys in Washington played hard and played for keeps. She waited her turn as others, people she had respected, went before committees and succumbed to the pressure. Clifford Odets, Sterling Hayden, Isobel Lennart, Lee J. Cobb, Budd Schulberg, and even Elia Kazan all named names. Judy thought of Woodie Broun's warning: "You never know how you'll react until the shooting starts." Judy wondered whether her strict personal code would turn out to be just so much hot air. Would she betray her friends? Would she betray herself?

Harry Cohn did what he could to cushion the coming ordeal. According to insiders, he reached Nevada Senator Pat McCarran through contacts in Las Vegas and was assured the hearing would be held in closed session. There would be no television or newspaper coverage, no instant dramatic release of testimony for a splash in the headlines. Cynics at Columbia thought Cohn was merely playing for time—*The Marrying Kind* was due to open shortly after Judy's appearance in Washington. Some thought he was hoping to wring one more movie out of his new star in case the hearing went poorly and the star was no more. Those close enough to know Cohn's genuine fondness and regard for Judy saw his maneuvering in another light: if the brilliance of *Born Yesterday* was braced by a second success, the public would be less willing to forsake Judy, no matter the eventual revelations from the Committee. Cohn spared no expense. In addition to the costly Bierly investigation, he arranged top legal counsel and picked up the tab.

Simon H. Rifkind was a widely respected attorney and legal scholar who served ten years on the federal bench. He met with Judy and was struck by her dignity and unpretentiousness. He had seen others brought low by political difficulties, but this was clearly not humility come of nerves. Judy's lack of vanity might make her less susceptible to the Committee's scare tactics. On the other hand, she was visibly upset, and that could make her unpredictable as a witness.

Other attorneys were drilling their clients, preparing questions the Committee might ask and coaching responses. As one seasoned veteran of HUAC observed, many actors delivered their finest performances in Washington. Judge Rifkind did not operate that way. He devised no specific strategy for Judy, gave her none but the most general instructions. She had not been a party member, nor had she done anything illegal, and so there were no grounds for taking the Fifth Amendment, which practically speaking was considered an admission of guilt and guaranteed blacklisting. However, once the witness waived the Fifth and agreed to talk about himself, he could also be compelled to answer questions about others that he knew, under threat of contempt.

Still, Judge Rifkind felt that as long as Judy made a fair and honest presentation of herself and her beliefs, there would be no need for extreme measures. They went over the text of the statement she wished to read before the Committee. She was willing to announce her opposition to certain Communist methods and her support of patriotic ideals. But she was determined to come down hard against censorship, political harassment, and the grave threat to freedom posed by blacklisting and repression. The prepared statement had to be carefully worded. HUAC had shown sharp disfavor with the practice, since it took away some of their inquisitional initiative. The Senate Internal Security Subcommittee, or SISS, did not yet have much of a track record, but odds were they would be just as touchy as their House colleagues.

Judge Rifkind was given a copy of the dossier prepared by Bierly. This was his guide to the handling of the case, and as far as he could gauge, it contained only one potentially damaging item of information. The FBI had long made a practice of gathering evidence through confidential informants. The methods varied from actual infiltration of alledgedly subversive organizations to what amounted to little more than the repeating of malicious gossip. Red hunting had become a national obsession. Informants were under pressure to produce, and so they sometimes offered information that was at best highly conjectural.

Yetta had an apartment in Knickerbocker Village in lower Manhattan where she entertained regularly. Apparently among those attending a large party in late 1950 was a person secretly employed by the FBI. It seems this informant had looked over the bookshelves at the apartment and out of some 2,000 volumes found a few titles which might be considered leftist literature. Based on that alone, the informant later reported to the FBI that it was possible, but not probable, Yetta was a Communist. This was hardly reliable evidence, but in the current climate, opinion could count as heavily as fact. Judy told Judge Rifkind she had no knowledge or part of Yetta's political sympathies. Judge Rifkind told Judy she should be prepared to answer questions about it just the same.

Judy was far more worried about particulars that hadn't shown up in the dossier. She knew the names of several show-business heavyweights who had had a flirtation with the party in the past. If SISS did their homework better than Bierly, this was the sort of sensational disclosure they would be after, not some obscure employee of the NYPD. Foremost in her mind were the documented contributions made to organizations which the attorney general cited as Communist-dominated. Judy was not afraid for herself, but for Helen. There was no telling how the Committee might exploit that, and Judy trembled at the effect that shock could have on her mother. She would not, could not, implicate Helen, whatever the cost. That alone could give her questioners awesome leverage to force other revelations.

There was little more to do than wait. Worse than the waiting was the isolation. Judy said nothing to Helen except to underplay the seriousness of the situation. She could not confide in Yetta, because if Judy were later made out to be a political leper, that could jeopardize Yetta's career. Yetta meanwhile regretted that she had somehow added even a paragraph to Judy's dossier, no matter how flimsy and conjectural the reference. In this sense the Committee's work was done before a word of testimony was spoken. The subpoenaed witness was virtually quarantined, immobilized, rendered untouchable.

Judy could not have survived this period without David. He was everything to her—friend, family, lover, confidant. He alone knew the danger she felt and the depth of her anguish. David stuck by her every step of the way. He comforted her, reassured her, and even solicited lawyers before Columbia hired Judge Rifkind. Since the start of their marriage, Judy had always devoted herself to David's career. Though she disliked public appearances, she attended all of his concerts. If her presence threatened to distract from his glory afterward, she hid herself. When David made the move from musician to executive, she supported him and endured the kind of work-related social affairs she normally detested. She even risked alienating Harry Cohn by demanding a contract that would allow her to remain in New York, where her husband's work was.

Now David could return the support. For the first time he was in a position to truly help Judy, and he made the most of it. He arranged to go with her to Washington and spoke to a mutual acquaintance, public-relations man Robert L. Green, about lodging so Judy would not have to run the risk of being discovered at a local hotel, which would blow the lid on the closed session. Close friends of Judy's who had once viewed David as selfish and self-absorbed were the first to admit he was selfless and saintly in his handling of an extremely delicate situation.

On March 24 Judy spent the evening with David, Judge Rifkind, Woodie Broun, and Sam Jaffe, who had experienced political troubles of his own. Judy thought perhaps she should make a more defiant statement. They worked through a few different drafts before deciding to go ahead with the original. It was really just a way to work off nervous energy. Woodie and Sam kissed her and wished her luck.

On March 25 Judy and David slipped into Washington and arrived at Green's apartment on the top floor of a Victorian mansion. By this time Judy compulsively asked the advice of everyone. Green, no political savant, imparted his understanding of the mentality she was about to confront: "Let me tell you about congressmen and committeemen—you must remember that you are a star, and, honey, they don't translate that you have an IQ at a level that you do. They just think you're Billie Dawn. If I were you, I'd play Billie Dawn. How can they take you seriously as a political figure then? They'll be charmed. Their wives will want to know what you were like, what you wore."

Judy could scarcely believe she was listening to him, although in her present state she probably would have listened to the man who emptied the Committee's ashtrays. "What should I wear?" she asked Green.

"What you don't want to do is appear intelligent. You represent a mistress, an absolutely darling piece of fluff. I would dress in dark clothes, a little sexy, not trashy. They'll be thrilled, they'll say, 'She's exactly what she is on the screen.'"

Green might have published a tract, "Dressing for the Inquisition." As superficial and outlandish as his advice was, there was also a pathetic grain of truth in it. Congressmen were image brokers who played to constituencies the way actors played to audiences. Many of them felt a fascination and perhaps a distasteful kinship with show business, which bred a virulent resentment. That's not to say that HUAC hauled in Larry Parks because Chairman Wood secretly wanted to do a time step and croon "Mammy." Rather the Committee was the ultimate image maker and breaker and was eager to impress that fact upon those in media. That was the implicit morality tale being played out. If a witness conformed to the Committee's image of what an actor should be, this confirmed their wisdom and power and inclined them toward forgiveness. The dominant stereotype was the actor as man-child, easily misled, an unthinking illusionist who changed political sympathies as often as he changed roles. The Committee played the stern parent who threatened and scolded the child and extracted the tangible token of regret, names. That was where the scenario broke down for Judy; whatever else went on in that hearing room the next day, she would call on her last ounce of strength not to inform.

On the morning of March 26, 1952, Judy and David met Judge Rifkind and proceeded to the Senate Office Building. Judy was conservatively dressed, visibly nervous, with an anxious knot in the pit of her stomach. They took the elevator to the fourth floor, walked the echoey corridor to the hearing room, and entered. The first thing Judy noticed was the senators and their legal staff perched on a raised wooden rostrum that stared down ominously over the witness table. The second thing she noticed, in neat stacks before each committee-man, was a copy of Bierly's dossier. At 10:30 sharp, Chairman Arthur V. Watkins gaveled the hearing to order.

The staff director was Richard Arens, a Kansas City lawyer who graduated from Missouri politics and came to Washington during the second Truman administration. He quickly made a name for himself as staff director of the Senate Immigration Subcommittee. He helped draft the McCarran-Walter Act, which greased the skids for deportation of subversives by taking cases out of due-process courts and leaving them to the discretion of nonelected immigration officials. The act also extended immigration quota systems based on national origin, which contributed to Arens' growing reputation for anti-Semitism. Of the four show-business people subpoenaed by the SISS that spring, three were Jewish.

Following some formalities by Watkins, Arens began the questioning by pestering Judy about her family name, which he was keen to establish was Tuvim and not Holliday. From there he went to family and professional background, as Judy choked down the tremble in her voice and recited the particulars with forced equanimity. Arens then began to inquire after specific activities and political associations. At that point Judy realized Arens was following the Bierly dossier item by item. She had all but committed the document to memory, and so after each response had the split-second luxury of anticipating the next question.

There were dangerous digressions, to be sure. An apparently harmless question could splinter into a half-dozen follow-ups, each trying to trip her up on some prior remark. Arens and Watkins kept circling, looking for an opening to hit her with a name. They were especially interested in Betty and Adolph, but that was no surprise to Judy. Judge Rifkind had guessed they were part of the lightning rod that drew the Committee to her to begin with. Judy weathered the early going. She answered directly when she could and waltzed around questions when she had to.

Arens kept peppering her with citings from the dossier, items that dated back to *Red Channels*. When that failed to get results, he changed tack and asked about Uncle Joe. Judy could answer candidly about his varied political and professional past, with an equally honest disavowal of his influence on her beyond her early teens. He was gone and there was no harm to be done to him. Besides, if she gave them what they wanted on Joe, they would be less likely to bring up Helen. This was a necessary gambit. Given Arens' past use of deportation, it was conceivable, if unlikely, he might bring that threat against Helen, who was a naturalized U.S. citizen. The point, of course, would not be to harass Helen but to reach Judy through Helen. It was no more than a remote possibility, but the mind throbbed with possibilities as the hearing passed into its second hour.

Arens droned away with alleged front activities, and Judy chalked them off to innocence, ignorance, or misreporting. Her answers were for the most part truthful, but the Committee was impatient with denials. When Watkins expressed skepticism about these assertions of naive virtue, Judy decided to toss him a morsel and said she could tell him plenty of other activities not listed. Watkins rose to the bait, but Arens ignored it and suddenly asked Judy what she thought of the McCarran Act, the nominal source of these hearings.

There was an absurd exchange as the two men jockeyed back and forth following two separate lines of questioning. Judge Rifkind challenged Arens' right to ask about the act, and Watkins deferred in order to inquire after Judy's other activities. Judge Rifkind offered to answer for Judy, and Watkins became incensed. "Let her tell. Judge Rifkind is not to tell you. He is not to coach you in any way."

Judy tried to straighten things out. "You started by saying,

'You didn't admit most of your associations.' In my mind it was that I had admitted most of my associations." She could see he hadn't believed a word she said. "I am telling the truth as far as I know the truth."

"I am not saying that you are not," Watkins retorted. He could see he was getting nowhere, so he let Arens proceed. That exchange went no better.

"Have you ever urged directly or indirectly the repeal of the McCarran Act?"

"No."

"You knew that the general idea was to register the Communists?"

"Now you told me. Frankly, I was wondering whether it was about deporting people." Judy tipped her hand, but Arens didn't seem to notice. He abandoned his line of questioning, as Watkins had; still, the detour had cost her. Judy had intended to offer Watkins a conciliatory scrap, but he and Arens had fought over it like a couple of terriers and now they were exasperated with her and Judge Rifkind. Judy's anxiety soared as Arens returned to the dossier.

When he walked through her association with the Stop Censorship Committee, Judy knew precisely what came next.

"Do you know a lady by the name of Yetta Cohn, C-o-h-n?" Arens asked significantly.

"Yes, she is my best friend."

"Has she had anything to do in any respect with your signatures and affiliations with these Communist-front organizations?"

"None at all."

"Has she ever counseled with you on this?"

"No, she has no interest in that sort of thing." The dossier flashed through Judy's mind. The informant's accusation was there right before Arens' eyes. Judy ran a lightning inventory of options; her fright was near the breaking point. She decided to preempt and soften what she felt was sure to be his next question. "I was told that she was a Communist."

Arens seemed genuinely surprised, if not especially interested. He continued with his interrogation, and Judy realized he
had not intended to ask about Yetta after all. Judy had
drastically miscalculated. She was desperate to rectify her
mistake. She steered the testimony back to Yetta, insisted she
was blameless, and concluded with an impassioned protest, "It
is a dreadful thing that she should be even mentioned simply
because she is penalized by knowing me and I am penalized by
knowing her, and it just never ends anywhere."

Judy was near tears and Arens was coldly unmoved. The slip
about Yetta was small potatoes, not the major revelation he was
seeking. He lifted more questions out of the dossier, but Judy
had difficulty regaining her composure. Arens and Watkins
asked if she thought she was being mistreated by the Committee. Judy told them no, which of course was grossly untrue. She
thought they had been condescending to her, and worse, rude to
Judge Rifkind. But Judy was in no position to lecture them on
ethics; the hearing had already gone beyond the usual time for a
lunch break, and that was a bad sign.

Watkins asked once more about the other activities mentioned
earlier, and Judy finally explained to his limited satisfaction that
she had meant contributions to charities and the like. She went
on to recant her past front connections and spoke strongly
against the party and the threat of world Communism. She
genuinely believed this, but she resented being forced to
announce her beliefs. Arens could see her discomfort with such
public affirmation and sadistically rubbed her nose in it, asking
whether she believed in God. It was a shabby trick, a gratuitous
exercise of power which Judy did not want to dignify with an
answer. But there was no way not to answer, not without
branding herself a godless, unreconstructed Communist sym-
pathizer in Arens' small, hateful mind. Yes, she believed in
God. No, she did not attend church.

The Committee indulged Judy's prepared statement with
obvious displeasure. When she professed her opposition to
Communism, Arens as much as called her a liar. He could not

grasp the fact that she saw shades of political meaning or that she might defend the civil rights of alleged Communists without being one herself. Arens saw white or black, truth or deceit, anti-Communism or Communism. He denied there was any middle ground, and anyone who said so was a dupe. This was a time of labels, and that was to be Judy's.

She played the role, not Billie Dawn per se, but that of the misguided innocent. It wasn't a conscious decision, more a protective shell she drew up around herself. Throughout the morning she had conducted herself with dignity, answering her questioners as she might a reporter. But the constant sniping, the snide remarks, the nasty tone, the pious presumption of her guilt, wore her down. Even after the committee members despaired of coercing names from her, they kept up the pressure. If Arens could not make her inform on friends, he would have her inform on herself. This was his specialty, the are-you-still-beating-your-country school of interrogation. Judy stood up under the browbeating for the better part of two solid hours. When she could take it no longer, she quietly slipped into character. She affected wide-eyed wonder through their lengthy lectures. She nodded through their smarmy characterization of themselves as merciful and just. She agreed when they told her how lucky she was that they were withholding the proceedings from the press for now. Judy had prevailed; that much was apparent. She only wanted the nightmare ended.

Watkins gaveled the hearing closed at 1:10 amid warnings that Judy leak no word of her testimony. Judy and David thanked Judge Rifkind, then made their way back to Robert Green's apartment. Judy called Helen, then Woodie, then had a drink or two; she was feeling extremely wound-up. As the three of them sat down to dinner that evening, Green told Judy it seemed she'd won, though she thought of it more as having survived. In 1952, survival was something.

12

~~~~~~~~~~~~~~~~~~

*A*fter Washington came purgatory. Judy had been cleared of any criminal wrongdoing, but the undisclosed testimony had the manipulative force of blackmail. The simple fact that she had been called would mean a stain on her public image. Actual disclosure would leave her at the mercy of partisan columnists who were free to quote responses out of context. Judy was never more vulnerable.

She could take some solace from *The Marrying Kind*. With its New York premiere in mid-March and its national distribution a few weeks later, the film was creating an encouraging stir. It was not likely to win the widespread popularity of *Born Yesterday*, but it wasn't meant to. *The Marrying Kind* was a comment on middle-class life and the hopes and dreams embraced by marriage. It showed how marriage could be not the cause but the receptacle for disappointment and broken dreams.

Judy was absolutely convincing as Florence Keefer, the modest wife of modest intelligence but good sense. She did not play down to the character or give her a contrived common nobility, but rather found in her a kind of working-class aesthetics. This was not the sneaky glamour of the shopgirls Joan Crawford used to play. Florence was realistic with traits that ran from annoying to endearing, and a slightly bewildered pathos that was quietly fascinating. Judy showed critics and the public that she was not a one-note comedienne but an actress with sensitivity and range. The film displayed her to excellent advantage: she had a shattering dramatic scene in which her young son drowns at a family picnic. She even got to sing the catchy "Dolores" while accompanying herself on the ukulele. The performance gave every indication of initiating the transition from Billie Dawn that Judy wanted. She was so good that she even made a better actor of the callow Aldo Ray, whom she generously helped on the set but thought little of personally because of his drinking and apparent low opinion of women. Harry Cohn was immensely pleased with his discovery Aldo Ray, but was less forthcoming about Judy. Judy's fate at Columbia was about to suffer another setback.

Judy was pregnant. She had found out shortly before going to Washington, and some friends had even suggested she use that as an excuse to avoid appearing before the Committee. She flatly refused, but the fear of testifying was soon replaced by a fear of childbirth—her hypochondria had become such that she fretted over everything from colds to hangnails. She had no tolerance for pain, and the mere thought of labor terrified her. There was more to it than that. This was not a planned parenthood, and the timing could have been better. Her career was in limbo, and this would further forestall a decision from Columbia about her future in films. Then too, Judy and David had enjoyed their carefree life together, and the responsibility of a child would drastically change that. Still, they were loving adults with a healthy marriage, and the initial shock gave way to heartfelt happiness. Following the Christmas episode with Abe three years earlier, Judy had entered psychoanalysis. There was still much more to unravel, but she had come to an understanding and acceptance of her father which eased her apprehensions

about parenthood and the irrational fear that she might somehow repeat the mistakes that she had suffered as a child. All
things considered, Judy was well prepared for motherhood. She
was not prepared for the family's reaction to the news.

Since Joe's death Harry Gollomb had assumed the role of
paterfamilias and he was playing it to the hilt. When Uncle
Harry learned of Judy's condition, he paid a visit to David and
without so much as a handshake castigated him, "How could
you do this? How could you get Judy pregnant?" It didn't occur
to him that this was no more David's fault than Judy's. Besides,
it was absurd to speak of it as a "fault" at all; it happened, and
the couple was already happily adjusted. Harry was convinced
that this would ruin Judy's career if not her life, and that David
was the culprit. On subsequent visits Maude was just as critical
and chilly. David remained as calm and courteous as he could,
but the damage was done. The truth of Yetta's family caveat hit
home with a bang: the in-laws were meddling, they even had
the audacity to criticize David's private life. It did not immediately affect his feelings for Judy, but there was the disturbing
sense that she would eventually have to choose between him and
her family, if in fact she had not already done so.

Judy was having problems of her own. Helen's reaction to the
news was also negative, but unlike Harry's, her anger turned
inward as depression. Judy launched a major campaign to boost
her mother's morale, constantly telling her, "You're going to be
a grandmother, think how wonderful that will be. You're going
to have a lot of responsibility, you'll have a child to look after."
But all Helen could think was that she would be replaced in
Judy's life. The room she often stayed in on Waverly Place
would become a nursery. She wouldn't be able to drop in as she
pleased; her daughter would have no time for her. The more
Judy tried to cheer up Helen, the more depressed she became.
By late spring Helen began to suffer crying fits. By early
summer she grew disoriented and once was found walking
dazed around Seventy-fifth Street.

One night Judy woke up with a start. David asked her what
was the matter, and Judy said she could feel something was

wrong with Helen. She called, and there was no answer. It was conceivable Helen was with Harry and Maude or simply sound asleep. Judy's foreboding grew. She threw on a housecoat, drove uptown, and arrived at Seventy-fifth Street in time to pull Helen's head out of the oven.

All the old fears seemed to be coming true. Judy took Helen to a psychiatrist and he confirmed that she had suffered a breakdown. The doctor recommended immediate treatment and suggested a private institution on Long Island. Arrangements were made, and Judy drove Helen the long two hours there. Shock treatment was begun at once, and with proper medication, the suicidal urge passed. As was customary, the procedure severely jarred Helen's memory. She had difficulty remembering simple things, even Judy's name. The psychiatrist there spoke with Judy and said repeated visits were doing neither her nor her mother any good. Helen was beyond danger and showed strong signs of recovery; Judy was well along in her pregnancy, and long hot rides were not an especially good idea. Judy tried but was unable to stay away. It was as if with Helen's current therapeutically regressed state, Judy had become the mother. She could not sit idly by.

It was a blistering late summer, but Judy faithfully made the arduous trip to the hospital. Sometimes Yetta would join her, sometimes Ruth Buffington. Once or twice she went alone. She would sit and chat with Helen or take her to Jones Beach. As Judy's pregnancy progressed, Helen's recovery also accelerated, as though she were experiencing a kind of rebirth. The breakdown was certainly not consciously calculated, but the aftermath could not have been more uplifting for Helen had it been. It was plain the maternal bond would remain no matter the events of her daughter's life. Judy was pregnant, with the first hints of marital strain and a career teetering on the edge of ruin, but Mama still came first.

Of course it was a two-way street. By scrupulously tending to Helen's needs, Judy could sidestep her own problems. More and more this was becoming the pattern: everybody came to

Judy with personal woes, and she could solve everybody's troubles but her own. It was deceptive even for her closest friends. Because she showed such mastery of other's dilemmas, it seemed impossible she could be so lost in her own. Besides, there wasn't all that much anyone could do for her; Judy's habit of withdrawing under personal stress made her less accessible to help or advice. Yet, for all the emotional camouflage, there was one sure yardstick—her weight. When Judy was anxious or depressed, she ate; the more she ate, the more upset she became, and so the cycle spiraled. She was pregnant, and according to lore, a pregnant woman was permitted dietary extravagance. But Judy's eating was something more. By the end of summer her weight was nearly 190 pounds.

Helen was discharged, and Judy took her to Nantucket with Ruth. They stayed at an old inn and walked to the public beach each day. Judy was restless and nervous; she ate and read and worked word puzzles. Her self-consciousness worsened as word spread of her presence and strangers hovered for a glimpse of the star. Ruth and Helen became Judy's phalanx, escorting her to and from the water, encircling her as she sunned herself on the sand. Judy made herself comfortable by digging a hole and easing her belly into it like some nesting bird.

One morning the beach security was breached when two young Harvard students approached Judy and remarked at the double-crostic she was beginning. This was the connoisseur's word game which ran in the *Nation* and later *Saturday Review* and commonly took experts a day or more to solve. The Harvard boys sat by speechless as Judy whipped through the puzzle in thirty minutes. Afterward they shook their head and repeated "My God, my God." Judy was no intellectual snob, but she enjoyed her command of language and the scope of her reading and knowledge, and she especially enjoyed exploding the myth of actresses as vacuous sorts who mouthed the words of others. Beyond that, the puzzles were her mental calisthenics, a way to burn off anxiety and keep loneliness at arm's length.

Other interactions on Nantucket were not so harmless. Each

day more people searched for Judy and circled her like so many vultures. Under normal circumstances she was not fond of being star-gazed. Eight months pregnant, with the figure of a professional wrestler, the last thing she wanted was to be on view as some celebrity specimen. This violation of privacy reached its low on the third night of the vacation. The threesome went out to dinner and a woman at the neighboring table coarsely exclaimed, "She's got a nerve coming out in public in her condition." Judy was embarrassed, as she always was in the face of rudeness. But more than that, she was reminded that the public felt a certain license where stars were concerned. This was especially true in Judy's case, since she played earthy, decidedly familiar characters. Although fans more often respected the patrician reserve of a Hepburn, they felt free to approach a Holliday as they might a beautician or a woman in the market. She was one of them. Judy was partly flattered by this, and partly alienated. She did not think of show people as a special class aloof from the common folk. That look-but-don't-touch attitude was something she found pompous and distasteful. Then again, Judy scrupulously respected the privacy of others and expected as much in return. She could shrug off the more innocent invasions, but there was the odd discourteous incident, such as the remark at the restaurant, that upset her. The gap between her public image and personal identity was a kind of psychological pressure point. She protected it as best she could.

Judy returned to New York and Waverly Place and prepared to while away the last five weeks of pregnancy. There had been no further word on her political status, but the prolonged lull was considered a very positive sign. At six A.M. on September 24 there was a rap at the door. Judy hurried downstairs and was greeted by two somber-looking men who identified themselves as FBI agents. They handed her a bound copy of her Committee testimony and told her that precisely twenty-four hours later identical copies would be distributed to all major newspapers and magazines along with that of the other three McCarran witnesses, Philip Loeb, Sam Levenson, and Burl Ives. The pressure had been great on all four, especially Loeb, who had been forced from his role as Papa Goldberg on Gertrude Berg's popular television series *The Goldbergs* and whose testimony had been particularly defiant of Arens. Still, Judy was by far the best known of the four, and given the proportionate nature of the redhunt, she was sure to receive the most publicity.

An hour after the men left, Judy phoned Yetta. "I think you better get over here, something's happened."

Yetta dressed and grabbed a cab for Waverly Place. Judy sat her down at the kitchen table with a cup of coffee, handed her the transcript, and said, "I think you better read this."

Yetta read it and almost fainted. Judy had told her little of the substance of the hearing and nothing of the slip about Yetta's politics. She honestly thought the document would not be made public. Judy explained how Arens had used Bierly's dossier as a guide to questioning and how she had jumped the gun as he reached the informant's item. Judy felt horribly guilty about her miscalculation. Yetta felt guilty about having added to the dossier and giving the Committee that extra bit of ammunition. But the self-recrimination was getting them nowhere. Judy had one day of grace before the news became public, and she was determined to use it to protect her friend. She asked Yetta to take the day off from work, and then the two of them made a list of every New York newspaper. The national press was less likely to latch on to Yetta's name. Judy then placed one call after another inviting columnists to say what they wished about her but to keep Yetta's name out of it since she was an innocent bystander and the mere mention might compromise her position on the police force. The newspapermen were amazingly cooperative, and Judy and Yetta breathed a sigh of relief. In their momentary triumph they forgot to double-check their list. If they had, they might have noticed a small evening daily they had overlooked.

The timing of the disclosure could have been worse. Vice-presidential candidate Richard Nixon—who had gotten untold political mileage from the red scare—had just delivered his "Checkers" speech denying the existence of a secret campaign slush fund. The master stroke of that televised address intensified the campaign between Eisenhower and Stevenson, and, with reports from the Korean front, moved the McCarran Committee's release off the front page. In the items that appeared, Judy was, as expected, repeatedly singled out; her picture was run with every article, and her name decorated each headline or kicker. The news stories were relatively gentle in tone. They extolled the virtue of the Committee, not once mentioning Arens' brutal tactics. It was accurately reported that none of the witnesses had ever belonged to the Communist party, but much was made of their front associations and characterization as dupes.

The editorials were not so kind. The *Times* lectured about the need to discriminate between good and bad liberal causes. The *Daily News* portrayed the four as cowards and fools and described Judy as "the dumbest of the bunch."

The conservative columnists were vicious. They went after Judy with undisguised zeal, dismissing her defense of unwitting complicity and painting her as something of an evil genius who outwitted the honorable Committee. Robert Ruark called her a pinko who played "footsie-footsie with organized Commie fronts," adding, "She just rolled them big dumb blue eyes and said she was too irresponsible for words." He did not say that the eye-rolling was the product of his own fertile imagination, or that her eyes were brown, not blue. Ruark was too filled with righteous fire to be distracted by such incidentals. Victor Riesel went one better by implying that Judy owed her success to the encouragement of other industry left-wingers. This was patently preposterous. If anything, she had encountered repeated resistance within the business, and the ultimate success of *Born Yesterday* was due to the general public which attended in spite of the pickets and alleged subversive content.

The columnists fed on their own pieties and attacked Judy from every imaginable angle. Several of them mentioned her advanced pregnancy, and one implied this somehow increased her debt to America. That alone was unforgivably malicious. Far from her portrayal in the press, Judy never regarded herself as a privileged person and had her name and number listed in the Manhattan phone book. The calls came the instant the columns hit the streets. One said, "I hope your baby is born dead." Another said, "I hope you die in childbirth." A third said, "I hope your baby has two heads." Judy wept and David had the phone disconnected and an unlisted number installed.

The cruelty was more than she could bear. Judy had faced the Committee and, in effect, was cleared. The subsequent release of the testimony could have no conceivable constructive end. It was a cheap play for political publicity and brought further pain to witnesses who had already suffered immeasurably. It was high among the events that would cause Philip Loeb to take his own life three years later.

The columnists greedily did the dirty work of character assassination and freely interpreted and distorted the transcripts. The presumed political irresponsibility of the four was nothing next to that of the columnists. They played a dangerous game of demagoguery, catering to the public's ill-informed fears and contributing to the atmosphere of hate that spread like a cloud across the country.

Yetta's name showed up in the overlooked evening daily, and her phone was immediately tapped. Friends who knew only what they read in the paper called and complained, "How dare that Holliday woman get you into this mess! Why didn't she keep her mouth shut?" Yetta would answer blandly, "I think the Committee is doing a splendid job, I'll get back to you." She would hang up and race downstairs to a public phone, call back the friend, and explain that Judy had tried to protect Yetta and keep her name out of the papers. It was a vivid example of how easily reputations were damaged by a biased press. Yetta heard nothing from the police department, but it was a smoldering silence.

It would be months before the full effects of the transcript release could be gauged. Meanwhile, Judy's thoughts turned to the imminent concern of childbirth. Despite the twin crises of politics and Helen's breakdown, the pregnancy itself had been uneventful. True, Judy's weight ballooned, but she was otherwise healthy and resilient. And though the prognosis was for a trouble-free delivery, she became increasingly obsessed with the inevitable pain of labor. Her friends did what they could to distract her, playfully guessing what the child would look like, even starting a pool at a dollar a shot for the precise date of birth. Judy was fully looking forward to motherhood; getting there was the hard part.

Judy went into labor on November 10, 1952. David rushed her to Doctors Hospital and had to be reminded later that he'd won the pool. Her physician was Norman Pleshette, and he saw her through long hours of labor. Judy's pelvis was narrow, and the extra tension come of pain only prolonged the labor. Finally Dr. Pleshette decided to take the child by cesarean. Judy gave birth to a healthy baby boy, Jonathan Oppenheim.

Yetta came to visit later that day and asked Judy about the operation. Judy was blasé about the entire procedure save the cost, which at $1,500 she considered a bit pricey. Still, she liked Dr. Pleshette and fairly glowed with pride.

"Where's Jonathan," Yetta asked.

"In the nursery."

"How will I know which one he is?"

"You'll know," Judy answered impishly.

Yetta walked down the hall to the nursery thinking that all newborns looked the same—shriveled and ugly. Could Judy have already succumbed to the silly vanity of new mothers? Yetta came to the glass, took one look, and knew at once why Judy was aglow. Jonathan had a wide smile that reached to two round red cheeks, and a full head of blond curly hair that made him look like a miniature Greek god. She had never seen a more beautiful baby.

Judy came home to Waverly Place after a week and hired a nurse, whom she quickly fired. For the next several days she went through nurses almost as fast as Jonathan went through diapers. When she finally found one she liked, she hovered about and all but scared her off. Judy was a very fussy mother; also a bit touchy. Friends filed through and raved about the baby. Leonard Bernstein dropped by and teased, "He looks just like his father—he looks like a gorilla." David laughed, Judy exploded. She chased Lennie from the place and told him never to come back again. Others there at the time told her that was just Lennie's way of paying a compliment. Judy said she didn't give a damn about Lennie's way of doing anything, and though she continued to see him socially, she never really forgot his minor indiscretion. Judy had felt unprotected as a child, and Jonathan would have nothing but protection.

Harry and Maude were thrilled with the new addition to the family, but that did not repair their rift with David. Helen shared Judy's happiness and at last came to see that far from competing with Jonathan, she could help in his upbringing, which, in turn, would cement her place in her daughter's life. This presented some logistical problems. The Waverly Place apartment was peculiarly designed with a good deal of social space and relatively little bedroom space. Jonathan could have his own nursery, but that would leave Helen no place to stay overnight. Judy and David discussed moving.

There was an unexpected benefit from Jonathan's birth. Abe, who in recent years had been persona non grata, was delighted to have a grandson and paid frequent visits to Waverly Place. Judy was the wiser for her time in analysis, and although she was not entirely rid of resentment for her father, she was better able to accept and welcome him. Abe was still working as a fund-raiser for Zionist causes, but his best days were behind him. He lived alone in a brownstone apartment on the East Side. The place was strangely decorated with Mexican artifacts and snapshots. If he had no romantic life to speak of, he still had many friends. But Abe was lonely for the sort of family life that might enrich his declining years. And though his leave-taking years before had meant a practical end to his role as husband

and father, the new role of grandfather seemed to fit him well. He was soft-spoken and cuddly, and his voice had a rich, reassuring pitch. Above all, he deeply loved Jonathan and seemed committed to giving him many of the things he had denied Judy. In a real sense, the baby was a centripetal force that brought the extended family closer than it had ever been.

With her own house in order, Judy could concentrate on her best friend's problems. Just after the first of the year, Yetta received a notice to appear in the chief inspector's office. She was seated in the center of a large room and questioned by a tribunal for over three hours. In step with the times, the NYPD was conducting its own purge, and their methods were as intimidating as the worst Washington had to offer. Yetta was asked whether she raised money for the Loyalists during the Spanish Civil War, whether she marched in any May Day parades, what her political affiliations were, whether she had ever received Moscow gold. The hearing turned up nothing of substance, and Yetta returned to work the following day. But the stress was intolerable; she couldn't be certain of her fate in the department, and she feared that a widening investigation might create trouble for her sister and brother-in-law, both of whom taught in the city schools.

Judy took Yetta to see Judge Rifkind. After a few minutes he told Yetta she couldn't afford him. Judy was in no position to help out financially, besides which there was probably little Judge Rifkind could do for Yetta; departmental decisions were not necessarily open to legal review. Judy and Yetta left the office and ran into Adlai Stevenson, who just weeks before had lost the presidential election to Eisenhower. This was a man Judy greatly admired, and forgetting herself and the mood of the moment, she fished a pen and pad out of her purse and shyly asked for his autograph. Stevenson obliged, smiled, and went on his way.

The ongoing departmental purge wore away at Yetta. She had not been targeted for further investigation, and as far as she could tell, her phone was no longer tapped. But the residual anxiety was oppressive: she couldn't sleep, her mouth was dry, she sometimes shook with fright. Judy had been after Yetta to quit the force for years, certain that the talents she had developed editing the police magazine could be put to better use in business. Yetta had saved some money and so would be spared the immediate burden of job hunting. With Judy's blessings she finally resigned and left for two months' vacation in Europe.

There was still the matter of where to live. The Village was not known for spacious apartments and parks, nor was it the kind of residential neighborhood Judy wanted for raising a child. The East Side was pleasant and unarguably chic, which was all the more reason Judy needed to reject it. That left the Upper West Side, where Judy spent most of her youth. There were some dangerous blocks, and it was hardly the height of fashion. But there was access to Central and Riverside parks, a friendly largely Jewish middle-class population, and Broadway had a certain grimy charm. There was an added feature: it was close to Helen's place.

Judy and David decided on the Dakota, a stately Victorian building on the corner of Seventy-second Street and Central Park West. The rooms were enormous, with towering ceilings, ornate molding, and deep-grained mahogany doors and trim. Judy loved the location and the idea of living in an antique building, but she had reservations about the scale and the opulence of the place. The day she signed the lease she phoned the Buffingtons, who lived minutes away on Seventieth near Broadway. She asked them to come over, and they arrived to find her in the middle of the formidable drawing room curled up on a lone wicker chair. No other furniture had arrived, and the vast emptiness dwarfed Judy.

Ruth looked around and gasped, "Look at this place."

Judy repeated forlornly, "Yeah, look at this place. Oh, my God. How can I live here?"

The move was made, and slowly the cold rambling apartment assumed some of the warmth of the Village place. It would be a while before Judy could truly make it her own, but she was quickly quite pleased with life at the Dakota. It was a status symbol in which she took no small pleasure.

In the past hectic months Judy's life had been a frenzy of problem-solving. She had gotten Helen back on her feet; she had survived a congressional hearing and a thrashing in the press; she had given birth to a healthy baby boy; she had helped Yetta through an ordeal; she had begun to patch things up with Abe; she had moved to a new apartment. The one remaining cipher was her future at Columbia. In March she learned that Garson Kanin had written a new comedy script which his wife, Ruth, saw as a perfect comeback vehicle for Judy. There was only one catch—Judy's weight.

With Jonathan's birth Judy went from 190 pounds to 172 pounds. She was sure the scale was broken; she felt quite slim. With token willpower she managed to work her way down to 164. The new film was scheduled to start shooting on May 1. On March 24 Harry Cohn let it be known that unless Judy was back to her normal weight in two months, the picture would be scrapped. She was in no position to argue. Given the events of the past year, Cohn's patience, never known for its elasticity, had been stretched to the limit. He might have used any of a dozen loopholes to escape Columbia's contractual commitment to Judy, and still could. Besides, she knew she was not fully back in the boss's favor, since on Jonathan's birth she received only a dozen roses, whereas other Cohn stars received much more lavish gifts. Finally, she was, for all practical purposes, still blacklisted.

Judy confined her diet to hard-boiled eggs, celery, tomatoes, grapefruit, the usual V-8 juice, and small portions of broiled meat. It was hell, not only for Judy but for those around her. When Judy dieted, the world dieted. No one was to discuss fattening food around her, much less eat it. Judy was serious about losing the prescribed weight by deadline, but Harry Cohn was leaving nothing to chance. Each morning at nine she was visited by a studio doctor and a lesser studio executive. Judy would lead them to the bathroom, shed all but her slip, and step on the scale. They would record the results and wire the figures to Cohn on the coast.

Nothing depressed Judy as much as dieting. She was not narcissistic, and so vanity was no incentive. She was not fashion-conscious, and so clothes were no incentive. She was social, and she loved socializing over a good meal, which only compounded her sense of sacrifice. As in many ethnic households, food was love. The pantry was stacked high with goodies and the refrigerator overflowed fine food. Helen was an excellent cook. Judy was a better eater than she was a cook. Food was the joy of the family, and the diet descended like a plague. The pantry and refrigerator were stripped bare, Judy grew listless and irritable. One day she caught Helen at the door hiding a cylindrical object in brown wrapping. "What's in the package?" she demanded. Helen said it was nothing, but Judy was adamant. Helen peeled back the paper to reveal an enormous kosher salami. Judy screamed, "I can't stand it another minute. I'm starving!"

On the thirty-eighth day Cohn's diet patrol reported an astonishing 127 pounds, three pounds under the goal weight. Judy was ecstatic. Her analyst's office was on Madison Avenue in the Eighties, not far from a discount clothing store. After that day's session Judy went out and grabbed every size-ten dress she could lay her hands on.

The movie would go on as planned. There was just enough time for a quick trip to the country. Judy and Ruth went up together; Buff had a performance to play and arrived later that afternoon. He got out of his car and Judy stepped out of the front door in a snug pink jump suit.

She struck a cover-girl pose. "Ta-da!"

Buff hadn't seen her in weeks; he couldn't believe his eyes. "Judy, I didn't know you had a body like this."

Judy nearly matched his disbelief. "Look at this. I'm never going to eat again."

13

~~~~~~~~~~~~~~~~~~~~~~~

The wardrobe test was not going well. Columbia had found a new leading man who had worked extensively in television and appeared in a recent Broadway revival of *Room Service*. His name was Jack Lemmon and he had all the makings of a fine comic actor. The studio had carefully screened him over a period of months but inadvertently overlooked one thing—his size. Jack was trimly built, maybe five-feet-ten in height. Judy, even in her slender condition, was broadly built and in heels also stood about five-ten. This violated the Hollywood rule by which a leading man had to at least appear larger than his leading lady. Judy thought it was foolish but she had long since learned to expect such foolishness in movies.

Jack was handed a pair of lifts, which left the matter of bulk. He was then given a special sports coat with shoulders that were padded and built out with all the subtlety of a football uniform. Jack told Judy he felt like an asshole. She made pleasant conversation to put him at ease. Toward the end of the afternoon Jack was thinking of a way to express his gratitude to

Judy and in a moment of forced nonchalance he ventured, "What are you doing for dinner tonight?" He couldn't believe he had asked. Why would this star want anything to do with an upstart from television?

Judy casually took the cue. "So where we going?"

Jack couldn't believe his luck. "I don't know. You tell me."

Judy lowered her voice conspiratorially. "There's this wonderful little Italian place that I shouldn't go to but I love. I'll pick you up. Where you staying?"

"I'm at the Hollywood Roosevelt, but I'll pick you up."

Jack took down her address and set a time. He went out and rented a car and promptly got lost. He arrived at Judy's place twenty minutes late and she proceeded to navigate him to the restaurant, a clear case of the blind leading the blind. They were on a dark winding road in the Hollywood Hills when the car blew a tire. Jack instructed Judy to roll up the windows and lock the doors and he took off in the direction of some distant lights hoping to find a gas station. He had run perhaps two miles and the lights seemed no nearer. He started to worry about Judy and ran back to the car, afraid she had been hurt or abducted. He returned sweaty and breathless to find her sitting calmly in the front seat. "I'm sorry. I'm sorry," he apologized. "We'll have to drive down, I'll probably ruin the wheel."

"Do you have a handkerchief?" she asked.

He handed her one. "What happened?"

"I changed the tire."

Jack had come west reluctantly, expecting to find an absurd "star" system full of phony hauteur and overblown egos. He looked admiringly at Judy, chuckled, started the car, and thought to himself: She isn't a star—she changed the fucking tire!

They were friends from that moment on, and it was only part of the rare family feeling that soon surrounded the production. Judy had brought Jonathan and Helen along and both were quite popular with the company. George Cukor was directing and he had Judy over often for dinner, which had become the norm when they were working together. It was also his way of keeping a watchful eye on her diet. Helen was always a welcome addition to these gatherings, with her refreshing, quirky personality. During one meal at Cukor's she was seated next to Cole Porter. She had not been introduced and did not recognize him, so she tried to break the ice. "Tell me," she asked, "what do you do for a living?"

Porter answered modestly, "I play the piano."

"So do I," Helen chirped.

The warmth extended to the cast's other leading man, Peter Lawford. Peter knew Betty and Adolph from their work together a few years before on the film *Good News*. He had never met Judy and was the least bit wary, half-afraid she might look down her nose at mere movie people. Before shooting they bumped into each other on the set and without the least hesitation or awkwardness Judy offered her hand and introduced herself. They chatted and clicked right away.

The occasion for all this togetherness was a story premise Garson Kanin had stumbled upon months before. He was driving past Columbus Circle in New York when he noticed that Ruth was in low spirits. He looked up at an empty billboard and playfully asked how she'd like it if he had her name printed there in full view. She didn't think much of the idea. Ruth's mood passed, but Gar's notion lingered and flowered into a story about a young man who comes to New York bent on success. He fails and as a last resort rents a sign and has his name put on it. For no better reason than that, he becomes known and his celebrity snowballs. Gar tried out the idea on Ruth, who liked everything except the gender of the protagonist.

"It feels like Judy Holliday to me."

"Fine," he allowed, "but it's going to be Danny Kaye."

By the time Gar completed the script, he had come around to Ruth's way of thinking. Judy was the exclusive property of Columbia, and so Gar prepared for another collision with Harry Cohn. Cohn approved the script but not the terms, which included Gar as director with final cut. The dickering was more belligerent than usual, and it ended with the author selling the work outright and angrily departing for Europe. Cohn lined up Cukor, ordered Judy's crash diet, and readied *A Name for Herself* for early summer.

The plot was about Gladys Glover, a young woman who comes to New York in quest of fame and becomes a girdle model. She loses the job after becoming a bit thick through the hips and is about to despair of her dream when she hatches the idea of renting a billboard on Columbus Circle and posting her name. She encounters a suave young soap scion who wants her billboard to promote one of his products, and after much wooing she swaps the one space for several located strategically around town. Meanwhile she gets to know a second suitor, a young documentary filmmaker who loves Gladys but disapproves her pursuit of celebrity. Gladys has her day in the sun, decides that fame is not all it's cracked up to be, and throws over her corporate Romeo for the filmmaker.

The story was light on substance and heavy with contrivance. It lacked the sparkle of *Born Yesterday* and the drab realism of *The Marrying Kind*. In fact Gladys Glover was not Garson Kanin's most original or inspired character, but more a weak sister of Billie Dawn. Nor was the dialogue especially crisp. With the director's help, the cast would have to read between the lines and breathe what life they could into the script.

Shooting began in early summer, and it was a happy set. Jack was somewhat tight to begin with, and Judy did what she could to relax him, including not complaining about repeated takes that Cukor requested. They were playing long scenes, sometimes three or four pages at once. Jack was sure it was great, and Cukor would tell him, "Wonderful, wonderful, don't you know. However, let's do it just once more, shall we, and, Jack, less. Less, dear boy." This went on for days; they would complete a scene and Cukor would say, "Once more, and less, dear boy, less." Judy worked closely with Jack, who grew anxious trying to decipher the repeated direction. Finally he could take it no more and when the next "less" was requested, he blew up.

"Are you trying to tell me not to act?" he demanded.

"Oh, God, yes," Cukor sighed. "Oh, yes."

Jack was learning what Judy had learned when shooting *Born Yesterday*. On film, stage technique came across as stagy. It was necessary to pare down a performance, to think and behave and let technique take care of itself. Judy might have told him, but she never interfered with Cukor's direction, and anyway, she knew Jack had to discover this for himself.

After that Judy and Jack's work together went from good to excellent. They both had sharp minds and their timing was precise and almost musical. Judy in particular seemed to think in sixteenth notes, sensing whether to come in on, just before, or just behind the beat. Their theater training showed in that they played to each other and not to the camera. They were responsive and inventive and their dialogue crackled with energy.

Cukor wisely used that rapport to good advantage. One day Judy was killing time on the soundstage and found an old upright tucked away into a corner. She mentioned it to Jack, who liked nothing better than to noodle at the keyboard. Judy, Jack, and the piano were inseparable. The bane of moviemaking is delay; there are sound checks, set changes, lighting setups, camera run-throughs, and occasionally acting. Ordinarily Judy would pass the time reading or working puzzles, but with Jack it was like having a second Buff around. She would sing standards or listen as he felt his way through new tunes. Cukor could not help but notice the fun they had, and as a scene approached, set in a bar with Gladys and her filmmaker friend Peter Sheppard, he suggested they find a way to use the piano.

It worked beautifully. Jack sat at the piano picking out random melodies and humming. Judy joined him and they sang a few bars of "Let's Fall in Love," which was exactly what was supposed to be happening between Gladys and Pete. It was a tender, sexy bit of business that said more than a page of dialogue. For an otherwise slick and obvious comedy, it was an intimate human moment which reveals rather than broadcasts emotions. It was a wonderful example of the way a sensitive open director could utilize the special talents of gifted actors.

Later in the shooting there was another outstanding instance of this. There was a heated fight between Gladys and Pete in which he criticizes her lust for celebrity and she tells him it's none of his business. There is a false note of finality after which they wait a beat and Pete asks if their date for the next day is still on and she says yes. It was a very funny scene and it played well in rehearsal. Only, Jack had an idea: if Pete not only waited a beat before confirming the date but actually stormed out the door, then returned, the tag line might play even better. On the other hand, he was afraid Cukor might veto the suggestion or, if he agreed and rehearsed it, the bit of business might lose its spontaneity. Jack decided not to mention his idea.

The cameras rolled, and Judy and Jack took their places. The argument built naturally through her line, "Do me a favor and butt out." Jack answered, "Great," but instead of waiting a beat and going on to the tag line, he turned and left and slammed the door behind him. Cukor said nothing, but kept the cameras going. Another actress might have broken character and grumbled that the exit was not in the script. Judy responded to the exact stimulus. When Jack left, she kicked a nearby chair to kill the beat, then he reappeared and growled, "So is it still on for Friday lunch?"

"Yes."

"Thank you."

"Don't mention it."

Jack exited again, and Cukor called, "Cut, print." They all had a good laugh at the sudden improvisation, and later, when they saw the scene in previews, the false exit received the biggest laugh. This was Hollywood moviemaking at its finest.

Jack was not Judy's only admirer. Peter Lawford, as the debonair Evan Adams III, was impressed with her consummate skill and unselfishness on camera. Judy was in a film written for her and directed by a man with whom she had worked thrice before and who had a reputation as a woman's director, and yet there was not the least trace of star ego. Peter realized that here was a superb actress and director doing their jobs to the best of their ability and that none of the other paraphernalia of stardom applied. Judy enjoyed acting with Peter and adapted to his sophisticated style. Her scenes with him were as soft and smooth as her scenes with Jack were feisty and electric.

Peter's fondness for Judy did not stop at the set. He enjoyed her fresh, unaffected manner, which was unique among actresses he had met in Hollywood. More than that, he delighted in her lively sense of humor, her witty incisive remarks, her bemused way of looking at things. The attraction was mutual. Judy found him utterly charming and attentive, with an almost boyish sense of fun. They both appreciated the company of interesting, imaginative people.

Peter met Jonathan and adored Helen, whose relationship with Judy struck him as genuinely caring and respectful. Peter took Helen and Judy to the Beachcomber for dinner and following egg rolls and various Polynesian exotica, the waiter brought out three plates with rolled hot towels for cleaning the fingers. As far as Helen could see, this was just another unfamiliar eastern delicacy, and she raised the towel to her mouth and tried to take a bite. Judy leaned over and said, "Mother, you don't eat that." They all laughed, and Helen laughed the loudest.

Betty and Adolph were in Hollywood to begin work on their next film, *It's Always Fair Weather*. In recent years they had collaborated on the screen versions of *On the Town* and Peter's *Good News*, as well as *The Barkleys of Broadway*, *Singin' in the Rain*, and *The Band Wagon*. They had taken the town by storm and moved in a stylish social circle much like the one they had entered in New York. Judy and Peter spent time with Betty and Adolph making the rounds and spending most weekends at Gene Kelly's house, which was a nonstop party with a guest list that read like a Who's Who of Hollywood. Judy either played poker, badly, or charades, well. More often Judy and Peter kept to themselves. They were private and discreet and almost no one suspected they had become involved in an affair.

In June the production moved to New York for location shooting. One morning Yetta got a call from Judy. "Come over, we're going out to lunch."

"We?"

"Peter Lawford and I."

"Judy," Yetta said, "I haven't seen you for a while. Why do I want to see Peter Lawford?"

Judy called Peter and put him off till dinner, then met Yetta for lunch. Yetta asked Judy what was going on. Judy told Yetta about her involvement with Peter. Yetta was nonplussed; as far as she knew, there had been no serious trouble in the marriage, and even if there were, this was drastically at odds with Judy's strict moral code. And yet she seemed so innocent of it all, as though it were no more than a schoolgirl crush. Judy had said nothing to David, nor would she. As to how long this might go on or where it might lead, Judy didn't say and Yetta didn't ask.

Over a period of months Judy had been under unrelieved strain. There was the subpoena, the hearing, the pregnancy, Helen's breakdown, the release of the testimony, the difficult labor and delivery, the abrupt end of Yetta's career on the force, the blacklisting and uncertainty over Judy's career, her near-obesity, her heroic diet, the move into a new apartment. It was reality like a vise, and for once Judy welcomed the never-never land of Hollywood. It wasn't as if she believed she owed herself a wild time. Rather she seemed to want to convince herself that she had come through her many trials intact, that she was still a vital, attractive woman. And what better way to prove that than to spend time with a dashing, desirable Englishman? The fact that it became more than simple companionship was due to a strong mutual attraction and affection. As far as Peter knew, Judy and David were separated. For her part, Judy was willing to forget the reason and control that had always driven her and give way to impulse and fancy. She did not try to explain it to friends; she could not explain it to herself. Later when another friend was introduced to Peter, she took Judy aside and remarked, "He's so good looking. He looks like he ought to be an actor."

It was a sweltering New York June. The daytime temperature never dipped below one hundred degrees and the sticky air was like a Turkish bath. One scene in the script required Judy and Peter to drive around Columbus Circle in a convertible sports car. Traffic was horrendous and several retakes were required. Judy practically collapsed from the heat.

Another scene was set in Central Park, where an already despondent Gladys gets into a tiff with a cranky stranger who accuses her of trying to pick him up. It was a hilariously caustic encounter and Judy asked Cukor to cast Woodie Broun as the stranger. Woodie arrived in the morning and the temperature was already a hundred and two. Cukor ran the scene and afterward turned to Woodie and asked, "Were you afraid of getting venereal disease in conversation? What is all this disgust? It's just an argument in the park. We'll do it again." The next time Cukor asked Woodie, "Where is your disgust? Are you used to chatting with whores?" There were repeated runthroughs, and after each one Cukor gave Woodie the opposite direction of what he had just done. At length the director excused himself for a minute, and Woodie took Judy aside. "I'm sorry. I appreciate you getting me this job, but it's just not working."

"Oh, no," Judy reassured him. "He likes you. If he doesn't like what an actor is doing, he either immediately gets another actor or he cuts the scene. He likes you."

Cukor returned and ran the scene for the cameras. After each take Woodie walked to the shade and dabbed at his face with a cold wet towel. At length Judy approached him and muttered, "You son of a bitch, you prick, you bastard."

Woodie wondered what had happened to her consoling attitude. "What's wrong?"

"You get to use those damn towels. I'm all made up. I can't stand watching."

There were several more takes, and finally Cukor announced, "Wrap." He then summoned Woodie, who expected a lecture or a lambasting. Instead Cukor told him, "I was a friend of your mother and father. Perhaps you will join Miss Holliday and myself for lunch at the Plaza."

"Mr. Cukor, I'd love to, but I'm not fit to go into anyplace."

"You can take a shower in my suite. I'll lend you a shirt."

The three of them went to Cukor's room, Woodie showered, and this time Judy would not be denied. She was due to return to the park after lunch for a scene with Jack; still, she slipped into a cold bath without removing hat or makeup. When she returned to the park, it was much as it had been that morning, incessant retakes, only by now it was several degrees hotter. Judy never once complained to Cukor. She trusted him implicitly and knew that if a scene was reshot, there was a reason. That was the greatest source of their personal and professional kinship: they were both perfectionists.

Location shooting was concluded in just under two weeks. Helen and Jonathan stayed behind as Judy returned to the Coast to wind up her studio work. Principal photography ended in July, but Judy took a place in Malibu and lingered on through August. She and Peter discussed the possibility of doing a nightclub act together and went as far as to meet with Betty and Adolph about material and arrange a tentative November opening at the Sands in Las Vegas. Peter lost interest and the plans floundered. Judy then tried to convince him to join her in a play, not for Broadway but for a small regional theater. Again Peter was uninterested. Judy began to talk about staying west for another picture, though nothing was available at Columbia. Mostly she was playing for time.

On August 12 Judy got a phone call from Hearst gossip Louella Parsons. She bluntly stated that *A Name for Herself* was finished and that Judy had been seen repeatedly in the company of Peter Lawford. Judy did not deny it but insisted it was all in preparation for their nightclub act. Aware of the insinuation, she offered a postscript. "If you ever saw my husband, you would know how nice he is and that I am really in love with him." Parsons' reply was transparently sarcastic. "Okay, Judy, any girl who talks as sincerely as you do must mean it." The next day the exchange appeared in the gossip's column, which was syndicated across the country, including the New York *Journal American*. Judy left shortly after that; she made no further plans to see Peter, who felt the parting was friendly. He dearly valued the time he spent with her.

Judy was not long home when she heard that Peter intended to marry Pat Kennedy, daughter of industrialist Joe and sister of the newly elected senator from Massachusetts, Jack. The news jolted her. Judy had never seriously considered leaving David for Peter, but she was not at all aware that Peter was even seeing anyone else. She quickly got over the shock and the next time she saw Ruth Buffington she wisecracked, "Can you believe it? He's going to marry one of those from that horsey set." Judy did not object to Pat so much as her brothers, whom she saw as political opportunists. Jack had allowed himself to be swept along in the redhunting tide, and Robert had just signed on as legal counsel with Joseph McCarthy.

David suspected the affair with Peter, but Judy said the rumors were untrue, and he had no choice but to take her at her word. Still, the marriage had fallen on hard times. The accumulated weight of family interference, Judy's revitalized career, and David's feelings of neglect led to a predictable stress. They remained together, but friends could only wonder how long.

A Name for Herself was released in late January of 1954 as *It Should Happen to You* and it was a commercial success. Not only did it introduce Jack Lemmon to the moviegoing public but it also provided Judy with an invaluable comeback vehicle and officially ended her blacklist exile. Although McCarthy was at the very height of his power, Judy received no flak from redhunters. A month later she made another significant break-through with her first major television appearance in a thin little

On *The Marrying Kind* set with, from left, George Cukor, Ruth Gordon, and Garson Kanin. *(Author's collection)*

As the blushing bride in *The Marrying Kind*. *(Author's collection)*; *Right*, Judy singing with her mother, Helen. *(UPI)*

Judy with her six-month-old son, Jonathan. *(Wide World Photos)*

Judy arriving in New York with co-star Peter Lawford to film *It Should Happen to You. (UPI)*

Upon being named one of the twelve smartest women of the year. *(Wide World Photos)*

Above, with Woodie Broun and Jack
Lemmon in *It Should Happen to You*;
Right, Judy and Jack Lemmon sing
"Let's Fall in Love." *(Alfred Eisenstaedt,*
Life *magazine,* © *Time Inc.)*

On vacation in Paris, 1955. *(Wide World Photos)*

With Helen and Jonathan, Judy leaves for Hollywood to film *Solid Gold Cadillac*. *(Wide World Photos)*

Judy with Jule Styne rehearsing *Bells Are Ringing*. (*Wide World Photos*)

Judy with the Tony award she received for *Bells Are Ringing*. With her are fellow Tony winners Rex Harrison, Margaret Leighton, and Fredric March. (*UPI*)

Judy toasting the success of *Bells Are Ringing*. *(Wide World Photos); Right,* with co-star Sydney Chaplin, celebrating the first anniversary of *Bells. (UPI); Below,* a saddened Judy tries to avoid photographers in Paris after her abrupt break with Sydney. *(UPI)*

Judy with jazz musician Gerry Mulligan. *(UPI)*

Judy in a rare public appearance not long before her death. *(Bob Gomel, Life magazine, © 1962 Time Inc.)*

farce, *The Huntress*. As the *Times* television critic Jack Gould attested, the show was less important for itself than for the fact that it brought Judy back to the medium that had banned her only a short time ago.

Judy was certainly glad to have survived the blacklist, but she knew that she had not come through unscathed. Despite the triumph of the picture and further work on television, a disturbing pattern was taking shape. Before the release of her testimony she had begun to stretch as an actress. *The Marrying Kind* amply displayed her promise and versatility for material that was not exclusively comedic. Since the release, however, she had gotten nothing but Judy Holliday roles—variations on or throwbacks to Billie Dawn. She was fully aware that Harry Cohn had gone out on a limb for her, and she was morally if not contractually obligated to accept whatever scripts he offered. She expected no better of television, which was little more than a rubber stamp of personalities and images built up through film.

Judy had beaten the blacklist, but for now it was something of a Pyrrhic victory. She was mired in typecasting.

14

~~~~~~~~~~~~~~~~~~~~~~~~

Judy was ill-suited to public life, which she found at once shallow and intrusive. She had entered a kind of career backwater, but rather than fight the inevitable, she devoted herself to her private life. Jonathan was a special joy. He was alert and smart, and Judy treasured the time she spent with him, which was considerable. She was also getting along well with Helen, who had readily adjusted to her expanded role in the family. These things fortified Judy and helped cushion the fact that her work was sagging and her marriage was faltering.

In what had become a regular cycle, Judy left for Hollywood in the spring of 1954 to make another film. Columbia had been pleased with Judy and Jack Lemmon's rapport in *It Should Happen to You* and teamed them again. The sequel had the ungainly and nearly unpronounceable title *Phffft* and was the first screenplay of George Axelrod, who was fresh from the success on Broadway of *The Seven Year Itch*. The director was Mark Robson and the cast included Jack Carson, Luella Gear, and Harry Cohn's answer to Marilyn Monroe, Kim Novak.

It was not a good script. The premise was familiar but workable—a kind of seven-year itch between a stuffy lawyer and his wife who is a writer of radio soap operas. At first glance, Judy's was a mature role with appealing womanly possibilities. But Axelrod did not develop his characters, who remained two-dimensional and static. Instead he extruded laughs from situations, which meant the story operated at the gag level and quickly wound down like a two-dollar watch. Had a director of George Cukor's excellence and elegance been on hand, something might have been salvaged from the mediocre writing. After all, the very best moments in *It Should Happen to You* were due more to acting and direction than to writing. But while Mark Robson was a creditable director, he had no comedy background, and it showed. Dialogue that might have played better in two-shot was crosscut. Labored reaction shots slowed the pace. Sight gags that would have benefited from judicious cutting were repeated ad nauseam. In general what might have been a gently daft screwball comedy spilled over into over-wrought farce. Judy, Jack, and Jack Carson, each capable of light understated comedy, were wasted on a film that resorted to such cartoon devices as a hideaway bed that went "whoosh" and a title that went "phffft."

Judy did not sulk, even though the character Nina Tracy gave her nothing to work with and the film's release brought her the dimmest reviews in years. She was not passive, just realistic about the fact that she was a contract star toiling in the studio system with no contractual right to script approval. Judy was a thoroughgoing professional—she invariably contributed to her scripts and offered ideas about how certain scenes might best play. But once the shooting started, she delivered herself totally to her director. She did not storm off sets or invent eleventh-hour ultimatums. She was punctual, affable, cooperative, and she gave even the worst material her best effort.

Judy's loyalty did not go unnoticed. Harry Cohn knew that she had endured *Phffft* stoically and he was eager to reward her with a more fitting vehicle. Cohn purchased the rights to the

George Kaufman/Howard Teichman Broadway hit, *The Solid Gold Cadillac*, about a minor idealistic shareholder who uncovers corruption at the top rung of a major corporation. The principal role of Laura Partridge had been performed by septuagenarian Josephine Hull, a wonderfully fey comic actress who had recently passed away. Cohn hired Abe Burrows to tailor the role for Judy, which mainly consisted of lowering the character's age and contriving a romantic interest. Burrows had his first brush with the irascible mogul, but aside from a few disagreements on specific lines and casting, the association was remarkably peaceful.

Judy was given the completed script and thought it was a brilliant adaptation of the play. It asked her to do nothing comedically she hadn't already done before, but the character was well-conceived and the dialogue well-crafted, even if the plot was somewhat pat. Judy was further encouraged when she learned that the film would be directed by Richard Quine, a former actor with a solid track record in comedy. She didn't even mind the fact that her leading man would be Paul Douglas. Time had healed some of the wounds from *Born Yesterday*, and she did respect the man as an actor.

Judy started work on the film in the fall of 1955 and was joined by a friend at one point during production. The shooting was going well until a particular scene, set in the corporate boardroom and requiring close to two hundred extras. The friend arrived shortly before six and watched as Judy repeatedly fumbled a simple line of dialogue, something she rarely did. At precisely one minute of six she got the line right and Quine called a wrap for the day. The friend walked Judy to her dressing room and noticed she seemed mildly agitated. "What was that all about?"

"They were throwing me the wrong line," Judy complained. "They wanted me to fluff the line, because if shooting goes one minute over six o'clock, they get two hours' extra pay."

The friend saw nothing awful about that. "What the hell do you care?"

"It's not right," Judy insisted. "And I hate to say it, but I don't like extras. They'll do anything to get their faces on camera, including knocking you down," she said, remembering her rough treatment years earlier as an extra in *Greenwich Village*. She had no desire to deny these people their rightful day's wage, but admitted, "It distresses me to see people behave in this manner."

What Judy might have meant was she was wearying of moviemaking, the interminable waiting, the constant battle against mediocrity born of studio commercialism. No single experience stood out as negative, but then, it had been some time since she felt really positive about her work. It was all so workmanlike: wait for a call from the studio, head west for three months of filming, return east, look for the release and the notices, then hope for a better vehicle next time. She was not growing as an actress, she was not given the chance. The roles fell safely within her established repertoire, and if some were better than others, none really expanded her craft. Were she any less of a pro, she might simply have walked through the performances. Only an unyielding sense of dedication and concentration kept her from apathy. Yet, it was a waste of her energy, fighting boredom instead of tackling a truly difficult or different part. It had been nearly five years since she last set foot onstage, and she longed for the chance to build a role and communicate with a live audience. For the present, she could only plow through the tedium and keep her mind limber between takes with word puzzles.

Judy continued to pass many of the long Hollywood nights with the regulars at Gene Kelly's house. She joined in such parlor games as charades but preferred poker, for which she had more enthusiasm than skill. One evening Judy was seated at the table next to Oscar Levant. The game was seven card stud and the betting was heavy. Judy folded, a card or two too late as usual. She glanced at Oscar's hole cards and saw a strong concealed hand. She also saw that he trembled more with each successive round of betting. Several half-smoked cigarettes later he suddenly threw in his cards. As another player happily scooped up the large pot Judy said to him, "Oscar, how could you fold? You had the winning hand!"

"I know," he answered, lighting another cigarette, "But if I'd stayed in one more second I would have had a heart attack."

Toward the end of shooting on *Solid Gold Cadillac* Columbia gave Judy her next script, called *Full of Life*, written by John Fante from his novel of the same name. It was a dreary maudlin story of a woman (Emily Rocco) married to a writer who is a lapsed Catholic. His devoutly religious father comes to stay, and in the course of Emily's pregnancy, the young couple discovers true faith. It would be hard to come up with a theme more anathema to Judy. She showed the script to Yetta, who read it, winced, and nearly gagged. "Don't do it," she advised. "I have no choice," Judy replied. Her political difficulties had long since passed, so this was no sop to the Catholic War Veterans. But she still had two films to go in her contract, and if this was what they wanted next, she had little choice in the matter. *Full of Life* was not due to go into production for a few months, and in the interim she would do what she could to make revisions.

Judy came home to the Dakota just before Christmas 1955. It was a cozy holiday with friends and family, a tree, piles of presents, and Jonathan cheerfully running about in a western getup twirling twin toy six-shooters. The outward contentment could not mask the mounting tension between Judy and David.

After the first of the year Judy received a call one evening from David. He had to entertain a client and wouldn't be home for dinner. This was nothing new; David's work often required him to socialize after hours. But Judy could hear music in the background as he spoke, and she asked where he was.

"I'm at a bar," David said. "We're having a drink before we go to dinner."

"What are you drinking?" she asked, appearing to make conversation.

"I'm drinking a martini."

Judy said good-bye and hung up. Something struck her as

strange about the call. Then it occurred to her that David always drank Scotch. Either he had changed suddenly or he was too distracted to think what he was actually drinking. Judy's eyes filled with tears. Somehow she knew David was having an affair.

There was a succession of stormy confrontations. David had in fact gotten involved with Ellin Adler, the attractive and accomplished daughter of actress and drama teacher Stella Adler. Friends had seen it coming but were powerless to prevent it. Some thought the burden of Judy's fame and greater income had been too much. That may have been a factor, even though she had always taken pains to avoid publicity and play down the importance of money. Certainly her periodic pilgrimages to Hollywood were no help; in seven years of marriage Judy had appeared in six films, each requiring prolonged absence from New York. Even the sturdiest marriage might have trouble withstanding such repeated incursions on time.

But as David would later confide, two separate episodes had pushed him beyond the breaking point. First was the family's reaction to the news of Judy's pregnancy. Harry's outlandish lecture and Helen's breakdown graphically proved their immersion in Judy's life, as well as Judy's refusal or inability to do anything about it. Second was the affair with Peter Lawford. No one had confirmed it to David in so many words, but then, no one had to. At the very least the semipublic nature of the affair hurt his pride. More than that, the experience must have underscored the extent to which Judy's work and the separations it necessitated made him vulnerable. The relationship had been an isolated incident, the peculiar offshoot of events and emotions too intricate for even Judy to fully grasp. But it was a disconcerting precedent; it had happened once, and could happen again.

David came to Judy and asked for a divorce. It turned into a bitter confrontation during which Judy struck David with a large antique photograph album. Shaken and enraged as she was, she took care not to hit him in the mouth. The argument resolved nothing. David walked out and Judy vowed she would not give him a divorce.

Through the many tantrums and tears that followed, one thing became painfully clear: Judy still dearly loved David, she would do anything to save the marriage. But it seemed just as clear that David had no intention of coming back. Judy's moods swung between depression and anger. She shielded Jonathan as best she could, but in the back of her mind was the terrible truth that he might have to face the same trauma she had faced as a child. Judy had wanted nothing more than to spare her son the pain she had experienced. And yet the scenario was fearfully similar—a somewhat insecure but loving husband alienated in large part by meddlesome in-laws. That realization made her cling stubbornly to self-control. Judy would allow herself to be upset, to be regretful, to be angry as hell. But no matter how bad she felt, she would not go to pieces as Helen had.

Judy's friends saw her through the first shock of the separation. Yetta spent every spare moment at the Dakota, and when she was away, talked to Judy by phone at all hours of the day and night. The Buffingtons were loyal to Judy, although they had known David longer. Only two years before, Judy had helped see Ruth through a nearly fatal premature birth, rushing her to the hospital, spending the night in the waiting room until Buff could get there. Judy had even taken time out a few days later on New Year's Eve to drop by with roses as the hospital workers gawked at this famous star dressed to the teeth, with Adolph in tow. When Ruth came home from the hospital still weak but with a healthy new daughter, Judy insisted on a nurse and paid the fee. Ruth and Buff were steadfastly there for Judy when she needed them, knowing it meant a virtual end to their friendship with David. Helen also rose to the crisis, comforting and caring for Judy and weathering some misplaced anger. If any immediate good resulted from Judy's pain, it was the profound awareness that she had the complete love and trust of several exceptional, totally devoted friends.

By late spring of 1956 Judy was feeling well enough to go

back to work. The occasion was the less-than-promising *Full of Life*. She went west with Jonathan and Helen and rented a house that belonged to Sylvia Sidney. It was an unusually social stay for Judy, possibly because she found the film so objectionable. She had made numerous changes in the screenplay and had transformed her character, Emily Rocco, into a level-headed thinking woman who not only keeps house but is widely read and plays chess. But these were essentially cosmetic additions to a plot run through with cheap sentimentality and a frightening helping of ethnic schmaltz.

Former Metropolitan Opera star Salvatore Baccaloni played Judy's father-in-law, and while he reduced his technique somewhat for film, his performance was broad in the extreme, given Richard Quine's uncharacteristically flaccid direction. Papa Rocco was annoying to begin with, dispensing unwanted advice, repeating dubious old-world wisdom, lamenting that his prodigal son has many books but no Bible, many pictures but none of Christ. It was like a message from the Vatican. Judy made the best of a bad situation, and even engineered one or two endearing scenes with Baccaloni. For the most part she did her day's work and hurried home each night to be with her mother and son.

One unexpected pleasure from the film was the friendship Judy developed with her leading man, Richard Conte. He had trained at the Neighborhood Playhouse in New York and began making movies toward the end of World War II. He was affable and perceptive and he shared Judy's doubts about the current production. He dropped by the house often for a drink and a chat. What Judy liked most about him was his down-to-earth manner; he was wonderfully un-Hollywood.

This was the direct opposite of her feelings for Humphrey Bogart, whom she met again through Lauren Bacall. A Jewish holiday was approaching, and Bogart remarked to Judy that he'd never had a real Jewish meal. Judy invited the couple to dinner and, with Helen's help, prepared a spread that was sumptuous even by Gollomb standards: matzo-ball soup, potato latkas, pot roast, honey cake, and plenty of everything. Afterward they retired to the living room for drinks and Judy played bartender. Instead of complimenting his hostess on the monumental introduction to Jewish cookery, Bogart began a long harangue on what he saw as her failure to conduct herself properly as a Hollywood star. She avoided parties and for those few she attended she dressed plainly and camouflaged herself behind friends and industry outsiders. What's more, she allowed herself to be seen in public wearing blue jeans and workshirts and no makeup. This was carrying idiosyncrasy to the brink of iconoclasm, and he vehemently disapproved. Didn't she realize she had a debt to her fans, an image to maintain?

Bogart was so insulted by her flagrant lack of propriety and class that he tried to make an example of her right then and there. "I'll bet you don't even have any green Chartreuse." This to him was a mark of status, stocking exotic liqueurs.

Judy glanced at the liquor cabinet and reported, "You're right, I don't."

There was a frosty interlude after which Bogart and Bacall left. Helen witnessed the entire bizarre evening. On impulse she went to the bar, grabbed a bottle from the front row of the cabinet and held it up to Judy. "You have green Chartreuse."

"Yeah," Judy steamed, "but I'd be damned if I'd let him know."

In Judy's mind Bogart already had two strikes against him for his frequently public drunkenness and inexcusable verbal abuse of Bacall. This evening's behavior was a colossal third strike. His repulsive preachments were not only tactless, they were positively boorish after the trouble she had taken to feed him. Judy repaid her fans by delivering the whole of her talent to each and every performance. The debt ended there; what she did with her personal life was her concern, and she was not about to be lectured by a man she regarded as boozy and basically misogynistic, no matter his accomplishments as an actor. With that, Judy shut the book on Humphrey Bogart.

*   *   *

Ruth Buffington was on tour with the Robert Shaw Chorale. She had written Judy and mentioned she'd be in Los Angeles for a brief stay. Ruth knew Judy was in production and figured at best she might have time for a quick drink or bite to eat. Ruth was a bit nervous opening night. The orchestra was onstage, and knowing nothing about stage makeup, she painted herself up with a flair more befitting Ringling Brothers. The performance was splendid and backstage was a madhouse. She was talking with several other musicians when over the din she heard, "Ruthie, Ruthie, where is Ruthie?"

The crowd parted magically as Judy approached, kissed Ruth, then laughed. "What have you got on your face?" Ruth explained she was new to stage makeup, and Judy offered to give her lessons later. Judy then said, "Come on, let's go hear some jazz. We're meeting Sydney Chaplin, you'll like him."

Sydney was the second son of Charlie Chaplin, a hilarious free spirit who diverted himself with bit parts in B westerns and supported himself with his father's ample trust fund. Judy first met him when she came to town as a Revuer, and again over the poker table at Gene Kelly's house. Sydney was best known as a one-man traveling party; he liked to drink and eat, and he had a vocabulary that could raise a blush in the Seventh Fleet. Judy had been seeing some of him, and though their personalities could not have been less alike, they had a good time together.

The three of them went out for drinks and music, Judy said good night to Sydney, and asked Ruth where she was staying. "Oh, some motel in town." Judy told her she had rented Sylvia Sidney's house and that it was far too big for her, Helen, and Jonathan.

"The master bedroom has this huge round bed. I'm so terrified of sleeping in that bed by myself. Come on and stay with me."

Ruth depended on the musicians' bus for transportation. "How am I going to get around?"

"I'll give you one of my cars."

It was settled. Ruth spent the night and they giggled like two schoolgirls. Ruth left the next morning for rehearsal and Judy invited her to bring back some of the musicians that evening. Ruth followed instructions and returned with a handful of colleagues, including Robert Shaw's kid brother. They were joined by Helen and Shelley Winters, whom Judy had befriended, and the lot of them sat on the plush carpet and played penny poker late into the night. Bogart could have his propriety—this was Hollywood Holliday-style.

There was still a month to go on shooting when Judy was permitted another diversion. A year earlier she had gotten together with Betty and Adolph and kicked around the idea of a Broadway musical. The writing team had collaborated on a musical version of *Peter Pan* two seasons before, but despite a popular and profitable sale to television, the show had a disappointing run on Broadway. Betty and Adolph were eager to reestablish themselves and they thought they had the perfect idea for Judy—a story about a good-hearted operator at an answering service who is able to solve everyone's problems but her own. The resemblance of the character to Judy did not end with her stint on the Mercury switchboard, but extended to her growing habit of wisely counseling friends while her own life often teetered on the edge of disaster.

In May Betty and Adolph were on the Coast for a job and they presented Judy with the first draft of their libretto. The reunion was awkward at first. The three of them had not worked together in over ten years and in that time they had enjoyed resounding separate success. They were no longer three peers in an act of four. Betty and Adolph were among the leading writers of musicals onstage and in film. Judy was a top star. They were slow penetrating the distance of years, careful to avoid hurting one another's feelings. Much of the uneasiness vanished once Judy read the script. There was no score, but the character and story were skillfully wrought and played to her strengths.

Judy agreed to do the show, and the three of them decided there was no time like the present to begin looking for a leading man. Judy's shooting schedule left only lunchtime free, and she arrived each day for auditions in full costume, which at that point in the picture meant she was eight months pregnant. They weren't having much luck turning up suitable male leads, and Judy finally suggested they give Sydney a chance. Betty and Adolph knew him well and liked him very much, but they also knew he had no stage experience, let alone musical experience. Furthermore, his well-earned wild reputation did not inspire faith for the rigors of Broadway. Judy persisted, and they relented. Sydney auditioned but was unimpressive. Betty and Adolph returned east to find a composer and resume the search for a leading man.

Judy finished *Full of Life* in late June and cheered herself with the observation that she was only one film shy of completing her contract with Columbia. Back in New York, Betty and Adolph had joined forces with Jule Styne, who had written several of the songs for *Peter Pan*. Judy had been lobbying for Alec Wilder, but Alec's music was unconventional and unlikely for musical comedy. She was not especially fond of Jule, but she respected his talent, and that was enough.

Betty and Adolph were turning their thoughts to possible directors when they learned that Josh Logan was interested in the show. Judy heard the rumors, along with word that if Logan directed, he might want his star from *South Pacific*, Mary Martin. Judy phoned Yetta and asked her to come to the Dakota for lunch. Yetta went directly to the bedroom, a friendly spacious room with a large king-size bed where Judy spent more and more of her time and where she regularly entertained her closest friends. Yetta listened to the story about Logan and Mary Martin and exploded. "Judy, get on the phone right now and call Betty and Adolph and say, 'That was written for me and I want it.'"

Judy took the advice and called Adolph. "The show was written for me, I think it should be mine." Adolph, who had never been much good at standing up to Judy, agreed, and the rumors soon ceased.

Jerome Robbins, an alumnus of *On the Town* and *Peter Pan*, consented to direct. Betty and Adolph and Jule played a backers' audition for Armina Marshall and Lawrence Langner of the Theatre Guild, and quickly had a producer for the show.

There remained the question of a leading man. Further auditions had been fruitless, and with a production schedule fast taking shape, everyone was growing edgy. Judy continued to push Sydney, but Jerry Robbins was no more sold on the idea than Betty and Adolph had been. Under duress from Judy, they eventually granted him a second chance. Sydney flew east and Judy coached him in the part. This time the audition went better and Betty and Adolph were won over to Judy's side. But Jerry was unconvinced, admitting that Sydney had the looks for the part, but not the voice. Several arguments later, Jerry agreed to give Sydney as long as the New Haven tryout to prove himself. If he failed, a replacement would be found, and not another word would be said.

Sydney was signed on September 12 and the show, now known as *Bells Are Ringing*, was readied for rehearsal. Aside from the New Haven compromise, two grave doubts lingered. First was Judy's singing, which in the past had been confined to patter songs as a Revuer and lubricated crooning in the parlor with Buff at the keyboard. Second was Judy's feelings for Sydney. Throughout the auditions it had become increasingly apparent to all that she was casting more than just a leading man.

15

~~~~~~~~~~~~~~~~~~~~~~~

*H*erbie Greene sank his fingers into Judy's throat, and something like a howl filled the room. She looked at him as if he were out of his mind and demanded, "What the fuck is that?"

He explained that he was manipulating her larynx in order to enlarge the size of her voice. This was Herbie's specialty—transforming actors not so much into singers as into actors who also sing. He preferred actors to singers. He considered singers narcissistic and unimaginative, mannequins relying on a single tool, the voice. Singers could upset the fragile logic of a musical, abandoning character and reducing the show to little more than a concert.

Actors, on the other hand, employed an entire array of tools and worked strictly within character and plot. The trick was not turning them into virtuosos but helping them find and project the correct voice for the part. This was sometimes easier said than done, particularly in Judy's case. She had had no prior musical training and her fear of singing onstage was inordinate. Throughout the planning stages of the show she had, along with the rest of them, begged the question of her singing. When the time came to make good the assumption, she panicked. She stalled, she stiffened, she wept, she fought. Herbie matched her tantrum for tantrum. He knew that underneath all of the childishness was a tough professional and that pampering and coddling would only be self-defeating. Judy and Herbie fussed and brawled and, for it all, actually grew to like each other.

Herbie was less enthusiastic about her leading man. The first time he clutched Sydney's throat, Sydney threw up all over the studio carpet. Herbie announced, "I can't possibly teach Syd-ney Chaplin how to sing because he vomits when making a noise that doesn't remotely resemble singing." Judy had already stood off Betty, Adolph, Jerry, and the Theatre Guild, and she was not about to waver now. She sternly told Herbie, "I don't care if he does vomit on your rug. You do the best you can by him." It was not open to debate.

The songwriting was going much more swimmingly than the singing lessons. Despite having to discard five songs that didn't fit Sydney's limited vocal range, Betty, Adolph, and Jule were sequestered in Jerry's house and the bulk of the score was completed in a matter of days. There were many good songs, but the gem was a gentle soulful ballad, "The Party's Over." There was only one drawback: Judy insisted she could not sing a straight ballad and would not try. Betty remembered how Judy liked to sing decorative obbligatos over the few slower tunes Buff used to play down on Waverly Place. Jule devised a scheme: he taught Judy a vocal line which he said was the countermelody to the ballad. That relieved her anxiety and she quickly learned the part. When she asked who was going to sing the melody, Jule answered, "You, baby, you've been doing it for a week."

Judy was not always so handily outsmarted; on occasion it took brute force. She had been training with Herbie nearly two months and was growing quite comfortable with the score when he hinted it might be time to try a small recital. Judy said no. Herbie invited Betty and Adolph and Jule up to his studio one afternoon without telling her. Judy arrived and angrily took Herbie aside, "Why are all these people here?"

He explained patiently, "Because to begin with, it might be advisable for you to sing for somebody else besides me. And secondly, you're going to have to be performing for something like fifteen hundred people every night. So let's start with at least three other people."

"I won't do it," she stated.

He tried to provoke her into it. "Stop being a child."

"I'm afraid, and I won't do it," Judy replied in a squeaky Billy Dawn voice.

Herbie was running out of patience. "Find a way to do it, Judy, or else."

Judy marched to a corner of the studio, turned away and mumbled, "I'll try it this way first."

Herbie threw up his hands, sat at the piano, and played the first few bars of "The Party's Over." Once Judy was into the song, he ran to the corner and spun her around. "Now, sing it, goddammit!"

She sang and sang well. Her anger at Herbie helped her overcome her fear. It wasn't his favorite technique, but that's what they were paying him for, and he was determined to deliver.

The nonsinging rehearsals were far less traumatic. It was a strong cast which included Peter Gennaro, Bernie West, Jack Weston, George Irving, Dort Clark, Eddie Lawrence, and a wonderful comic actress, Jean Stapleton, whom Judy remembered from *In the Summer House* three years before and thought would be ideal as Sue, owner of the answering service. Jean was so thrilled with the prospect of working with Judy that she left the cast of the long-running *Damn Yankees*. She decided this would be a rare opportunity to watch a master at work and she wasn't disappointed.

Bells was about Ella Peterson, one of several switchboard operators at a New York answering service with the hoaky name of Susanswerphone. Ella is a kind, resourceful woman who not only serves her clients but also assists them in their respective hopes and careers. She becomes especially involved with a struggling young playwright, Jeff Moss, who is on the verge of giving up writing. At the switchboard she poses as a benign old lady with apple-pie optimism that keeps him going. But her involvement becomes more personal as she meets him and they fall in love, though she is afraid to reveal her true identity. There is a somewhat superfluous subplot as Sue's man friend, Sandor, surreptitiously turns Susanswerphone into a front for a bookie organization. In fact, the entire story was rather flimsy and contrived, but as Jerry Robbins explained to his company, it was essential to remain faithful to the logic of the book and not descend into farce or camp.

Judy followed her director's dictum to the letter. She brought no preconception to the role and at first there seemed to be no character at all. As with all plays, the cast started on book and read while seated. Jerry was fascinated by the way Judy worked. He had seen other actresses, especially those in musical comedy, who come in with an established personality or style, superimpose that on the current character, and then make the company react to that. Judy was just the reverse; she listened closely and reacted to the others. She approached it as she might a straight play, evolving slowly within the story context, tending to every last speck of the characterization. Her instinct told her that even the most makeshift musical might succeed if the audience could be made to care about the characters. As with Billie Dawn and Alice before her, she fashioned a recognizable personality, then tilted it, giving it individuality and life. Every last member of the company was won over by Judy's professionalism and unselfishness.

No less fascinating for Jerry was the way Sydney had begun to come up in his performance as Jeff Moss. His singing was little improved and his dancing was only slightly better than his singing. But his acting had the precise sexy insouciance that the part called for and his scenes with Judy had more spark than the standard musical-comedy romantic interest. It wasn't just acting.

Sydney had taken a place on West Eighty-first Street and was fairly constantly in Judy's company. Friends could not imagine a less likely couple. Whereas his older brother, Charles, Jr., labored under the burden of their father's fame, Sydney had long ago given up any notion of rivaling Charlie's vast accomplishments. He anesthetized himself with an almost fevered commitment to fun, a willful superficiality. He was raucous, bawdy, and unpredictable, with an irresistible zaniness. He had a feel for moments that was extremely charismatic in an odd, almost childlike way. He had matured from a somewhat roly-poly young man to a dark, manly handsomeness—his coloring and the soft contour of his face were not at all unlike Abe Tuvim's, or for that matter David's. Sydney had a way of sidestepping difficulty or unpleasantness. He could suddenly turn off or simply disappear, which more or less defined his history with women. His many affairs tended to end as suddenly as they started. He liked Judy, enjoyed working with her, and while he did not love her, saw no reason not to get involved.

Judy's involvement was not so easily explained. She knew David and Ellin were seeing each other openly, but it was doubtful she would have contrived a retaliatory affair. Certainly she had been lonely since the separation and she had strong needs for male companionship along with strong sexual needs. Sydney was no intellect, but he was uniquely entertaining in an outrageous way. Judy knew of his footloose ways and checkered past with women, and yet her almost maternal care of his career at the time seemed to give her a measure of control and protection. Above all she felt feminine with him, and that was a feeling she had sorely missed for some time. Different as they were individually, Judy and Sydney were happy together. Betty and Adolph merely chalked it up to another backstage romance like that with Peter Lawford, which would come apart mutually with time. More astute friends thought they saw Judy falling in love and setting herself up for a hard fall. As her sometimes poker partner Maureen Stapleton would later point out, you don't knowingly put your hand in a buzz saw and act surprised when you're hurt.

Bells moved to New Haven for more rehearsals and an October opening. As with all shows facing tryouts, it was nervous time with long hours and tempers near the flash point. Yetta attended one rehearsal and was pleased to find Betty militantly protecting her friend and star. During one dance routine the chorus boys nearly fumbled Judy, and Betty screamed, "Be careful, don't let her fall." Yetta was so impressed with Betty's concern that she sent her a bouquet of flowers with the note, "To a great woman, a great writer, thanks for taking care of Judy."

Yetta got a call from Judy the next day. She was offended that Yetta would send Betty flowers and not her. Yetta tried to explain it was simply a gesture of thanks for Betty's care, but Judy was not open to reason. She had been rehearsing ten hours a day with production meetings and rewrites going long into the night. She had not been under such strain since Philadelphia and *Born Yesterday*, but at least there she had the full attention of John Houseman and Nick Ray, to say nothing of her director, producer, cast, and crew. Here she was just one of many striving toward a common end. She had little time to give to Jonathan, and to make matters worse, she had torn a shoulder tendon and would have to open in a hidden sling. Yetta was sympathetic but she would not accept blame for what to her had been an innocent gesture. The conversation ended on a sour note.

Four hours before curtain on opening night in New Haven, Herbie Greene got a frantic call from Betty saying that Judy was refusing to talk to anybody and could he please go to her room at the Hotel Taft. He went directly over and asked what the problem was. Judy swallowed and said, "I don't think I'm going on tonight."

She was not being coy; Herbie could see that she was genuinely terrified. He considered commiserating but figured that would only feed her fear. He decided instead to appeal to her strength; he played it rough. "You don't want to go on tonight? So don't go on. It's not my career. If you want to fuck up your life, be my guest. I've already been paid for my services, and paid very handsomely. It doesn't mean a shit to me one way or the other except as an objective professional goal to have you sing."

Judy glared at him. "Where the hell do you come off saying these things to me?"

Betty and Adolph had often been cowed by Judy's anger, but Herbie wasn't giving an inch. "What the hell do you want me to say to you? That I'm very sorry you feel this way and that everything is going to turn out all right? I won't play that game. The only way to deal with you, Judy, is to deal straight. I've given you some of the tools, but you're the one that must employ them. And if you don't wish to employ them, fuck you."

The argument went on for nearly two hours. When it was over, she was tempted to slap him or storm out of the room. Before she could do either, Herbie left. The next time he saw her was in the wings of the Shubert Theater. The conductor, Milton Rosenstock, was running through the last strains of the overture. Judy's entrance cue came, but she seemed frozen in place. Herbie leaned over her shoulder and whispered, "You want to feel a funny feeling?" Then he shoved her onto the stage.

For all the fireworks beforehand, it was an excellent performance. Sydney played convincingly and Jerry Robbins admitted his mistake and agreed his leading man was in for the duration. Richard Rodgers had sunk a good deal of money in the show and heartily approved of what he saw. When it was over, the only one who was less than encouraged was Judy. Yetta visited her in her room at the Taft and thought she looked raddled. She handed her an expensive blouse she had purchased at Saks as a peace offering over the flower rift. Judy took one look at the gift and tossed it indifferently on the bed.

Yetta returned the following night with friends and afterward found Judy in a slightly improved mood. Judy drew her aside and confessed, "I'm very ashamed of myself."

Yetta said, "Why be ashamed? The show's a great hit."

"I'm angry that in the reviews that came out today, the play got better notices than I did. I'm ashamed of myself for feeling that way, but I thought I would tell you."

That went a long way toward explaining Judy's behavior. She was a perfectionist and she felt her performance was not up to her potential. The reviews and the loud applause for Sydney seemed to confirm her feeling that she was failing. At a production meeting earlier that day there had been a concession that the show was failing Judy in one respect: she needed a strong song toward the close of the show to rally the audience behind Ella and lay the groundwork for the inevitable happy ending.

The production proceeded to its next stop, in Boston, but Betty, Adolph, and Jule were getting no nearer to Judy's song. Several possibilities were written and rejected. Meanwhile the opening went smoothly; Judy needed no last-minute heroics to get her onstage and her performance was more self-assured. *The Solid Gold Cadillac* had recently opened in town to glowing reviews, and this seemed to warm critics and audiences alike. Judy's notices were much stronger than in New Haven. But there was still the question of that second-act song.

Jule's suite at the Ritz became the site of repeated pitched battles. Wanting outside inspiration, Betty and Adolph finally looked to their own libretto. Ella referred early in the show to her previous job at a lingerie manufacturer. Someone suggested it might get a laugh if it had been a brassiere company. Thinking of Fraçoise Sagan's current novel, *Bonjour Tristesse*, someone suggested it might get a better laugh if it were the Bonjour Tristesse Brassiere Company. Betty and Adolph remembered that in the days of the Revuers Judy had always done well with full-bodied bluesy numbers. Jule pounded out a tune and, like the instant tunesmiths of Hollywood legend, they had their song an hour later. The song was rushed into the closing Boston show, and it brought down the house.

Bells worked out some wrinkles with a successful two-week stay in Philadelphia and moved on to New York for previews and a November 29 opening. Hopes were running high for the show, and Judy's relationship with Sydney seemed surprisingly stable. Still, Judy was anxious about her pending Broadway singing-and-dancing debut and her anxiety level climbed when David again asked her for a divorce. From where he stood, the timing was propitious. Judy was totally involved with another man and a show that was sure to triumph. He was eager to marry Ellin, and as far as he could tell, there was flatly no hope of resurrecting the marriage with Judy. He did not know that for all the anguish and bitterness, and despite her love for Sydney, Judy would have taken David back in a minute, not just for Jonathan's sake but also her own. Yet it was plain the marriage was beyond repair. Judy turned matters over to her attorney and good friend, Arnold Krakower, and instructed him to work out the legal details for a divorce.

Opening night, the only chill was in the overcast November sky. The audience reception for *Bells Are Ringing* far exceeded Judy's expectations. It was not the response of a crowd that had been dazzled by flossy production numbers, catchy tunes, and general pyrotechnics. Rather it was a human response to an unusually human performance within the musical-comedy idiom. Ella Peterson was not a singing-and-dancing Billie Dawn, but a fully formed character in her own right with just enough vulnerability to capture and hold audience sympathy. It was a far cry from stock musical-comedy romance. Judy gave what was in many ways an ordinary old-fashioned show an added layer of joy and pathos. Which is not to say her performance lacked showmanship. With the help of Jerry Robbins' and Bob Fosse's inspired choreography, Judy danced with an appealing natural grace. But the key to the evening was her singing. It was not an elegant or rich voice, but it was the right voice. As with, for instance, Fred Astaire, the voice flowed believably and honestly from character. Judy made the audience accept Ella, and her singing style only affirmed that trust: if a woman in real life actually did burst into song at a moment's notice, this is the way she would sound—a thin, slightly nasal, ingratiating soprano, not an operatic coloratura that shook the rafters and shut the audience out of the character. Judy made the deceivingly difficult transition from comedy acting to musical comedy.

The opening-night party was held at the Hampshire House and Judy, fresh from an obligatory stop at Sardi's, was resplendent. The notices came in one by one, and all were raves. Ironically, the critical pendulum had swung since New Haven, and most reviewers thought Judy's performance was superior to the material. Judy could see Adolph was distressed by the news, and she took him aside and said it was absurd to think there could be an excellent performance without excellent material. She did not let it rest at that; in subsequent interviews with reporters she would make special mention of Betty and Adolph's work.

Yetta and the Buffingtons attended the party and presented Judy with a beautiful negligee. Judy thanked them in a somewhat distracted, offhand manner. Ruth thought it was understandable under the circumstance, but Yetta thought it was high-handed. She phoned Judy the next morning and fumed, "What's the matter, you going Hollywood? Don't have time for your friends?" Judy apologized, and once Yetta cooled down, she realized that this had not been a snub. In fact, Judy was as un-Hollywood as ever. When she was told of the Broadway practice of not inviting the pit musicians to the opening-night reception, she protested loudly. When they were still excluded, she arranged a lavishly catered affair for them the next week at the Dakota. Judy was not suffering from a bloated ego; there was something else going on.

Judy had fallen hopelessly in love with Sydney, and as in the past, she was absorbed in the relationship to the point of distraction. Judy admitted that the depth of affection was not returned by him. Good friends cautioned, "You're letting yourself in for a lot of trouble." But Judy was too infatuated to care. She had companionship, her family, and the first really fulfilling role in years; trouble was the farthest thing from her mind.

If it was a fantasy romance, it was no less alluring for friends. There was a deliriously festive Christmas party at the Dakota, with an immense tree and piles upon piles of gifts. Sydney gave Judy a lovely pair of diamond earrings, and she seemed to be floating on air. Even skeptical friends had to admit it was a magical day.

The momentum of it all helped carry Judy through the long-delayed and poorly received release of *Full of Life*. It also dulled the aftershock when the divorce was finalized in early March 1957 with a decree obtained in Juarez, Mexico. The terms were fairly amicable, given the stormy history. David allowed Judy to divorce him, and Judy asked no alimony or child support. She retained the house in Washingtonville and David was permitted to visit Jonathan at the Dakota. Arnold Krakower saw to it that the divorce was handled tastefully and quietly, without scandalous play in the press. Judy did experience a last wave of regret; she couldn't help wondering whether things might have been different. And like most new divorcées, she felt pangs of failure over the official end of a relationship that once seemed so perfect. Judy was saddened, but she did not torment herself. She was soon able to accept the conclusion of the phase in her life that David had represented.

There was one minor relapse. That spring marked the first Casals Festival in Puerto Rico, an event that attracted classical musicians the world over. Buff was playing in the festival orchestra, and Ruth, who was then playing in the orchestra for Broadway's *Most Happy Fella*, arranged leave to join him. David had just married Ellin, and since he was scheduled to oversee the recording of the concerts for Columbia Masterworks, he combined business with pleasure and the trip doubled as a honeymoon. There were countless parties, and Ruth could not see the point of avoiding the newlyweds. They had several polite interactions, none of which Ruth mentioned in her letters home to Judy.

Ruth came home to New York and called Judy right away, but the conversation was awkward. Two days later she dropped by the Dakota, and Judy's face seemed drained of color. They chatted idly, but both were aware that they were dancing around the topic of the festival. At length Judy asked, "You saw them?" Ruth said she had, and little more was said. There was still a residue of pain, and the simple fact of being in contact with someone who had been in contact with them was difficult. Judy explained she did not consider this a breach of trust. Ruth understood that divorce only begins with the signing of papers and that Judy was feeling a normal emotional lag. There was no harm done to her friendship with Ruth and Buff, and when it came time to record the cast album of *Bells*, she saw to it that they were in the studio orchestra for her moral support and their finances.

Bells began what was sure to be a long run, and Judy faced the rigors of eight performances a week. Already Sydney had been troubled by a bad throat. Judy also had intermittent throat problems, along with an assortment of minor aches and pains and recurring bursitis. Through it all, she never slackened her work. If there was a dead house, she considered it her fault and worked that much harder to win them over. Sydney had a habit of walking through tough nights, but never Judy. Her intricate mind went after an audience like an anagram, adjusting a gesture, a pause, an intonation, experimenting and reshuffling until she solved it. At times she was overly self-critical, but she had a thirst for approval and her awesome powers of concentration won her the results she wanted.

It was more a matter of professionalism than egotism. Judy felt a real debt to her audiences, and their applause was the only available measure of whether the debt had been paid. The urge for recognition and praise ended each day with the final curtain. Offstage and out of costume, Judy saw herself as just another New Yorker, and so she was always a little amazed at the crowds that lingered at the stage door after every performance. She was never one to make a quick exit from the theater. She retired to her dressing room, visited with friends, poured a drink, talked with her dresser and confidante, Elizabeth White, and often received a massage. Yet, fully an hour after curtain she would step out the stage door into an inevitable orderly throng. They were mostly women, mostly middle-aged. A few were autograph seekers, but largely they were content just to get a glimpse of Judy and offer greetings and thanks.

This was the greatest tribute to her performance, that people were able to closely identify with a character in a musical. To them Judy brought a certain aesthetic sense to the ordinary. Ella was a working girl without benefit of education or particular beauty. But she represented a generosity and decency of human spirit, and though unfortunate things befell her, the kindness ultimately came back to her as happiness. The audience identification had far less to do with the writer's conception than with Judy's sensitivity and art in realizing the part.

The extent of her dedication was evident in her attitude toward matinees. Many actors go half-speed on Wednesday afternoons. There is a second show that evening, and besides, the crowds get in for reduced rates and are decidedly inelegant. There are theater parties in town for the day, drowsily full of lunch. There are the loud whisperers, the fidgeters, and those who slowly open hard candy with cellophane that crackles through the theater like a brush fire. And yet, as Judy told Ruth, "I love those old ladies. They don't come because it's chic or because they're going to be seen in gorgeous dresses. They come because they really need to come. They have a good time, and I play my heart out for them." Her dedication was formally acknowledged when she was awarded that season's Tony for outstanding performance by an actress in a musical. Her pleasure was no less at the Tony that Sydney received for his supporting work, which convincingly vindicated her casting acumen.

As much as Judy appreciated the public's appreciation, she

had certain reservations. More than once she commented about the fans outside the theater, "It's nice, but they could turn on you, too." She may have been thinking of the ubiquitous pickets of a few years ago. Or she may have been referring to a fear of crowds and a marked ambivalence about celebrity. More likely it was Judy's special brand of pessimism, which seemed to suspect that every good implied its opposite. Acclaim and fame could be wonderful, but they could also be ephemeral. It was as if she were warning herself not to become overly attached to something so elusive.

Judy was not so cautious where Sydney was concerned. Despite ample evidence to the contrary, she invested her emotions totally in the relationship and hoped that it might lead to marriage. Sydney told her he did not love her, and he was rumored to be seen around town on occasion with other women. This led to several fights, but Judy's jealousy only crowded him more. If close friends waited for some outward sign of her concern, they had to look no further than her weight. At first it came in small ways: she interviewed with the *Times* over a large hamburger and fries with all the trimmings; she concluded her talk with *Theater Arts* magazine with a sirloin that could do justice to a football-training table.

The biggest binge was with Herbie Greene, no slouch either when it came to eating. One night he called Judy with the news that he had just signed to co-produce *The Music Man*. They agreed this called for a celebration and met at Lüchow's, a German restaurant in Greenwich Village. They had one complete dinner with a bottle of champagne, another with a second bottle, and finally a third of each. When it came time for the check, the owner walked over and announced, "It's on us. You just broke the house record for eating at one sitting." They dragged themselves out of the place and were waiting for a cab when Herbie said, "Why not go to my place? I know how to make the craziest tuna salad you've ever eaten."

Judy looked at him ingenuously and said, "No shit?"

So they capped the evening with a bowl of tuna salad. As

much as Judy enjoyed eating, friends saw the sudden gain in weight as a worrisome storm warning. Judy stubbornly ignored it.

In July Sydney signed a contract with the Theater Guild which extended his commitment to the show through June 1958. Judy's contract expired in October of the same year. It had been a happy company so far. Judy was on a first name basis with everybody, she had become friends with several members of the production staff, she and Sydney double-dated with chorus members, and she became especially fond of Doria Avila, the chorus swing man responsible for escorting her on and off stage through the darkened, sometimes hazardous wings. Woodie Broun's recent replacement of Jack Weston strengthened the cozy feeling.

Judy and Sydney were due their first vacation that fall, and Sydney had invited her to Paris and Switzerland to visit Charlie, now in self-imposed exile. However, since making the plans the relationship had begun to falter. Sydney had long been accustomed to the high life of parties and nightclubs, but Judy preferred to do her unwinding at the Dakota. Needless to say, there was the usual array of relatives and Helen's older friends, Harry and Maude, and periodic appearances from Abe. For a long time Sydney seemed unbothered by the radical change of life-style. He would drop by late afternoon and watch cartoons and westerns with Jonathan, keeping a running commentary with the television all the while. He would enliven otherwise drab family dinners with his antics, telling off-color jokes or suddenly reading a strand of spaghetti as if it were a Wall Street ticker tape. But the domesticity began to take its toll, and Sydney gave every indication of wanting to ease out of the relationship. Though this was apparent to Judy, she insisted they travel abroad as planned, hoping that might somehow revive his affections. Sydney acquiesced, though it was more to fulfill a promise than anything else.

They arrived in Switzerland amid rumors they'd come to seek Charlie's approval for marriage. From there they went to Paris, and the fragile peace was shattered. Sydney started to openly see several old girlfriends, and when Judy protested, he walked out, leaving her alone in the hotel room. She stayed a few days, caught a flight home and went directly to a summer house she was renting in Darien, Connecticut. Yetta received a frantic call from Helen. "You've got to come up right away, Judy's hysterical."

Yetta had never seen anything like it. Judy sobbed uncontrollably for hours at a time. She refused to say exactly what had gone on between her and Sydney, only that he had abruptly abandoned her in Paris. Judy was depressed beyond description; she either wept or was silent and dazed, in a near-catatonic state. She had taken the breakup with David hard, but her reaction then was primarily anger. This time all the anger was internalized as depression, and there was even some concern that she might try to kill herself. She made little progress over the next couple of weeks, and when she was due to return to the show, she begged off, claiming a bad throat. It was the first time she had ever willingly missed a stage performance.

Sydney had since come back from Europe with every intention of continuing in *Bells*. Judy finally went on for a few shows in late September, but it was too painful seeing him and she missed ten days in early October, claiming a flu virus. After that she returned to her role for good, but the onetime happy mood backstage turned into a virtual armed camp. It was a credit to Judy that her private life never once seeped into her performance onstage. For all audiences could tell, she and Sydney were as chummy as ever. Behind the scenes was another story. Judy drew up strict battle lines; she had nothing to do with Sydney, and any friend of hers who did had a lot of explaining if he intended to remain a friend.

Woodie tried to remain above the infighting, but it was hopeless. He felt sorry for Judy but figured she was a big girl and knew what she was getting into. That didn't mean he excused Sydney's behavior; Woodie also was the child of famous parents, yet that didn't give him license to go around hurting people. Then again, Sydney's reputation had preceded him into the affair, and Judy had no one but herself to blame for blindly going ahead. One day after the Saturday matinee Sydney invited Woodie to Sardi's for a bite to eat. Woodie returned to the theater for the evening show and was greeted by Elizabeth White. "She's very angry, she wants to see you."

He walked to Judy's dressing room and imagined a chill in the air. "I hear you had dinner at Sardi's with Sydney. How could you?"

"Judy," he explained gently, "if Sydney is behaving badly, that's between you and Sydney. Sydney didn't behave badly to me."

With some coaxing she was willing to pass it off as an innocent isolated incident. Judy was less forgiving when she learned that Betty and Adolph were continuing to socialize with Sydney, inviting him to parties with dates while she sat home nights in the throes of depression. Ruth Buffington was visiting at the Dakota one night when Adolph showed up unannounced. Judy ran to the bedroom without saying a word, and Ruth quickly followed. They sat there silently for several minutes, and Ruth at last spoke up. "Come on, Judy, let's go back in."

Judy turned to her grimly and said, "Lovers have a right to betray you. Friends don't."

Judy continued to see Betty and Adolph after that, but it was never quite the same. She felt they were too consumed with their status-conscious social life to ever again count among the truly loyal. Perhaps she was overreacting, demanding too much. But if they couldn't put their long-standing friendship with Judy ahead of a party list that might have added luster for Sydney's presence, then she could not consider herself entirely safe with them. Betty and Adolph felt she had unrealistic standards of friendship, but these were Judy's standards and you either met them or were banished from the inner circle of her life. With time she softened over what she saw as their betrayal. Recalling how thrilled Adolph once had been to attend a gathering with the famed theatrical producer and director

Gilbert Miller, she remarked to Woodie, "I love Adolph and I know that Adolph loves me. And I also know if I'm dying and Gilbert Miller is giving a party, Adolph would call an ambulance for me before he goes to the party."

It was still rough going for several months with *Bells*. Yetta regularly received phone calls in her office around midafternoon. It would be Betty. "Judy's having hysterics, she says she's not going to work tonight, please go and talk to her." Yetta would answer, "You know damn well she's going to work tonight," but to make sure, she'd stop by the Dakota for dinner. Throughout the meal Judy would maintain she wasn't going on. About thirty minutes before curtain she'd look at Yetta and say, "I think I'll go. Let's drive down to the theater."

This became the pattern: in times of stress, the show was the best way for Judy to step out of her misery and feel loved, if only by a houseful of strangers. It was an important emotional outlet, but it wasn't enough. What remained of her anger and frustration she sometimes took out on Helen; the meal wasn't right, she hadn't laid out Judy's clothes properly, she'd given the wrong instructions to the maid. It came to a head late one night when Judy and Helen had a fight and Judy ordered her home to the place she still kept over on Seventy-fifth. At two in the morning Yetta's phone rang and it was Helen. "Judy threw me out." Yetta told Helen not to worry, got dressed, and drove uptown to the Dakota. By the time she got there, Judy had already invited her mother back. Helen was asleep in a back bedroom; Judy joined Yetta for a snack in the kitchen.

After sandwiches, Yetta said, "Judy, you mustn't—"

But Judy interrupted, "Don't say it."

"I'm going to say it," Yetta continued. "Your mother's very old, and you mustn't treat her that way."

"I thought you were going to say that. I don't want to hear it!"

Yetta was in no mood to put up with Judy's childishness. She had already rushed out in the middle of the night to referee a fight that never quite materialized. The least Judy could do was indulge some friendly advice. Yetta left, and it was several days before they talked again.

Judy decided to go back into psychoanalysis. She had liked the previous analyst but quit when he seemed to develop a somewhat more than clinical interest in her. She did not much care for the new analyst; he was a strict Freudian, and as far as Judy could tell, he did no more than nod, sigh, and tell her when her time was up. But at least she could vent her anger without hurting her mother or her best friend.

Judy slowly pulled herself back together, and while it was still difficult working with Sydney, she endured and tried to defuse some of the backstage tension. As a gesture of truce she invited Woodie up for an evening at the house in Washingtonville. Woodie was now married, and one of the show's stage managers went along as a chaperon of sorts. The stage manager went off to bed, and Woodie and Judy sipped drinks and talked.

Judy lit a cigarette and mused, "Remember the White Cow?"

It had been over fifteen years since they had frequented the Village hamburger joint. Woodie remembered.

"Remember we sat around and talked about what we were going to do when we were stars. Okay. I'm a star. Six thousand dollars a week. I am not going to go any higher. When do I get to be happy?"

Woodie knew what she was saying: she could no longer blame her problems on circumstances, she had to accept full responsibility for what went on in her life. He looked at her wistful face and her tired fawn eyes and recalled the irony of an ancient Chinese curse: "May all your dreams come true." He wanted to say he understood, but couldn't find the words.

16

~~~~~~~~~~~~~~~~~~~~~~~~

"Yetta, guess who I went out with last night?"

"I don't want to guess. Just tell me."

"Okay, okay. Frank Sinatra."

"No kidding?" Yetta remembered that when she and Judy lived together on Fifty-eighth Street, every time Sinatra played the Paramount, they would go, sit through the movie, and stay for a second show. "What did you do?"

"The usual, dinner, drinks. Then he takes me home in his limousine and, get this, he starts crooning in my ear. Right there in the car. All I can think is that fifteen million women in the United States would give their eyeteeth to be in my place and I'm sitting there so bored I can't wait to get home. Can you believe it? I was bored to death."

She saw no more of Sinatra, but at least she was starting to circulate again. She spent one or two evenings with Billy Rose, and that too went nowhere. A weekend in Washingtonville with a film director fared only slightly better. Friends were looking after Judy, and when she casually mentioned she'd like to have a date with Adlai Stevenson, the grapevine relayed the news and within days he called to ask her out. He met her backstage after a performance of *Bells*, they exchanged pleasantries, and Judy asked what he'd like to do. Stevenson admitted he'd had a murderous work load lately and he'd like nothing better than to go back to her place, loosen his tie, kick off his shoes, and talk. Here was a man after her own heart.

They arrived at the Dakota and Judy handed him a drink and parked him in a living-room chair. She then ran back to the spare bedroom, where Helen was asleep. She shook her. "Mother, Mother, Adlai Stevenson's here." Helen woke up with a start; she had long been an admirer of his. Judy returned to the living room, and Helen followed a moment later in slippers and a robe. She walked directly to Stevenson, proudly extended her hand, and with utter conviction said, "Mr. President, how nice to meet you." Helen realized the slip and they all broke up laughing. The three of them spent the balance of the evening talking politics.

Judy's recovery from the Sydney debacle suffered a serious setback, however. In recent years Judy had reestablished her relationship with her father. Her first period of analysis set the reconciliation in motion and the birth of Jonathan concluded it. Abe was welcome to visit the Dakota whenever he chose. He came to dinner several nights each week and spent hours playing with Jonathan. He bought him presents and on two occasions wrote him long stories in verse which he had recorded on 45's. Abe was cordial with Harry and Maude and comfortably friendly with Helen. Although Helen continued to hope that they might yet get back together, their interaction was more that of brother and sister, and the two seldom talked at length. Abe had done well professionally and was now eager to make up for lost time with his family.

One day Abe showed up with an enormous Erector set. Judy said it was much too elaborate for young Jonathan; Abe replied it was not a gift for Jonathan but for Judy. For the better part of a week, Judy and Abe sat on the parlor floor putting the set together. They laughed and talked, and if either of them was aware of trying to recover lost moments from Judy's childhood, neither of them said so.

A short time later Sylvia Regan and her husband were spending a weekend at Kutsher's resort in the Catskills. They stepped out of their room one noon and saw a familiar face emerge from the neighboring room. It was Abe, and Sylvia, who had not seen him in years, had to stifle a gasp. He was stooped and pale and looked much older than his sixty-three years. He joined them for lunch and saw them off and on throughout the weekend. He was there alone, and on Sunday returned to the city.

Abe made an appointment with his doctor, who immediately ordered him to Mount Sinai Hospital for tests. He was found to have stomach cancer, but it had already metastasized and was inoperable. Helen dreaded hospitals, and so the full burden fell to Judy. Judy saw him every day as the disease rapidly spread. Abe kept talking about getting out, and one day after the first of the year told Judy, "I'm going back to work." That same day he slipped into a coma. Judy called Yetta. "Can you come to the hospital? My father's dying." Yetta sat with Judy through the afternoon and asked if she planned to work that night. Judy said she didn't think so. Around six the doctor came out and said there was no point staying, Abe was still comatose but stable.

Judy went to the theater, did the show, and returned to the hospital at 11:30. She sat with Yetta till two in the morning, when the doctor came out and told them it was all over, Abe was dead. Judy wept and went home. The next morning she could not bring herself to tell Jonathan, saying only that "Grand has gone away." It was a Wednesday. Judy performed the matinee, then attended Abe's funeral. At the last minute she decided to go through with the evening performance. It was not so much an escape as a way to assuage her grief. She had to choke back tears when she sang "The Party's Over."

Judy was pleased that she had made peace with Abe before his death. The hours spent with him in the hospital helped expiate some of the guilt she felt for her prolonged bitterness and sometimes harsh treatment of him. Abe left a surprisingly substantial estate to Judy and Jonathan. He left another legacy. In the course of conversations with Helen, Judy learned for the first time that Rachel had also died of cancer. Judy had long felt hounded by nameless fears, as though the tranquil veneer of life could in an instant give way to the demons of suffering and sorrow. All these fears were now consolidated under the dread label of cancer. It was both real and symbolic, and it fixed itself firmly in her mind.

Judy again became reclusive. She slept late, spent afternoons with Jonathan, dined with the family, did the show, came home, unwound, went to sleep, and started over once more. This went on for months, and finally a friend, Janet Woolf, initiated a small conspiracy to break Judy's joyless workaday rut. Janet visited Judy after a Saturday-night performance and asked her to name men who interested her. She mentioned comic Mort Sahl, who happened to be performing a one-man show not far from the Shubert. Janet scurried down the block and found Sahl in his dressing room. Janet announced, "Judy Holliday's working right across the street and she'd like very much to meet you." He seemed flattered and answered, "Well, I'd like very much to meet her." By the time the two of them got back to Judy's dressing room, she had been joined by Helen, Harry, and Maude. Introductions were made and Judy suggested, "Why don't we *all* go to the Russian Tea Room." Sahl looked at the relatives and blanched. "I'm terribly sorry. I just remembered I have another engagement." Janet chewed her lip, determined to say nothing she might later regret.

The haze of depression gradually lifted. Judy looked after herself, rested, and lost weight—not the frantic crash diet of the past, but a slow, healthy reduction. She was even coaxed into attending a party at Lee Strasberg's home, a gathering of some two hundred show-business elite. Judy walked in wearing a dark green sequined dress, and the guests were dazzled. Emboldened by the reception and a few cocktails, Judy left with a friend for a smaller party at Arlene Francis'. She knew whom to expect—Betty and Steve; Adolph and his new wife, who was also Judy's current understudy, Phyllis Newman; Jule Styne; and Sydney. She was greeted warmly by everybody except Sydney, who simply gazed at her and said nothing. Jule walked Judy to a piano and asked her to sing a song from the show. She sang "Just in Time" and departed a short while later. Seeing Sydney had been difficult, to say the least, but it was a decisive moral victory for Judy.

Sydney left *Bells* when his contract expired in June 1958. He was replaced by the understudy, Hal Linden, and everyone backstage at the Shubert breathed a sigh of relief. There was a noticeable change in the show; Hal sang better than his predecessor, and he did not have Sydney's maddening habit of sleepwalking past lifeless audiences. He was fond of Judy and somewhat awed by her intelligence. He hoped to get to know her better, but she had insulated herself with assorted cast and crew members and the protective circle seemed impenetrable. Woodie Broun noticed the same thing and came to refer to the entourage as Judy's Broken Wings, as though she had despaired of finding companions on her own level and so turned to those with their own foibles and frailties who returned Judy's attention with an almost cultish devotion and admiration.

Judy was open to their flattery, and one member of the circle talked her into recording an album of ballads and blues. It was a torturous experience for Judy. Although she had survived the cast album for *Bells* without undue stress, those were songs she had performed for over a year. The current selections were unrelated to story or character. She idolized such singers as Billie Holiday and especially Judy Garland, but she doubted her own ability to put across a cold lyric. Judy saw to it that the Buffingtons were among the studio musicians, knowing they could use the money but more that she could use their support in a sea of unfamiliar faces. The recording session was extremely trying and went on till four in the morning. The album was issued a few months later and had modest sales to faithful fans, though it did earn Judy a nomination in that year's *Playboy* jazz poll.

Judy was fighting the inertia that had seized her since the breakup with Sydney. She was relieved to have the backing of an ongoing Broadway hit, but she still had mixed feelings about the sort of visibility that brought in public. She might be walking down the street with a friend and a stranger would pass and gurgle, "Oh, Miss Holliday!" Judy would smile, say hello, walk a few more steps, and playfully mumble, "Fuck you." One afternoon she was shopping with Yetta along Madison Avenue when a dumpy middle-aged woman approached and shouted, "You're Judy Holliday, aren't you?"

Judy looked at her straight-faced and said, "No."

"You are so," the woman persisted.

"Really, I'm not."

"Gee, you sure look like Judy Holliday."

Yetta couldn't take much more of this. "Oh, Judy, for Chrissakes, tell the woman who you are."

"All right," Judy conceded. "Yes, I am Judy Holliday."

The woman studied her intently and concluded, "Naw, you're not Judy Holliday, can't be," and went on her way.

Judy didn't mean to be rude to fans, she just didn't see herself as anyone special and had a hard time facing strangers who held an exalted image of her. She led a quiet life, spending most of her time at the Dakota with friends, family, and the Broken Wings talking or playing Scrabble. These streetside disruptions caught her off-guard, and she never quite knew how to handle them.

Judy partly filled her time with regular poker games at Maureen Stapleton's apartment, but her urge for male company soon reemerged. She started to go out with Arnold Krakower, the attorney who saw her through the divorce and later handled Abe's estate. Arnold was single, successful, intelligent, entertaining, and good-looking. He loved Judy and treated her sensitively. He lacked David's moodiness and Sydney's wildness. He shared Judy's preference for quiet dinners, casual socializing, and relaxed evenings at home. They made an attractive couple, and after only a short time together they had the easy rapport and easygoing manner of two people who had been together for years.

Arnold wanted to marry Judy. Yetta, Helen, Harry, and Maude wanted Judy to marry Arnold. Judy was not so certain; there was no question she loved him or that he would care for her. Arnold was secure enough in his own ego not to be threatened by Judy's career, and confident enough in his love to know he would never mistreat or abandon her as Sydney had. Judy knew that Arnold would make a perfect friend and model for Jonathan, and that was a serious consideration. She was completely devoted to her son, in ways perhaps too devoted. As un-athletic as she was, she would even take him over to Central Park with a catcher's mitt and play catch. Still she knew it was important for Jonathan to have regular male companionship to balance the constant attention he received from his mother and grandmother.

But Judy sensed something missing in the chemistry with Arnold. One friend speculated that he was not neurotic enough for Judy, that she couldn't dote on him as she had the others, that she couldn't participate in his career, that there would be none of the danger she had come to expect of relationships. It was not unlike her reaction to Woodie Broun back in the days of the Village Vanguard. She loved Arnold and always would, but she needed him more as a friend and could not risk spoiling that with marriage. They remained extremely close and continued to see each other. It was a rare relationship which Judy would turn to for strength and sustenance in times of stress.

Judy wanted to get back on friendly terms with Betty and Adolph after her falling-out with them over Sydney. She had them over one evening with Jerry Robbins, Jule Styne, Herbie Greene, and a few others. The conversation veered, as it always had, into show business. Judy's threshold for shop talk was lower than normal, but she played along, content to have even a semblance of reconciliation with her estranged partners. Adolph was passing on an item of theatrical gossip when Herbie stopped him in mid-sentence, looked at Judy, and said loud enough for all to hear, "What the fuck am I doing here wasting my time?" He grabbed his coat and headed for the door.

Judy overtook him in the hallway, and before Herbie could explain that he meant only to insult the others, not her, she told him, "You know, you're the only one with enough balls to say that it is a fucking bore in there." She helped him on with his coat and returned to her ruffled guests.

As part of her continuing social renaissance, Judy attended a party given by Bobby Lewis, who had recently directed Lena Horne in the Broadway musical *Jamaica*. Judy's escort was Ralph Roberts, an actor who between jobs worked as a masseur for select celebrities. Ralph had on several occasions helped knead out the kinks from Judy's back and shoulders collected in eight weekly performances of *Bells*. They were just friends who got together for Scrabble and conversation.

Judy arrived late and gravitated to a corner where Marlene Dietrich was holding forth on the mysteries of femininity. When Judy had an earful she drifted across the room to where a tall, lean, blond, angular man stood chuckling at the idea of Dietrich lecturing women on womanhood. He was introduced to Judy as Gerry Mulligan. She was no jazz devotee but she recognized the name as one of the standouts in the field. Gerry was a baritone saxophonist, writer, and arranger who had worked his way up through several big bands in the late 1940's, graduated to smaller groups as a hard bebopper, and lately with Gil Evans and Miles Davis was in the forefront of a new postbop trend known as "cool." He was friendly, articulate, different, and he and Judy hit it off immediately.

Gerry was staying at the Algonquin Hotel, and the following week he walked over to the Alvin Theater, where *Bells* had been transplanted, and joined Judy for drinks. They were soon inseparable. Judy did not conceal the fact that she had started to see him regularly, she just did not go out of her way to reveal it. A few Sundays after Bobby Lewis' party, Judy and a woman friend went to an evening theater benefit. Afterward Judy mentioned she was meeting somebody at a favorite actors nightspot, Downey's at Forty-fourth and Eighth. They arrived and the friend met Gerry. She knew of his music and thought he was very handsome and sexy. She also saw that Judy and he were something more than casual acquaintances. The friend asked around and found Gerry had a well-deserved reputation as a ladies' man. The smoke had scarcely cleared from the Sydney calamity, and now Judy was getting involved with a jazz musician with a roving eye. This promised to be Judy's fastest romance yet.

But there was much more to it than first met the eye. As was not at all uncommon then in the jazz subculture, Gerry had had a history of drug use. With the help of a friend he had kicked the habit once. When Judy met him he had given up drugs for good but was enmeshed in a messy divorce from his second wife, who was succeeding in keeping him from his young son, Reed. What with these matters and living out of a suitcase at the Algonquin, he felt very much a transient.

Far from wanting more turbulence and uncertainty in his life, Gerry was ready for the sort of tranquility he had lost in his own failed marriage. He not only loved Judy, but as time went on, he readily accepted her family. He was fond of Helen and delighted in her malapropisms and balminess, while showing great patience with her recurrent depressions and intricate dependency on Judy. He didn't even seem to mind Harry and Maude. Most of all he enjoyed spending time with Jonathan, now seven, who was interested in baseball and hockey, whereas Gerry's interest in sports ran from indifference to ignorance. They found much to talk about and often ended up in healthy if heated arguments. Gerry liked history, and he was impressed with Jonathan's phenomenal memory for events and dates. In a real sense they met certain important needs in each other's lives; what with assorted pressures, Jonathan was not getting along with David all that well at the time, and Gerry was able to experience some of the fatherly companionship he missed with his own son.

Gerry found a place uptown and came to the Dakota almost daily for dinner. If he was playing in town, he would meet up with Judy later in the night, and since his work was in clubs, he had no need to go out nightclubbing as Sydney had. On off nights he was perfectly content to spend a quiet time at Judy's visiting with friends or noodling at the piano as she sang.

Judy loved Gerry and she loved the world he moved in. There was something about the community of jazz musicians that intrigued and attracted her. She boned up on the music and one night asked Gerry to show her around some of the city's many jazz spots. They were joined by alto player Cannonball Adderly and went from club to club. Over the course of the night Judy made special note of Gerry and Cannonball's genuine pleasure with the playing of their peers. Later she told Gerry, "You know, whenever somebody played a really good solo tonight, something wonderful happened. You and the others were pleased. That's so different from actors. Actors see somebody do well and they become threatened and critical. You and Cannonball were delighted."

Judy might well have been thinking of current gyrations with Betty and Adolph. There was no question Judy had been the mainstay of *Bells:* when she was away, the box office slumped; a London company of the show opened without her and closed quickly. Her contract expired in mid-December 1958, after which she planned to rest, then go to Hollywood for a scheduled film version. With luck the shooting would be done by early summer and Judy could retire Ella Peterson as she had Billie Dawn and then prowl around for the straight dramatic vehicle she increasingly craved. She had been saddened by Harry Cohn's death the previous February; they had become quite close, and he took on Judy as a confidante, visiting her regularly when he was in New York and talking for hours while cruising the town in his limousine. It was a measure of Judy's compassion that she was able to see through Cohn's ornery exterior to the pitiful loneliness that lay beneath. Still, his passing accentuated Judy's belief that she and Columbia had outgrown their need for one another. The studio lacked the incentive to give her fresh viable material, and she lacked the ego to endure another *Full of Life* just to be back in pictures. Neither party seemed interested in pursuing the unfulfilled seventh picture in her contract, and so Judy was looking forward to more artistic freedom than she had known in nearly a decade. All she had to do was get past the filming of *Bells*.

Betty and Adolph were not being particularly cooperative. Their enthusiasm for the show seemed to wane. Although MGM had already purchased the movie rights, Arthur Freed, who had produced all but one of their many film collaborations, questioned whether Betty and Adolph were the best ones to adapt the show. Given their flagging interest, another writer might inject new vitality and transform what was old-fashioned, almost outmoded musical comedy into something cinematic. Judy demanded that Betty and Adolph handle the adaptation, and Freed acceded. But instead of resolving potential problems, it was only the beginning.

To start with, Betty and Adolph had decided to get back on the boards and devised a showcase of their old parlor routines, some tunes from their Broadway and Hollywood shows, and even a smattering of Revuers material. They called it, appropriately enough, *A Party with Betty Comden and Adolph Green*. They ran off-Broadway, and encouraged by the response, opened the show on Broadway on December 12, 1958. There was one complication: they had promised Freed a clean first-draft screenplay of 110 pages by December 31. The script they delivered ran forty-three pages over and contained no lyrics, but did contain a request for an extension to accommodate their Broadway run. Freed was agreeable, but that only led to a succession of extensions and missed deadlines.

Judy's hands were tied. As long as the filming of *Bells* languished, she could not commit herself to a new play or film for fear of interruption. Perfectly aware that Betty and Adolph were frustrated showmen, she did not want to deny them the satisfaction of a Broadway run, nor could she ignore the fact that she had gone to bat for them and so far had only inconvenience to show for her trouble. Judy had already consented to stay with the show through March 7. But the way things were going, there was little hope of starting work on the motion picture before late summer.

A compromise was reached. Judy would close in town on March 7, 1959, then tour for five weeks in Washington, D.C., six weeks in Los Angeles, and finally six weeks in San Francisco before returning to Los Angeles. By then Betty and Adolph would have had enough time to scratch their performing itch as well as come up with a shooting script for *Bells*. It would mean disrupting her home life, but that was preferable to sitting idly by in New York, where Judy would do nobody good, least of all herself. Besides, she had several friends in the company and so the tour would just be a second family on the hoof. Judy was not at all pleased when Woodie told her he did not want to go on the road. She explained that Freed had granted her certain casting privileges and that he would be passing up a part in the picture. Woodie still declined, which Judy took as disloyalty, which Woodie in turn took as nonsense, with the result that they had yet another falling-out.

Two nights later Judy was playing Scrabble with Ralph Roberts and some friends and was, as usual, beating their brains out. She knew that Ralph was in need of work, and between turns said, "I wish there was something in *Bells* you could do."

Ralph perked up. "There is something. Francis," the comic detective role Woodie was about to abandon.

Judy had always liked to secure work for friends; she had done so with Woodie, Sydney, and the Buffingtons. It was no mere nepotism, but rather an applied personal perfectionism. Her choice of Woodie and Sydney was more than justified, and as for the Buffingtons, Judy actually got more than she gave— their impeccable musicianship and durable friendship through two stressful recording sessions. Judy never placed loyalty above professional standards; she did not think Ralph was right for the part, and she said as much. "You could never play Francis in a million years."

"I've been playing Francis for years," he countered, and asked her to come see him in a minor production of *Desire Under the Elms* he was performing in at Fort Lee, New Jersey. That Sunday Judy drove across the George Washington bridge with Jonathan and Helen, arriving in time to catch Ralph in one short scene. She found him afterward and said, "Okay, you can do Francis."

The tour went beautifully. Audiences were seeing a polished Broadway production with its original star, and the reaction was tumultuous. The blissful backstage mood that had resurfaced since Sydney's departure actually improved on the road. The principals continued to learn from Judy's meticulous and conscientious work onstage. All were drawn to her gentle ways offstage. Toward the end of the run in San Francisco Judy approached Hal Linden and asked a favor. She knew that before becoming an actor he had played saxophone with several big bands. She would be seeing Gerry in Los Angeles—would Hal be willing to teach her a few bars from one of Gerry's compositions? "Sure," he replied. "On what?" On the baritone sax, what else?

Judy got hold of a secondhand baritone sax, and each day for a week Hal would come up to her hotel room and run through the musical phrase she had selected. Aside from dabbling on a song flute, she had never played a wind instrument, but she made rapid progress. When Judy got to Los Angeles, she sat Gerry down and played her half-minute recital. He was completely charmed, not just that she would take the time to learn one of his tunes, but at the irresistible sight of Judy, her cheeks puffed up and her eyes almost crossed, trying to push a sound through this horn that practically reached to her knees. As it happened, it was merely the lull before a storm.

Betty and Adolph had yet to come up with a workable shooting script, and Judy felt ill-used after all she had done to adjust to their schedule. It was already August, and Freed stalled for time by dispatching his director, Vincente Minnelli, to New York with a second unit to shoot location exteriors.

Meanwhile Judy saw to it that Jean Stapleton, Hal Linden, and Ralph Roberts were cast for the movie. Her misgivings about the entire production were apparent, and Freed made the reassuring gesture of giving a small part to Gerry, who was appearing in yet another Freed film, *The Subterraneans*. But by the time studio work finally began on October 8, the production was doomed to discord.

For one thing, Judy thought Betty and Adolph had embarrassed her with Freed and was upset with them for that. Worse, she thought their adaptation was lackluster, and aside from a few new songs, did little to turn the show into a film. She was also concerned about the casting of Dean Martin as Jeff Moss. Judy liked Dean but he seemed to just walk through the shooting, and since she was as much a reactor as an actor, she feared the entire romantic interest might come across as hollow and disconnected. Worst of all was the tension that developed between her and Minnelli. Since this was Judy's vehicle and since she had performed it more than nine hundred times on Broadway as well as seventeen weeks on the road, she thought she had certain insights that someone new to the material might not. She would explain how a gesture or a reading had gotten laughs, and he would stare blankly and ask, "Why is that funny?" Like the proverbial jazzman, she might have replied, "If you have to ask what it is, it ain't."

The strain between Judy and Minnelli grew to the point that he automatically rejected her suggestions. There was none of the diplomatic give-and-take of a Cukor set. Minnelli viewed Judy as a threat to his authority and responded with more authority. Given what he saw as a troublesome star and a leading man whose consciousness was somewhere in the ozone, Minnelli worked around his principals. Judy thought she was being underrehearsed for key scenes while the extras, bit players, and even the sets were getting all the attention. When an actress is unsure of her material and director, the one thing she needs most is reassurance. But Arthur Freed was somewhat alienated, and Judy's pleas for support from Betty and Adolph went unheeded—they sided with Minnelli.

Judy's insecurity deepened. For all of the courage it took to sing in the theater, nobody stopped to think that she might require some patience and encouragement for her movie musical debut. She put on weight. She became hypochondriacal; the same bumps, bruises, and minor ailments that she had transcended onstage now sent her running from the set to her sickbed. There were whispers around the studio that she had grown temperamental, when it was really nothing of the sort.

Judy was wading into waters already muddied by others and was guilty of nothing more than trying to see that *Bells* became a worthwhile movie. She was not a mindless lovely mouthing lines and patiently awaiting the next cue. She had faithfully shouldered an unwieldy show for close to three years and had learned under fire what did and did not play. Granted, movie musicals presented a different set of demands from theater, and for that she gladly turned to the experts; but she would not be made to feel like a dog act being run through its paces. Even the notoriously autocratic Harry Cohn had given her more credit than that. If Judy occasionally overstepped her bounds on the set, it was forgivable—she had handed over a good portion of her life to that role and wanted it done correctly for film, if need be at the cost of some bruised egos.

Gerry offered some shelter. He and Judy took a house in Beverly Hills, and when time allowed, had people over for charades or poker. Sundays were reserved for jam sessions; a typical gathering would have Ben Webster on tenor sax, Gerry on baritone, Jimmy Rowles on piano, Mel Lewis on drums, LeRoy Vinnegar on bass, and Judy humming along or thumping a bongo drum. More than anything else, Gerry and the earthy camaraderie of the jam sessions saw Judy through the long days and nights between shooting. On the set, Judy found another way to pass the time.

Ordinarily Judy would amuse herself during long camera changes by working word puzzles, or, when costarring with

Jack Lemmon, singing songs. In a sense, she combined the two when she tried her hand at songwriting with Gerry. It was not as farfetched as even they first suspected. While modern jazz was largely free-form, Gerry's compositions and improvisational style had a strong, linear melodic side. Judy had an extraordinary feel for the form and nuance of language, which till now had been squandered on anagrams and the like. She and Gerry had a similar subtle way of thinking and a ready working rapport. Both were perfectionists, and the wastebaskets of the Beverly Hills home and the studio dressing room brimmed with wadded-up sheets of notepaper. Before long Judy and Gerry had three new songs to show for their efforts. It remained to be seen how good they were as songwriters, but as both of them were quick to admit, they were lousy song-pluggers. They shyly showed one tune, "It Must Be Christmas," to Dean Martin, who instantly arranged to include it in his upcoming album. They sent the same song to Dinah Shore, who asked to sing it for her annual network Christmas show. Whether the songwriting would prove more than a lark was anybody's guess, but at a time when some people seemed to be telling her she was just another troublesome actress, she showed she was something more.

Bells concluded principal photography one day before Christmas 1959. For all the delays, hard feelings, and frayed nerves, the dailies showed some very encouraging work. "Just in Time" and "The Party's Over" were fluid and affecting, with few cuts to break up the mood. Some of the less inspired numbers were staged imaginatively, although "Mu-Cha-Cha" looked like a dozen other stock Latin set pieces and "It's a Simple Little System" looked suspiciously like a castoff from *Guys and Dolls*. Jean Stapleton's performance was a masterpiece of comic character acting and Eddie Foy, Jr., Bernie West, Dort Clark, and Frank Gorshin showed well in smaller parts. The opening low-key slapstick scene with Gerry was among the funniest in the picture. Judy's growing fondness for Dean Martin did not disguise the fact that he was miscast, which for all purposes snipped the slender plotline of Ella and Jeff's tenuous romance. Still, a movie musical, like a stage musical, can get by on sheer momentum, and that was precisely what Judy provided.

Aside from her elusive turn in *Greenwich Village*, this was her first Technicolor movie, and at first that seemed to work against her. In black and white she had been all soft tones. Here her mustard-colored hair and red lips stood out against the pale white of her face, but that contrast was muted by the shy brown eyes, the honest smile, and Judy's uncanny way of letting the camera catch her off-guard and at odd angles. Her performance was skillfully tailored to the intimacy of film and ranged from antic to pathos without a false note between. Her knack for engaging the viewer, as though the eye were only a half-step removed from the character's inner workings, was abundantly in evidence. That the movie held together at all owed more to Judy's prodigious acting than to the writing or directing.

As with Billie Dawn, Judy saw Ella Peterson from stage birth to movie interment. And, as before, she was determined to leave the character and the entire category of comic blonds permanently behind. Only, this time, she had no pending political problems to box her into a stereotypic corner; she had no studio eager to press thinly disguised copies from the original. As she returned east with Gerry, Judy had the license and the will to change the course of her career. She also had the vehicle—her first straight dramatic play.

17

~~~~~~~~~~~~~~~~~~~~

Judy never saw herself as a star and so had no inhibitions about responding to others as a fan. When she read that James Mason wanted to give up acting, she dashed off a "Dear Mr. Mason" explaining how much she admired his work and imploring him to stay in the profession. At the few star-studded affairs Judy attended, she invariably took to the shadows and stole glimpses of the luminaries as if she were the hired help. But when it came to true artistic regard, Judy could be quite stingy. Among the select whose work she prized were Judy Garland, Laurence Olivier, and in a sense, Adlai Stevenson. No individual had a greater impact on her than Laurette Taylor as Amanda in Tennessee Williams' *The Glass Menagerie*.

Judy saw the show after it opened on Broadway in 1945 and came back to see it three other times, something she had not done before or since. In 1958 *Life* magazine ran a picture spread of top actresses in the roles they would most like to play. In the photo session at the Dakota Judy posed as Laurette in *The Glass Menagerie*. It was a rather solemn occasion for her, spoiled by the commotion over Marilyn Monroe, who was also being photographed at Judy's apartment. They had met a few years before, not long after Judy had done a Monroe imitation as part of a television special. Marilyn bumped into her on the street and said, "I hear you did a pretty good imitation of me." Judy said it really wasn't much and invited her over for tea. They spent a pleasant afternoon together, but it was an ironic study in contrasts. Both women had come to the public's attention for playing what were essentially, for want of a better term, dumb blonds. Judy's characters were more undereducated diamonds in the rough, whereas Marilyn's were overheated baby dolls. Marilyn bore a certain similarity to her roles, but Judy could not have been less like hers; however, they shared an impatience to break the images that had been imposed on them and pursue serious acting. As individuals they were virtual opposites, but as actresses they were both victims of cultural stereotypes that stamped women as unthinking, likable ninnies or childlike libidinal playthings.

Marilyn's second visit to Judy's place was less revealing—intellectually, that is. There were photographers and assistants swarming about, and word had circulated among the Dakota's maids, who collected in Judy's kitchen for a peek at the star. Judy was mildly miffed that the help would make such a fuss over Monroe when they had Holliday right under their noses. What distressed her most was the fact that Marilyn changed costumes in full view of Jonathan. Judy felt this was an imprudent eyeful for such a little boy. Minor complaints aside, Judy did welcome the opportunity to pronounce her awe and admiration in the pages of *Life* that April. The fascination was about to move beyond that point.

In 1955 Marguerite Courtney published a biography of her late mother, Laurette Taylor. It was a compassionate but frank account of the actress's rise from poverty to theatrical stardom, her subsequent obscurity and problem drinking, and her wondrous comeback in *The Glass Menagerie* before her death of a heart attack in 1946 at age sixty-two. Judy, whose constant reading seldom ran to biography, was captivated by the story and quietly shelved it in her memory. She was appearing on Broadway in *Bells* when she heard that Courtney had arranged to have the book adapted as a play. The playwright was Stanley Young, an academic, editor, critic, and novelist who over the years had written four Broadway plays, none of which fared well. Judy made special note of this and followed the project's progress.

In August 1958 Robert Mulligan was mentioned as a possible director, but there was still no play. By the time Young came up with a script, Mulligan had dropped out of the running as a director but retained a portion of the rights. Actually the issue of a director was less pressing than that of an actress to play the demanding title role. Judy was just completing her New York run in *Bells* when she decided to take matters into her own hands. Rather than sit by and hope against hope that her name would come up among those being considered for the play, she arranged a meeting with Marguerite Courtney, who had approval over casting. In nearly fifteen years as an actress Judy had never actively campaigned for a part. Even during Harry Cohn's celebrated Billie Dawn hunt, she had left the machinations mostly to interested third parties. For the first time Judy aggressively went after a role. She met Courtney, described her profound response to *The Glass Menagerie*, told how well she thought the biography had captured Laurette's complex personality, added that she was in search of a dramatic vehicle, and concluded by volunteering for the play.

The meeting went very well, and Judy departed a front-runner for the part. Negotiations continued in her absence, and while she was filming *Bells*, the deal neared completion. After the first of the year Alan Pakula became involved as producer, José Quintero was named director, and Judy was announced in the lead. Though Judy was pleased to have won Courtney's approval, the benefit was mutual. On the strength of Judy's name the producers were able to finance a play that so far had failed to spark much interest with investors, raising $150,000 in short order. Judy's terms were stiff but not unreasonable: she was entitled to fifteen percent of the gross, with a guaranteed weekly salary of three thousand dollars. Courtney and Young would divide the writer's royalty. Once the contracts were signed, casting could proceed and rehearsals were scheduled to begin in late summer.

Judy went about filling the intervening months. She and Gerry continued to improve as songwriters, though as song-pluggers they were hopeless. They spent a good deal of time up at the country house in Washingtonville, and that spring Gerry planted trees around the lawn. Judy caught the spirit and planted flowers, which for her initially consisted of scattering random seeds wherever she found a likely bare spot. Jonathan, Helen, and Yetta were up often, and the five of them visited a roadside bar in downtown Washingtonville, where Jonathan became the family expert on bumper pool.

All the while, circling Judy's mind was her approaching dramatic debut. She discussed it with confidants, some of whom doubted whether a biographical play about Laurette Taylor was really the right vehicle. Laurette was Irish, somewhat erratic, and alcoholic, all of which were alien to Judy's experience. Judy was quick to point out the similarities: a career start in a song-and-dance act, the relatively sudden rise to theatrical stardom, trouble with typecasting, an affair with a dashing movie star (in Laurette's case, John Gilbert), a failed marriage, career doldrums, and a problem with weight. But Judy was not one to live her roles. Laurette had been her greatest idol, and that by itself was reason enough to take the plunge.

As it happened, Judy was facing the production more alone than intended. Gerry was organizing his first big band—or concert jazz orchestra, as he called it—and the tour would require him to be away through most of the show's rehearsal and tryout phase. To make matters worse, Judy and Yetta had had a serious quarrel over several smoldering issues and by midsummer they were hardly speaking. The Buffingtons had since moved to New Jersey, and so Ruth was not available for impulse visits and talk. Helen was her usual oblivious self. The early signs were not especially auspicious, but then, Judy had seldom approached work from a state of serenity or equilibrium.

Judy had no contractual cast approval, but she did have considerable input throughout auditions. As with *Bells*, her director's instincts served her and the production well. The strong company included Joan Hackett, Nancy Marchand, Bibi Osterwald, Jack Gwillim as J. Hartley Manners (Laurette's second husband), and young Patrick O'Neal as John Gilbert. Given José Quintero's unassailable credentials as a strong director of Tennessee Williams and the leading director of Eugene O'Neill, Judy knew she had the backing of a sturdy production. There remained one monumental variable—the play.

Stanley Young had taken a decidedly literary approach to Laurette's life. The story was told in flashback, focusing primarily on the years from 1912 to 1938, though also requiring Judy to range from a sprightly young woman to a battered, boozy crone on the brink of death. The problem was not so much the epic or episodic structure as the tone. Young's text had the leisurely preciousness of prose instead of the aphoristic, economical, or oblique quality of spoken words. Judy and José had been aware of the problem from the start, but neither thought it insurmountable. Judy's experience with theater and film taught her that scripts generally evolved and crystallized as part of the larger collaborative venture. José recalled that Tennessee Williams virtually approached his scripts as a point of departure, raw material to be rewritten and refined through rehearsal and tryouts.

Stanley Young did not give an inch. He fought for every last word as if it had been chiseled in stone. It was not the sort of defensiveness born of lazy nattering from the players. In fact the requests for changes were handled very discreetly and funneled through José to the playwright. Yet, whenever there seemed to be some small understanding, the rewrites invariably worked around the proposed changes instead of with them. Rehearsal was supposed to be a time for invigorating, if sometimes fiery creation. Here there was a disturbing sense of stagnation. For someone with a valid reputation as a capable editor, Young was oddly unable to edit himself.

At first Judy accepted full blame for the play's dramatic anemia. Without Gerry or Yetta to talk to, she kept a journal, and the opening entry on August 29 was unsparingly gloomy:

> Totally disastrous day. I read like a stuffed owl, with as little familiarity with the English language. It's now seven in the morning and I've been walking up and down the hall alternately holding my aching stomach and wringing my hands. Oh, well, it's only humiliation.

The next day's rehearsal gave her more reason for hope. She was confident in José's direction and was willing to admit that she had made some progress with her part. She was especially fond of Pat O'Neal, who broke some of the tension with a sudden fit of giggles during one of the more passionate scenes. Despite these minor encouragements, Judy could not ignore the fact that the writing was failing the acting, not the reverse, as she'd first assumed.

> The writing, on reading aloud, turns out to be shoddy. It defies the actors to do anything but a stock performance. Pseudo-poetic *Ladies' Home Journal* circa '40—$10.00 and a little box in the middle of the page. Stanley alternates between writing vitally and pretentiously. Just when it starts going someplace, it sloshes over into conventional banal sentimentalism.

The concern over the writing spread with the growing evidence of the playwright's inflexibility. José pressed for revisions, and after a series of heated exchanges, Young brought in the Dramatists Guild in an effort to protect his script. There was a temporary standoff, with the result that Young stopped attending rehearsals. That eased the tension somewhat but also removed the possibility of rewrites, which by now were flagrantly necessary. The company struggled to inject life into the available text, but it was an uphill battle at best.

For all the squabbling at the upper levels, the cast did not break faith. They understood that the fault was neither theirs nor Judy's, and this formed a certain alliance. As usual, Judy was cooperative and generous, with none of the distance or imperiousness that might be expected of a star under such trying circumstances. One scene toward the end of Act II called for Laurette and John Gilbert to join in a romantic tango. And though Judy was no Pavlova, Pat was a downright tangle-foot. The two of them spent a few evenings at Roseland Ballroom watching the experts dip and swirl. The research was enjoyable but the results were dismal and the tango was dropped from the play.

By mid-September the impasse with Young stiffened and José threatened to quit unless he was given the freedom to make alterations in the script. Young finally backed off and producer Alan Pakula secretly hired Gavin Lambert as a play doctor. It was a peculiar choice, since Lambert, like Young, had a background as an editor and prose fiction writer. Although he possessed a handful of motion-picture credits, he had never written for theater. Unlike Young, Lambert was open to suggestions, but his rewrites were not much better than the original text.

In a play that was meant to signal Judy's full matriculation as a serious actress, she found herself writing. Rehearsals were followed by a dinner break, after which Judy, José, Alan, Pat, and a few others would gather back at the Dakota to wrestle with the script. Some improvements were made, but it was a cumbersome enterprise, trying to do by committee what should have been done by the playwright. For Judy it was an added distraction to an already exacting role. A script needn't be letter perfect by the close of rehearsals, but it should be sufficiently formed to allow the actors to concentrate on character without fear that random changes might undo or undercut their work. Judy was placed in the unenviable position of constructing an almost prohibitively complex part on the shifting sands of a problem script. The strain was beginning to show.

The script is hopeless. Stanley is staying away from rehearsals and Alan got Gavin Lambert to rewrite, but so far his stuff is very little improvement over the old. José has been heroic in standing firm and protecting me. We've all made a horrible mistake in assuming this play would be ready in time. We leave for New Haven Wednesday and we have only one good act, the climax of which I can't play. I'm trying to eliminate every vestige of my own personality, style, and approach and get into somebody else's skin. Sometimes I feel I've accomplished it, but when I don't, I'm nobody at all. These hours and days that pass with nothing maturing in the performance, but only stopping and starting because of the terrible dialogue— what torture. I'm afraid there just isn't time. And when will I be able to work on the *character?*

Laurette was due to open in New Haven on September 26, 1960. The production had continued its chaotic course, and during the afternoon run-through it came crashing home to Judy and Pat that there was no closing scene to the second act. This was the pivotal moment in the play when Laurette meets John Gilbert, and the entire encounter was staged in hollow pantomime and blackout, no dialogue, no curtain line. Judy and Pat approached José. She told him, "There's no end to Act II. We're going to give you one for tonight." José, who had Gavin Lambert stashed away in the Hotel Taft attempting rewrites, looked at them with a beleaguered expression and said simply, "Okay."

Pat and Judy spent the balance of the afternoon in her dressing room on the ground floor of the Shubert Theater. Judy wrote on a yellow notepad as they broke the scene into three parts. First was their chance meeting on a Hollywood studio lot. It was light, slightly clumsy talk, just the sort that might take place when two famous people meet for the first time. The second part of the scene consisted of lively banter and a few jokes—two strangers nervously sniffing around, sharing a comic sense of uneasiness. The third part was wordless, a sudden mutual attraction; a kiss, a clinch, lights, curtain.

The scene played perfectly that night. Unfortunately it was one of the few strong moments in an evening of lost moments. The cast fought hard, none more than Judy, but the bulk of the material was impenetrable. It was like trying to get a foothold on sheer granite—impossible and unpleasant to watch. The audience grew restless through the third act, and a few even nodded off. The final curtain was less a climax than a reprieve for those on both sides of the footlights.

The reviews were mostly unfavorable, yet kinder and more instructive than expected. The critics agreed that the play was extremely spotty and that Judy was toiling under a crushing theatrical burden. Still, there was a consensus that a decent play and potentially fine performance were lurking around, if only someone could pound the script into shape.

The company was not so optimistic. Morale was low, and during the New Haven run Pat finally pulled José aside and said, "We don't have a play here. Don't you know we don't have a play?" José conceded, "Yes, I know we don't have a play." Judy was painfully conscious of the fact as well, and when Gerry came up for an evening performance, she detected his disappointment despite his words of encouragement.

It was as though Judy were trapped in a classic nightmare—cue, curtain, audience, and no lines. She had suffered versions of this before onstage and in film. But there had never been this feeling of entrapment. Gavin's rewrites had been inadequate, and it was ridiculous to think that Judy and Pat could continue to construct entire scenes without eventually neglecting their acting. Ordinarily there was no particular shame in closing out of town or even in closing on Broadway after a brief, hapless run. This was not an ordinary play for Judy. This was her long-awaited transitional work, a gutsy attempt to break with her past forte and prove to herself and the public that she was more than a comic character player.

Audiences are not adept at distinguishing between substandard material and substandard acting. Either they like a play or they don't, and the most visible member of the production, the star, often becomes the target of their disfavor. Judy could almost anticipate the sniping: she's in over her head, she should have stuck with comedy, why is it clowns always want to play *Hamlet*, maybe *Born Yesterday* was a fluke after all. It was a constant disquiet, like rain on a tin roof. And if that were not enough, Judy's throat was beginning to give her trouble. Her voice grew husky, and at one performance she was barely audible. The audience fidgeted, some booed. Judy was devastated.

There was a closing-night party at the Hotel Taft and the company got down to some serious drinking. Judy stayed a short while, though long enough to sense an air of resignation. The cast hadn't given up, they were still doing more for the play than the play was doing for them. But they were convinced the play was a bomb, and in a curious way that seemed to relax them. Marginal productions can generate every manner of blame and bickering and back-stabbing, a kind of compulsive fault-finding to explain away possible failure. *Laurette* appeared to be a sure loser, and that left the company loose: there was no sense killing themselves over the unavoidable outcome.

Laurette was due to open in Philadelphia on October 7 before moving on to New York for an official opening on the twenty-seventh. What had become a virtual death watch had a sudden turnabout. The play was no less ragged, but Judy felt she was finally getting a handle on her character. After several productive rehearsals the director and producer seemed to agree. The play was never going to be problem-free, that much was obvious. But if the writing excesses could be held to a minimum, and if Judy's confidence continued to solidify, there was reason to hope that the show might yet survive. It was not at all uncommon for a mediocre play to ride on the strength of a powerful starring performance, especially a biographical play. Alan Pakula called the company together for a meeting and announced that he planned to stay out of town as long as it took to give *Laurette* a fighting chance. The defeatism of New Haven seemed to have been premature.

Judy had been in constant phone contact with Gerry, who was having a successful road trip with his band. He was in San Diego between gigs when she called with news of Alan's pep talk and her own progress on the character. For the first time Judy was enthusiastic and animated, and at her request Gerry flew in for the Friday opening. He arrived in Philadelphia and went directly to Judy's hotel room, expecting to find her cautiously hopeful. He was greeted instead by an edgy, troubled scene.

Judy had missed the matinee because of laryngitis. A doctor had gotten there moments before Gerry. Following a thorough examination, the doctor returned stone-faced to the outer room where Alan, José, and Gerry waited. He told them Judy could not possibly go on that night, and he recommended she return to New York at once. That seemed awfully extreme for simple laryngitis. Only then did the doctor explain that in the course of the physical he had found a lump in Judy's left breast. They were all stunned. Gerry could hear Judy sobbing in the next room. He approached the doctor. "Listen, can one day possibly make a difference? More than anything, she wants to open, she wants me to see this thing. Can't you let her perform it tonight?"

The doctor was unyielding. "Absolutely not. She has to go right away."

Alan once again summoned the company, and this time told them that Judy would have to leave the show because of a throat ailment. He had come to the difficult decision to close *Laurette*. He invited the cast to have a parting drink with him.

Gerry got in touch with Arnold Krakower, who booked a

room for Judy under an assumed name at the Gotham Hotel. Arnold thought it best to keep matters from the press, and especially Helen, until a definitive diagnosis could be obtained. Gerry rented a car, and he and Judy drove the excruciatingly long two hours from Philadelphia to New York. She was in a state of shock. She had swung through so many emotions in the last few days—dejection, optimism, and now utter dread. Gerry put on a brave face for Judy, but he could have cried right along with her; it was so cruelly ironic, so unfair.

Gerry had to leave early the next morning to catch up with his band in Chicago. He kissed Judy good-bye and promised he would be back in a day. Arnold arrived at the Gotham and called Yetta and David, who hurried over and were told what had happened in Philadelphia. Arnold was due in court later that day, and he asked them to take Judy through a series of medical examinations he had arranged. He too left and said he would be in touch with them by phone.

It was a strange reunion. Since the divorce Judy had seen David during his weekly visits with Jonathan at the Dakota. In the beginning she would take to her bedroom whenever he came. Lately they had become more cordial, and David stayed for dinner when circumstances permitted. Even so, there remained a kind of emotional partition between them, along with the distance that had grown between David and Yetta, despite her feeling that he had in many ways been good for Judy and that the divorce had been regrettable. Added to all the cross-tensions was the fact that Yetta and Judy were in the midst of a severe quarrel and had not spoken for nearly six weeks. Yet all the conflicts evaporated before the severity of the situation.

They visited three separate specialists that afternoon. Each doctor insisted Judy check into a hospital as soon as possible for a biopsy to determine whether the growth was benign or malignant. At five o'clock David went home and Yetta and Judy went to the Dakota. Arnold had seen to it that *Laurette*'s publicist reported Judy's illness to the press as a throat ailment.

Possible afflictions of the female breast were not discussed openly in 1960. Judy greeted Helen and repeated the story about her throat and mentioned a brief hospitalization for tests. In one sense, it was pitiful that Judy did not feel she could confide in her mother for fear of some extreme psychological reaction. But in another sense, Judy was simply doing what the family had always done—protecting Helen almost as a diversion, an exercise of control in troubled times. Judy probably needed to shield her mother less than she needed to substitute the manageable for the unthinkable. In that peculiar way, Helen was actually an asset.

Judy spent the next morning at home and was joined by Gerry, who flew in between performing dates. She kept a cheerful mask for Helen and Jonathan, but when she was alone with Gerry she could not hide her terror of cancer. The knowledge that Abe and Rachel had died of the disease weighed heavily on her mind. It was as though Judy had crammed her many phobias into a Pandora's box labeled cancer. Those still somewhat vague fears threatened to become reality as she checked into the hospital that afternoon.

Gerry and Yetta drove up to Columbia Presbyterian Hospital just after dawn. They were met there by David. Helen did not come; Helen did not go to hospitals. Judy had been prepped and sat in her room wearing a surgical gown. Yetta, David, and Gerry stood in the hall. Judy was wheeled past them headfirst toward the operating room and she could see the three of them. Fright surged like a current through her body, but she did not cry, she did not whimper. Instead Judy sat up, looked back at Yetta, David, and Gerry, and started blowing kisses, first with one hand, then the next, like some diva taking bows. They all laughed; they all fought back tears.

It was eight o'clock in the morning. If all went well, Judy would be out of surgery inside of two hours. Longer than that indicated malignancy and mastectomy. Yetta, David, and Gerry paced and made small talk. David and Gerry talked easily and politely without any trace of animosity or discomfort. They

avoided looking at the clock. By noon they silently acknowledged that their worst fears seemed to be coming true. Gerry,
who had gone without rest for days, retired to Judy's room and
dozed on a couch. Yetta and David went out for a cup of coffee.

In the nearly fifteen years they had known each other, Yetta
and David had been cool and reserved at best. But the growing
sense of foreboding seemed to break down the barriers that had
built up over time. They talked openly and freely without the
usual prickliness and sarcasm. David did most of the talking. He
puzzled out what he thought had gone wrong with his marriage
to Judy. He admitted that the family had been a terrible
handicap and that their reaction to the pregnancy had not only
angered him but also hurt him deeply. David then drew a deep
breath and said there had been one other decisive factor in the
breakup: he had always suspected that Judy had had an affair
with Peter Lawford.

Yetta set down her coffeecup and looked David straight in the
eye. "You're wrong." Whatever had gone on between Yetta and
David in the past, she could not deliberately hurt him; she could
tell he still loved Judy.

Yetta, David, and Gerry collected back in the hospital
waiting room. At four o'clock the surgeon came down and in a
hushed voice told them that the lump had been malignant and
that the left breast had been removed. Judy would be under
sedation for another hour. He was optimistic about a full
recovery, he felt the cancer had been completely removed. Yetta
sat down and let the words sink in. "He thinks they got it all,
that's what he said. That's what they always say."

18

~~~~~~~~~~~~~~~~~~~~~~~~~~~~~~~~~~

The papers reported a benign throat tumor, and some
theatrical circles whispered that Judy had found a psychoso-
matic way to slip through the cracks of a doomed play. The
company of *Laurette* knew better, and Pat O'Neal bristled
whenever he heard anyone imply that Judy had deserted the
show. Through nearly ten weeks of rehearsal and performance
he had acquired a deep regard and respect for Judy as an actress,
and more, as a person. There was no doubt in Pat's mind that
she could succeed as a straight dramatic actress, given a good
play. That was the awful crime of *Laurette:* most people
assumed Judy had let down the play, when the exact opposite
was true.

Nothing could be further from Judy's thoughts than the
small-minded gossip of the show-business community. Any
regret she might have felt about the play was fully eclipsed by
the shame and desolation she felt at having had a breast
removed. She could accept the surgeon's prognosis for a full life,
but she could not help but wonder what the quality of that life

might be. She feared beyond all reason that the public would discover the truth about her illness. In the bosom-obsessed culture of 1960 America, a mastectomy was the female equivalent of castration. The procedure had no physiological affect on sexuality, but the psychological implications ran to the core of Judy's identity. There was no public consciousness of breast cancer, no support system among women who had suffered the same agony. It was talked around, not about.

Judy had never totally believed in her physical appeal to men. There were any number of social gatherings where she turned heads, but she seemed to see this as fleeting and almost the product of cosmetic legerdemain. She knew that even on bad days she was attractive to men, but she saw that more as the result of her charm, her mind and wit, the gleam of some inner light. It was the outer beauty that concerned her. Judy had always delighted in low-cut blouses and gowns; this made her feel feminine, and that was gone. Her ego bowed under the weight of self-consciousness and doubt. She feared Gerry would no longer find her sexually desirable; she feared he would leave her.

After two weeks in the hospital Judy came home and took to her bed. She became introverted and withdrawn. Although she was well along in her recovery from surgery, she greeted visitors in her housecoat. She did not dress or make herself presentable. Her ordeal was known to only her closest friends, and they rallied to her side. Yetta, David, the Buffingtons, Betty and Adolph, Lennie, Alec Wilder, Doria Avila, Ralph Roberts, and others; they were all eager to help, to return Judy's many kindnesses over the years. But she was not in a state of mind to be helped, and there was only so much they could do to rebuild her lost confidence. That was Judy's personal struggle, though she was to receive invaluable support from some unexpected sources.

Helen had to be told of the mastectomy. Obviously Judy could not continue the charade of minor throat surgery. And as happened before in the bleak aftermath of the Sydney affair,

Helen held up sturdily. She nursed Judy, she looked after Jonathan, and she played hostess when Judy was too weak or depressed to entertain visitors. She tapped an inner strength she had been kept from using most of her life. In recent years Helen had more or less run the household, but it was mainly busywork, Judy's attempt to give her mother something to do. Now Helen could rise above the trivial, and she did so with a competence that exceeded everyone's expectation. Helen did not have great insight into what Judy was going through emotionally, but her instincts were humane and sound and she was instrumental in assisting the family through these potentially treacherous times.

Yetta, of course, was a mainstay. She spent every spare minute with Judy and in her special way trod the delicate line between sympathy and support. Yetta's no-nonsense style of friendship gave Judy something no one else could, an almost molecular depth of understanding and a challenge to avoid destructive despondency and self-pity. Even that was not quite enough. Judy still had to feel that she was a vital, attractive woman. On that count Gerry surprised everyone, including himself.

Gerry had never encountered a crisis even remotely like the present one. He had no empirical frame of reference, and so he simply followed his instincts, and that made all the difference. From the time of his visit to Philadelphia he did everything in his power to be with Judy. He repeatedly shuttled from his road tour to her side, pushing himself to the edge of exhaustion yet sensing that what Judy needed most was companionship.

By the time Judy was discharged from the hospital, the tour had ended and Gerry practically lived at the Dakota. He didn't try to rationalize or intellectualize with Judy, he didn't attempt to talk her out of her feelings. If she felt rotten or depressed, that was how she felt. Nor did Gerry ever give her the impression that he was with her out of pity or duty. His sheer presence was a tremendous lift for Judy. He was affectionate and, when it fit, funny. He was comfortable with her family and friends, and that cushioned the long weeks and months of confinement at the Dakota. With time, Judy and Gerry resumed their sex life, and that did more to mend her ego than all the flowers and sympathy put together. There would be difficulties and setbacks along the way, but for the first time Judy conceded that she might yet live a normal life.

Judy had sequestered herself for several months when she reluctantly ventured out of the house. Shopping had always been a pleasant diversion, but that too was complicated for reasons obvious and not. Added to Judy's self-consciousness about her body was a sensitivity about infection. As part of the surgical procedure, some glands had been removed from her left armpit, and that lowered her immunity. The minor annoyances of clothes shopping, zippers and errant pins, became mortal enemies.

Judy went to one shop, and while she was trying on dresses, a friend stood guard at the dressing room. She didn't want salesgirls flitting in and out; no one was to see her other than fully clothed. At length Judy found a dress she liked, and she stepped out to have a look at herself in the mirror. The clerk recognized Judy and was eager to be of assistance. She noticed that the zipper in back was undone and impulsively pulled it up, inadvertently pinching Judy's skin in the process. Judy angrily rebuked the clerk, something she had never before done. She had always made a point of courtesy toward working people, but her self-absorption was nearly obsessive. Try as she might to put her condition out of her mind, there were endless reminders great and small.

Judy was rightly concerned about herself, but not to the exclusion of others. It was the first Tuesday of May, and Helen was going through her morning routine. She saw to it that Jonathan was dressed and fed, then took him downstairs, where the two normally caught a cab for the short ride to school at the Ethical Culture Society a few blocks down Central Park West. The doorman stepped onto the street to hail a cab, and Helen and Jonathan waited on the curb, when an empty car parked temporarily in the Dakota's driveway slipped its brake and rolled over Helen. The doorman rushed over to find her pinned underneath but without apparent serious injury. Meanwhile, Judy was told of the accident, and she tossed a coat over her nightgown and rushed to the street, where the doorman was jacking up the runaway car off an incredibly calm Helen.

Judy was frantic as they waited for an ambulance, and by the time they arrived at Roosevelt Hospital, she was almost hysterical. The doctors examined Helen and found a slight fracture of the left ankle, plus assorted scrapes and bruises. They turned from their patient, who was in fine spirits, to Judy, who was distraught. With some effort they quieted her, though she insisted on spending the night in her mother's hospital room. After a few days Helen came home, and life returned to relative normalcy. The tie between mother and daughter was stronger than ever.

Judy made steady progress, and that brought about an inescapable conflict. She could not feel truly positive about herself unless she was working, but the lingering self-consciousness about her appearance left her unwilling to perform in public. Once again, Gerry came up with an ideal solution.

The Dramatists Guild had recently organized a symposium on the future of the musical theater. Among those on the panel were writer Anita Loos and jazz critic Nat Hentoff. The panelists agreed that Broadway musicals had begun to imitate themselves, losing the vigor that had long been their chief attraction. The culprit, it seemed, was music. In the past, musicals had always borrowed from popular song, which, with certain changes, had remained melodic and lyrical and served the narrative requirements well. But now the dominant popular musical idiom was rock-'n'-roll, which relied on driving rhythm and minimal melody and the virtual exclusion of lyrics, which tended to be repetitive, simplistic, or nonsensical. Hentoff suggested that the theater turn to jazz for inspiration, and he mentioned Gerry Mulligan by name as one of the more melodic practitioners.

Anita Loos acted on the advice and called Gerry the next day. "Would you be interested in working on a musical comedy based on my play *Happy Birthday?*"

"I'd love to try," he answered.

"Do you have a lyricist you like to work with?"

Gerry played it cool. "The only one I've ever had any success with is Judy Holliday. We work very well together. She helps out with the music, and I help out with the words."

"Well, do you think she'd be interested?"

Gerry said he'd ask, thanked Anita, hung up, and told Judy. Judy was thrilled. It was hard to think of it as more than a game at first, but it seemed the perfect remedy for her dilemma: she could work in theater, which she loved, and yet put off the issue of acting. She could fulfill the old ambition for writing, she could use her mind without being made to feel like some intruder among writers and directors.

Judy and Gerry had planned to drive out to Bridgehampton on Long Island to find a beach house for the summer. En route they read a copy of *Happy Birthday*, underlined possible song cues, and the ideas flowed. They rented a spacious house which overlooked the beach, then returned to New York and told Anita that they were ready to proceed. Judy suggested she join them in Bridgehampton, and arrangements were made for a summer-long collaboration. There was ample room for Jonathan and Helen as well. Considering the misfortune of the past year, Judy could scarcely believe her good fortune. She had her family, Gerry, and an opportunity to write with one of the leading Broadway playwrights.

It was like a page out of a Philip Barry play: a beautiful rambling beach house, an eccentric family, a devoted offbeat lover, a delightful and lively house guest, three bright and talented people with a common working goal. Judy and Gerry were night people. They liked to work far into the evening and then unwind with drinks and friends at home or out. Anita was usually up with the sun. She would visit with Helen or play with Jonathan, or go directly to a small cottage near the ocean's edge and type away for three or four hours. Judy and Gerry rose before noon, and Anita joined them at the piano in the main house. They compared notes and then got on with the afternoon's work.

The collaboration was thick with admiration. Anita thought Judy was one of the most thoroughly cultured people she had met in her many years in show business—she was well-read and knowledgeable of classical and popular music and made little of either fact. Anita was equally impressed with Judy's discipline and working speed, and most of all with the subtlety, freshness, and wit of her lyrics. Anita was also pleased with Gerry's music, although she liked to tease him with Judy about being a "far-out jazz man." Both Judy and Gerry were charmed with Anita and flattered that the author of such hits as *Gentlemen Prefer Blondes* and *Gigi* would so willingly work with two neophytes. They labored hard and soon had something to show for their efforts.

Happy Birthday had originally opened on Broadway in November 1946 while Judy was well into her run in *Born Yesterday*. The show starred Helen Hayes as a homely Newark librarian, Addie Bemis, who with the aid of a few drinks is transformed into an enchanting siren radiating personality and *joie de vivre*. Though she succeeds in tempting a shy bank clerk from a flashy barfly, the show is not an advertisement for the joys of liquor. In the course of a rainy evening at the Jersey Mecca Cocktail Bar, Addie mixes drinks with abandonment and goes on a bender that was surrealistically depicted by director Josh Logan.

The show ran for two years and Katharine Hepburn was eager to play the part in film but ran afoul of the Hollywood censors, who feared it would drive lonely girls to drink throughout the country. Garson Kanin suggested a way around the objections which would turn the inebriated evening into a fantasy sequence, but that seemed to drain all the life out of the plot. Nothing more was said until late 1957, when Anita was joined by Charles Gaynor and Jule Styne, fresh from his success on *Bells*. They met in Italy and set about adapting the play as a musical for Carol Channing. Carol decided she was wrong for the part, and the project lay fallow until the summer in Bridgehampton.

Judy maintained that her interest in the project was purely as a lyricist. But she would no sooner complete a song with Gerry than she would declare, "I can't let anybody else do that." Nothing more definite was said, but Gerry and Anita were increasingly aware that Judy was getting hooked by her own material and that was fine—she would make an ideal Addie.

At the end of six weeks *Happy Birthday* had eight songs and a presentable libretto. Judy did not entirely trust the ease with which it had all come, and feared they had slipped into a creative vacuum. The others agreed that they were probably not the best judges of their progress and thought it best to bring in a savvy outsider. Judy suggested her producer from *Born Yesterday*, Max Gordon, and plans were made for an informal audition.

Max had not produced a play on Broadway since *The Solid Gold Cadillac*, eight years earlier. He had dabbled in television and lapsed into semiretirement, but he was still one of the most highly regarded theatrical producers and was ever on the lookout for the right property to lure him back to the fray. Max was understandably fond of Judy; she had given him his biggest hit and he was only too happy to make the long ride out to the Island to hear her debut as a musical-comedy lyricist. He was probably also prepared to talk her into playing the lead, although that would have required very little persuasion.

Max was delighted with what he heard. There were flaws, naturally, there always were at this stage of creation. But the plot and characters were strong and the songs fit seamlessly within the text, advancing the story as they were meant to. One lyric stood out in particular, a whimsical number to be sung by the proprietor of the Newark saloon where the action occurs:

It's a turkey but it's mine
I like the way it looks.
No one comes in here to dine
There's nobody here that cooks.
There's not room enough to dance,
There's nothing to recommend,
It's not so very fancy
But it's a friend-ly neighborhood dump.

Another, more wistful song was "Something Lovely," to be sung by Addie before her sodden metamorphosis. Judy, who had to be bamboozled into singing a ballad in *Bells*, turned out to be a sensitive ballad writer.

I want something lovely to happen to me,
Some tender romance I can dream of.
As fresh as the springtime as warm as July
A love song that I am the theme of.

I want someone lovely to happen to me,
I want to be warmed by his laughter.
If I can remember the sound of his voice
Then I can rejoice even after he's gone.

I won't care if it's not meant to last.
I won't have a future,
But oh what a wonderful past.

Max thought that the next logical step was to bring in a director who might help polish the material and get it into shape for a backers' audition. Unfortunately Anita was due to travel abroad, but rather than break the momentum, she hinted that perhaps she had gotten too close to the original play over the years and that another writer might make the book more than simply derivative. She would retain an interest in the production and that was the understanding, even though no papers had been drawn up and no money had changed hands. Other writers were considered. Moss Hart was mentioned, and Joe Stein.

Anita took off for Europe and Max talked up the show back in New York. Judy and Gerry inquired after various directors and librettists but came up empty-handed. Summer ended and they closed up the beach house with the raw material of a show and no immediate hope for a production.

It was starting to look as if Judy and Gerry would become two perennially undiscovered songwriters. They had also taken four of their other songs along with some Irving Berlin and Cole Porter tunes and completed a recording session at the Olmsted Studios in New York. It was a lively session with few of the tensions that had marred Judy's past studio work. The musicians were drawn mainly from Gerry's big band and included Bob Brookmeyer, Nick Travis, Gunther Schuller, and Mel Lewis. The arrangements were excellent, the playing tight, and Judy's singing was generally strong. But the producer, MGM Records, chose not to release the cuts as an album.

The time in the studio was still time well spent. Judy felt perfectly at home with Gerry's band members and they adored her. There was lots of good-natured kidding, some quiet serious moments, and a healthy avoidance of show-business topics. Gerry found far less acceptance among some of Judy's friends. Certainly those closest to Judy liked him; that was a virtual condition of friendship. Yetta, Arnold, the Buffingtons, Alec, and of course Helen were very fond of Gerry and deeply grateful to him for guiding Judy through a nearly catastrophic time. But the outer ring of friends, some of whom had risen from the modest confines of the Village Vanguard to the very heights of uptown chic, seemed to hold Gerry at arm's length.

As Herbie Green was quick to point out, Betty and Adolph not so much threw parties as cast them. They gave careful attention to the supporting players, and that in turn further elevated the evening's star, who might be lesser royalty, a name politician, or a hot actor. Judy was invariably asked to attend, but she sidestepped the invitations as fast as they came. She detested the practice of image-mongering, since, by nature, she was more of an image-smasher, an iconoclast. Judy suspected that although she was invited as a friend, she was also wanted as a kind of cameo. Since she attended so few parties, any appearance was a minor coup. That too was a deterrent. She had no wish to greet strangers and serve up scintillating bits of the real Judy Holliday, no more than she wished to trot out her unshakable alter ego, Billie Dawn. With the band members, as with Yetta and Buff and Ruth, she was appreciated for herself and not some ill-fitting star persona.

Gerry was more gregarious than Judy. He liked to meet new and interesting people, he liked to learn by conversation and observation. Gerry could be opinionated, but his occasional debates were more a form of education and recreation than anything else. He believed Judy was far too reclusive for her own good, not just socially but professionally as well. What with possibly indefinite delays on *Happy Birthday* and a prolonged absence from acting, Judy's career was dormant. Though she hated to admit it, for all their repellent pettiness these fashionable clambakes did often lead to work; take a producer, a composer, a writer or two, sprinkle liberally with champagne, and the potential for deal-making is undeniable. Gerry told Judy it was one thing to avoid superficial socializing but quite another to cut herself off completely to the detriment of her career. Judy only grudgingly granted the logic of his argument.

Judy and Gerry were sitting around the apartment one evening when the phone rang. It was Adolph with an invitation to a party he and Phyllis were having for Peter Sellers. Judy made her usual excuses and said she would try to stop by, but when she mentioned the call to Gerry, her tone changed. "Come to think of it, Peter Sellers is somebody I really would like to meet. I admire him, and for a party for Peter Sellers, I want to go. This party we go."

"Terrific," Gerry replied. "That's great. I'd love to meet him too." He knew that Leonard Bernstein would also be there, and though he admired his music, they had never met.

Despite these dual incentives, Judy grew wary as the party approached. She thought back to all the dreary get-togethers she had braved in the past, and explained to Gerry how depressingly impersonal these things could be, especially when all were out to impress a guest of honor. Gerry would not let her back out, and Judy acquiesced but warned, "You'll see."

It was an after-theater party, and Judy and Gerry did not arrive at Adolph's until a little before midnight. They were greeted at the door by a tearful Phyllis. Judy was afraid something horrible had happened, an injury, a death. "Phyllis, what happened? What's the matter?"

She looked up gravely. "Peter Sellers cannot come."

To which Judy added without missing a beat, "Eeyi, eeyi, oh."

Gerry fell down laughing at the way Judy instantly turned this presumed social calamity into some idiot nursery rhyme. Phyllis was not so amused. Like a glum undertaker she showed them inside to a scene that was absurdly funereal. The grim topic of conversation was whether Sellers had in fact taken ill as reported or had simply stiffed them to attend another party. Gerry mused, "God forbid they should just be with each other," but he saw consolation in the opportunity to meet Bernstein.

But Lennie was consumed with the failure of the evening. He said he had given up another party to attend this one, and Adolph had not delivered the goods. Judy broke in to introduce Gerry, Lennie gave him a perfunctory greeting and went back to grousing. As the night wore on, Gerry tried repeatedly to engage Lennie in conversation but was pointedly ignored. Judy attempted to hide her shock at the discourtesy and the entire folly of the evening. Later she caught Gerry's glance from across the room and rolled her eyes. The message was unmistakable: I told you so. After that, they returned to Judy's style of low-key socializing.

In the roughly year and a half since her operation, Judy appeared to have recovered fully. Regular examinations indicated that the cancer had been completely removed. Her weight was down, her spirits were up, she looked and felt great. The only problem was her lack of work. Judy had overcome much of her recent trepidation and she not only wanted to perform, she needed to: it was intrinsic to her self-concept. By spring 1962 nothing more had come of *Happy Birthday*, and she and Gerry began to wonder whether anything ever would. One thing was certain; she was not simply willing to sit back and wait for the right offer. She wanted to pursue her songwriting, but she knew that acting was the surest and fastest and possibly most fulfilling way to get back to work. She instructed her agent at William Morris to start submitting scripts for her consideration.

Judy was approaching her fortieth birthday, and with that came an added measure of self-awareness. In her personal life she accepted herself as a single parent who would not try a second time to become a mother and wife. Neither she nor Gerry wanted more children, and both conceded they had failed once at marriage and were not eager to try again. Professionally she was likewise at peace with herself. Judy was philosophical about the disappointment of *Laurette*, for which she accepted partial blame for misjudgment, while sparing herself total responsibility. She was vindicated by the knowledge that a subsequent production with Siobhan McKenna under Stanley Young's watchful eye fared no better than the original. Judy meant to stretch and grow as an actress, but not by way of ill-conceived heavy-handed dramatic vehicles. Nor could she bring herself to attend the various workshops that were available to working actors looking to improve their craft. She could not see herself as a late-blooming method actor.

Judy knew what she did best, a kind of human comedy cum

pathos. That genre was not likely to transport her suddenly to great dramatic heights, but it could provide the necessary small gradual steps away from mere character acting, repetition, or worse, self-parody. Judy was mindful of the rumors of her desertion in Philadelphia. She was not the sort to bend to such backbiting, but she was no less determined to reassert herself as a performer. It might be a play, a movie, a musical; whatever it took to get her back to work. Judy knew that acting was a muscle that could atrophy without use. There would be plenty of time later for other dramatic experiments, songwriting, writing, or even directing, whose fascination had never left her. For now, it was first things first. She had to perform.

19

~~~~~~~~~~~~~~~

*T*he show was called *Hot Spot*, and it was being touted as
Judy's Broadway "comeback." It was a poor choice of words; it
smacked of death and resurrection. Judy had been away from
Broadway for only four years, from theater less than three years
counting *Laurette*. But talk of Judy's illness had filtered through
the theater community, and there was general relief that she was
well enough to return to work in a major musical.

The show was not Judy's first choice. She had spent months
reading stacks of scripts but found nothing even remotely
appealing. She had even gone so far as to purchase an option on
Ginny Brown's memoir, *Swans at My Window*, about an
American couple living in a boat on the Thames. There was talk
of an eventual film, but there were innumerable details to be
worked out, and the last thing Judy wanted was to act as
producer. She looked to theater, where the gestation period
from conception to opening was not nearly so long as pictures.
Her sense of urgency was not without justification.

Through the mid- and late fifties Judy's finances flourished.

She was never showy with money, least of all when married to David, who earned considerably less than she. But she sometimes handled cash like a kid with Monopoly money. She carried a big wad of random bills in a string purse whose contents she emptied on the nearest table whenever it came time to pay. Judy's generosity was legendary. She loved to buy gifts for others. She made substantial loans to friends and refused to be reimbursed. She was the sole support of Helen, who if anything was worse with money than her daughter. On more than one occasion Helen paid for a cab ride and told the driver to keep the change, only to realize later she had handed him a twenty- or fifty-dollar bill.

Judy wisely entrusted her financial dealings to Arnold Krakower, who counseled her well on some conservative investments, one of which was a California shopping-center development which was purchased in Helen's name. But at one point the money was coming in faster than it could be similarly invested, and when Judy mentioned a proposition told her by a friend, Arnold gave it serious consideration. It was a complicated financial arrangement which many in the entertainment field had used to good advantage. In essence it involved borrowing a sizable amount of money from a bank at what was then a small rate of interest. That money, along with other capital, was then used to purchase U.S. Treasury bills. The bills matured over a period of time and the yield was greater than the interest on the bank loan, and was tax-free. The borrowing interest, in turn, was tax-deductible, and between that and the differential of the loan and the bill rate, the gain was considerable. Judy knew nothing more than that it had worked for others and could work for her. She instructed Arnold to proceed.

However, in the early sixties the IRS ruled that the income from such speculating was to be taxed at an increased rate. The ruling was retroactive, which meant that investors had to make up the difference. Judy's financial plunge had been confined to 1957, but with penalties and costs, her tax bill was a whopping

$99,286. What with medical costs and unemployment, Judy did not have the funds to make good the debt. Arnold meanwhile appealed the ruling and felt he could hold up the assessment in court, though not indefinitely.

A musical entitled *Carte Blanche* had been planned for Tony Perkins and Carol Burnett, with lyrics by Martin Charnin and music by Richard Rodgers' daughter Mary. The project fell through and Martin and Mary got in touch with Jack Weinstock and Willie Gilbert, who had just collaborated with Abe Burrows on the book of *How to Succeed in Business Without Really Trying*, which won everything from the Tony to the Pulitzer, to say nothing of a hefty financial return. The four of them sifted through possible premises, when Mary turned up an item from the New York *Times* about a young female Peace Corps volunteer in Africa who wrote home a single critical postcard about the Corps's ineffectiveness, which caused a serious flap in Washington and led ultimately to increased aid to that country.

From that they spun a satire about a fetchingly inept Peace Corps volunteer, Sally Hopwinder, assigned to the small mythical kingdom of D'Hum (pronounced "dumb"). In an effort to obtain foreign aid from America, she invents a Communist threat, but the situation swiftly gets out of hand. By story's end she wins a handsome Ivy League consular official and D'Hum wins its aid. It was a rather wispy premise but it had many musical possibilities. The rights were purchased by Lawrence Carr and Robert Fryer, the second of whom had produced Betty and Adolph's *Wonderful Town*.

From the outset all those involved wanted Judy to play Sally. Judy read the libretto, which she liked but about which she had serious reservations. While she played for time to decide, the producers auditioned other actresses, including Dorothy Loudon, Karen Morrow, and a relative unknown named Barbra Streisand. Martin and Mary were all for Barbra. Weinstock and Gilbert and Morton (Teke) Da Costa, just signed as director, were flatly opposed. Teke felt that audiences would simply not accept Barbra in a romantic lead. "They won't believe that anyone, *anyone* would want to kiss that face." Dorothy Loudon became a front-runner.

Judy continued to fret over the decision. She invited Martin and Mary up to the Dakota to play the score and a short while later invited Fryer and Carr over and told them she would do the show. A mood of euphoria descended over all but Judy. She had doubts about some of the songs and would have preferred to hear them with Gerry, who was on the road performing. She also questioned whether her judgment hadn't been clouded by her impatience to work, the dearth of suitable scripts, and her tax dilemma. But there was little time for second-guessing. As soon as the backing was secured and the contractual particulars worked out, the show was to go immediately into rehearsal.

The William Morris Agency had come to think of Judy as family. Her agent was keenly aware of the various pressures on her and held out for terms that won her some respite. Judy was granted ten percent of the gross against a guaranteed weekly income of $3,500. She was also entitled to ten percent of eventual profits, which would go to Jonathan through a corporation bearing his name, Jonhol Enterprises. Judy was free to hire her regular dresser, Liz White, and in an unusual concession she was permitted to have Paul Davis along as an assistant to the producers. Over the past few years Judy had occasionally had Paul on retainer as, among other things, a companion to Jonathan. It was a peculiar arrangement which some of Judy's friends frowned upon; it seemed he had become a security blanket for hire. In addition to these many concessions, she was given a $25,000 advance, which she sorely needed at the time. The early signs were Judy was worth every penny of it.

A backers' audition was set for Steinway Hall. It was a very flossy event which Judy sat out. Mary played piano, Martin sang, and Teke narrated parts of the story. It took three-quarters of an hour, at the end of which the patrons rushed the desk to sign up for shares. The show had been capitalized at $400,000; half was raised that night, and the rest followed quickly. It had been a skillful presentation, but the chief attraction to backers was Judy's name. The setback of *Laurette* was long forgotten and people looked for a return to the glory days of *Born Yesterday* and *Bells Are Ringing.*

Judy wished as much, but she could not ignore the changes brought on by time and her illness. She had put on a substantial amount of weight in the weeks prior to rehearsal. In the past a combination of V-8 juice, broiled steak, anxiety, and Ralph Roberts' patented rubdowns shed pounds in a matter of days. But Judy had been on cortisone medication since her operation, and between that and a forty-one-year-old body that had become less resilient, the most rigorous diet showed scant results. Judy was weakened to the point where she became dizzy, and the producers told her that a full-figured star was preferable to no star at all. Judy relaxed her regimen but continued to take diuretics to remove the excess fluids that the steroids retained.

By the time rehearsals started in January, ten of the eventual fourteen songs had already been completed. The company had been filled with the last-minute addition of leading man Joseph Campanella, whom Judy had selected from a list that included Peter Graves, Kevin McCarthy, and Robert Sterling. The production was due to open in Washington the first week of February. It was an unsparing schedule which would depend heavily on Judy and Teke Da Costa, who had worked well together years ago on *Dream Girl.* By way of an added incentive, there were already signs of an enormous advance ticket sale, and barring unforseen problems, the prospects for success seemed bright.

One of the foreseeable hurdles of any play is the start of rehearsal. An assortment of distinct egos and personalities come together for what will be an intensive, at times exasperating few weeks en route to out-of-town tryouts. From this muddle must emerge a kind of power structure, with the director in unquestioned command. More than anyone else, he sets the tone, he mediates between the writers and the cast, he acts as custodian of the vision that will ultimately become the show.

At first there is customarily a degree of testing and uncertainty from the actors. The writers and production staff have been with the material longer. The actors are the latecomers, and the ones who visibly rise or fall with the show. If the director inspires confidence from the start, the cast will respond with faith. If the director wavers, the cast will begin to bolt.

Teke Da Costa had brought in more than his share of Broadway hits with *Plain and Fancy, No Time for Sergeants*, and *The Music Man*. He was a veteran director with fine credentials, and yet for some reason he could not seem to get a handle on *Hot Spot*. It may have been attributable to any of a number of factors, including troublesome stomach ulcers. But whatever the cause, the effect was a lack of conviction, and that was the kiss of death. Judy was acutely anxious for any number of reasons. The moment she sensed Teke's hesitancy, she became restless, challenging his direction and questioning the material. The situation quickly got out of hand, and the songwriters were the first to feel the backlash. Whether it was due to Judy's own largely frustrated attempts at songwriting or the actual quality of the tunes was unclear. But Judy simply refused to sing some songs, and others she treated so listlessly as to guarantee their exclusion. Almost overnight six of the original ten were dropped.

That alone was not cause for alarm. In musical comedy, rewriting is imperative. Still, the gulf between Judy and Teke rapidly widened, and that was cause for great concern. They never openly fought, which might at least have cleared the air. Instead they engaged in a sort of war of nerves. Teke would offer a direction, and if Judy disagreed, she would fix him with a dubious, mutinous glare. Whenever tempers neared the boiling point, Judy would pout or retreat to her circle of supporters as Teke hastened to his. Judy was not the least interested in power games; she wanted only to make the show work. She had no faith in her director to bring about that end.

Hot Spot hobbled out of rehearsal in worse shape than it had started and got to Washington in almost total disarray. Gerry arranged to go along for the duration, which did wonders for Judy's spirits but alarmed Martin and Teke. Martin was both the youngest collaborator and the only one without prior Broadway writing credits. With Gerry along, it appeared more songs were sure to fall. Martin feared he might be the baby who would be thrown out with the bathwater next time around. Teke predicted that Gerry's presence might further insulate Judy from his direction, and to a degree he was right. When rehearsals resumed at the National Theater, Gerry generally sat a few rows behind the director and Judy looked to him repeatedly for tacit support.

The production was shot through with rumors that at different times had the writers, the director, and even the star being replaced. Actually there was no sinister conspiracy afoot to dump one or another person, just enough paranoia to fill a good-sized asylum. The opening notices only fueled those fears. The book and music came in for heavy criticism, while Judy was cited as a courageous martyr struggling gamely if somewhat vainly against mediocre material. Critics were careful to point out the show's potential, but potential was like a bad check—for all the good intentions, it didn't count for much at the box office. Everyone crossed his fingers and waited for heads to roll, hoping to be spared.

The first to go was Teke Da Costa, and he left on a stretcher. In the wake of the dismal reviews, he collapsed and was rushed to the hospital with bleeding ulcers. While the producers frantically searched for a replacement, the show went through a phase that could best be described as director-for-a-day. Robert Fryer ran the company through rehearsal one time, as did Martin Charnin, whom Judy completely stonewalled. These stopgap measures continued until it was announced that Richard Quine had agreed to come in and save the show. The resulting hopeful mood somehow failed to take into account that despite success as a movie director, his theatrical experience had been confined to a few turns as an actor in middling Broadway plays. Quine appeared wearing a tweed jacket and a fresh Hollywood tan, slouched in the second row for a run-through, and promptly disappeared.

The next candidate for director-for-a-day was Arthur Laurents, who had written *West Side Story* and *Gypsy* and directed *I Can Get It for You Wholesale*, which became the springboard for Barbra Streisand's career. Laurents could, in effect, wear both hats as director and writer, and that met the show's two pressing needs. He was introduced to the company on a Saturday and delivered a rousing speech that finished to cheers. He planned to move into the breach beginning with rehearsals on Monday. On Sunday morning he had breakfast with Judy. It may have been a clash of personalities or basic artistic differences—neither of them was saying. Though the details were somewhat murky, the consequences were plain: on Sunday afternoon Laurents boarded a train for New York and did not return.

As the director sweepstakes intensified, the writing also came under scrutiny. A number of play doctors came to Washington, and each more or less offered the same prognosis: the production was in deep waters and sinking fast. Mary's father, Richard Rodgers, stopped by and gave a concurring second opinion. At Judy's request Betty and Adolph came down and went over the script, and though they wanted more than anything to help their friend, they said there was little they could do to untangle the mess. Without significant improvement of the material, the production foundered and the search for directors began to seem pointless: it was like changing captains on the *Titanic*.

Hot Spot opened in Philadelphia on February 28, and the reviews picked up where the Washington reviews left off. Judy's performance was seen as heroic, given the disheveled production. Only, this time there was more talk of the problem-riddled material and no mention of potential. For all the pessimism, Judy did not give up on *Hot Spot*. It may have been a deep-seated fear of closing a second show in Philadelphia but probably had more to do with her stubborn code of professionalism. In many ways she had contributed to the production's instability, and she meant to bring it in if it was the last thing she did.

Judy was unaware of rumblings back in New York. The producers did not lay the blame fully on her, but they did feel that a replacement might pump fresh hope into the show. One of the backers, who had recently been with the talent agency MCA, checked on Carol Channing and found she was available. The producers considered bringing her down to Philadelphia for a look, but that could be a huge gamble. If Carol declined and Judy discovered the intrigue, *Hot Spot* might be left with no director or leading lady. Besides, there were tremors from the Shubert office indicating that the contracts had specifically named Judy and that without her the use of the theater could be legally revoked. It was not hard to figure: no director, no star, no theater, no show. For better or worse, the producers decided to stick with Judy.

Philadelphia was not without its lighter moments. At various times Judy was visited by Yetta, Helen, Harry, and Maude. What with rehearsals, performances, and incessant rewrites, Judy was not able to spend much time with them, but they did manage to cheer her on and assure themselves that her health was holding up under the strain. Gerry arranged to pick up some gigs in town so he could both work and keep an eye on Judy. Even so, a good deal of the tension seemed to lap over into the relationship. One member of the production showed some interest in Judy, and he was chatting with her in her hotel suite one night when Gerry showed up. Judy excused herself, went to her bedroom, slipped out of her clothes and under the covers. A loud argument broke out in the adjoining room, and Judy impishly thought: How wonderful. At last two men are fighting over me. She listened and eagerly waited for the winner to come in and claim her. Instead she heard the door slam and realized she was alone. The next morning she learned the two of them had patched over their differences, which had nothing to do with her, then went out for a few drinks.

Chief among the show's many deficiencies was the opening

song. This could be the linchpin of an otherwise rickety musical. A stirring curtain-raiser would set the tone and encourage the necessary leap of faith. The current choice, "Over," fulfilled neither of those requisites, and Martin was not making much progress on an alternative. Mary suggested they bring in Stephen Sondheim, who had made his mark as a lyricist on *West Side Story* and *Gypsy* and composer-lyricist of *A Funny Thing Happened on the Way to the Forum*. Sondheim came down to Philadelphia and, working closely with Martin and Mary, helped write "Don't Laugh." It was just what the show needed—an up-tempo, fittingly befuddled song that introduced the plot and showed off Judy's mastery of a comic lyric. The producers did not think this would magically save the show. But it was the first true breakthrough in a disastrous tryout tour, and they were thankful for small miracles.

Hot Spot finally came to rest at the Majestic Theater in New York. It had been scheduled for a late-March opening, which was immediately postponed. As the show prepared for previews, Nat Lefkowitz of the William Morris Agency brought Herb Ross by the theater. Herb was confronted by a veritable theatrical Frankenstein, a hodgepodge of songs and scenes that lumbered menacingly about the stage. Herb had a sound theatrical background as a choreographer and director, he got along well with Judy, and he saw where the show's disparate parts might be trimmed and integrated. He was hired and made the director of record. His imagination and resolve brought a glimmer of hope.

Judy's outlook fluctuated between hope and gloom. Her experience told her that no amount of change could salvage the show. Yet her pride would not permit her to simply go through the motions. There had been nights as far back as the Village Vanguard when she performed for as few as six people, half of them drunk and the other half wishing they were. It was not just some mindless show-must-go-on credo, but a view of theater as a sacred trust. The people paid their money, and Judy did the very best she could with the material she had. Her perfectionism and her drive to please made her the most conscientious of actresses. She loved to work, she did whatever she could to make a show work. Her ethic had seen her through raves on Broadway and heckling in New Haven. It would see her through the present trauma as well.

Emotionally Judy steered an amazingly straight course. There were brief depressions, but she always snapped back. She sat in on production meetings, rehearsed to all hours of the night, and never missed a performance. She demonstrated remarkable stamina and for that alone won the admiration of the cast. Her one sin was a chronic questioning of the material. At the start it might well have been justified; there was room for improvement and enough time to accomplish it. But as time began to work against rather than for them, she should have shifted her concentration from revision to performance. Judy was going off in two directions at once, to the detriment of both. In fact one glaring difference between this show and her last was that in *Laurette*, changes were taboo; in *Hot Spot*, they were almost obsessive. It was like dressing for a party she dreaded—nothing quite pleased her, it was too short, too long, too tight, too loose, the wrong combination, the wrong color. Judy was escaping the general through the particular, and those closest to the production couldn't help but notice she was procrastinating.

Herb Ross made more constructive changes in a matter of days than his predecessors had in weeks. He was a surgeon doing whatever he could to save the patient. Whole scenes were lopped off between rehearsal and curtain. Musical cues and wardrobe changes were often overlooked, and on several occasions Judy and Joe Campanella found themselves improvising before packed houses while the conductor, Milt Rosenstock, steadied a pit full of bewildered musicians. At Judy and Herb's suggestion, the producers kept delaying the opening.

Previews are a grace period in which a production fresh from tryouts has a chance to prune and preen itself before facing the New York critics. Previews normally last from one to two weeks, by which time it is rightly assumed that everything that can be done has been done. *Hot Spot* played a record fifty-eight previews, and it became an industry joke, like a virginal bride lingering in the bathroom on her wedding night. It was, of course, no laughing matter. The longer they waited, the less tolerant the critics would be. An opening was at last set for April 17, 1963, and changes were made right up to the overture.

Most of Judy's friends declined to attend, anticipating the worst. They missed what in many ways was the most electrifying performance of her career. All the doubting and stalling gave way to total concentration onstage. Judy played even the most tired routines as if they were vintage Kaufman and Hart. There was no trace of hesitation on her part, and her energy seemed to invigorate the entire company. The curtain rang down to honest applause and at least one of the backers exclaimed, "My God, she pulled it off."

The reviewers were far less amenable. All of them praised Judy's work, and most admitted that the show had a clever premise. But they could not overlook the messy patchwork book and the absence of any really memorable song. The *New York Times* was the money review, and while Howard Taubman was charmed with Judy and pleased with the rest of the cast, he concluded, "It still has the confused air of a musical dashing off in pursuit of any and all promising lines and ideas. Too bad, because it should and could have been better." These were not the kind of comments that necessarily guaranteed failure. With the boost of substantial advance ticket sales, the producers decided to try to make a stand. But cancellations poured in, and it became evident that Judy's name and notices would not be enough. On May 20 the closing notice was posted. *Hot Spot* would have fewer performances than previews.

Judy spent most of the following summer at her country home in Washingtonville, where she planted an elaborate flower and vegetable garden of which she was most proud. She took little comfort in what had been, for her at least, a warmly received return to the New York stage. She was saddened by the failure of *Hot Spot*, and with the distance of time hinted she might have done more damage than good with her campaign for changes. But all the second-guessing in the world would not bring back the show. She knew she had given every last ounce of her theatrical gifts, and considering the production's rocky history, it did turn out to be a near-miss.

Judy could not merely sit back and ponder the recent past. Though she was unaware of the severity of her financial situation, she did know that Arnold was losing ground on the tax ruling. In fact, the Dakota had recently gone co-op and the tenants were offered shares at a low insider's price. Judy told Arnold she wanted to buy her apartment as well as one or two others as an investment. Arnold said the building was in disrepair and he considered it a bad investment. The truth was, Judy could not afford her own apartment, let alone others, and Arnold had pleaded with the landlord to allow her to remain on a renting basis. Judy could read Arnold's discreet evasions; she understood she had to get back to work soon.

As if that were not worry enough, her relationship with Gerry had fallen on hard times. They'd had their quarrels before, but this seemed to portend more. The events of the last three years had taken their toll on Gerry. He stood by Judy through the ordeal of her operation and the postoperative depression. More than anyone else, he was responsible for her emotional recovery, helping her believe she was not a cripple but a still lovely, sexual woman. When she was too self-conscious to perform, he encouraged her to experiment with songwriting. When she was ready to act again, he endured *Hot Spot*'s tempestuous road to Broadway. But by late fall he started to chafe at the strictures of Judy's possessiveness and dependency. Gerry started to stray.

It happened in subtle ways at first. Gerry would go out of town for a weekend job, then show up in New York on Tuesday or Wednesday instead of Monday. Judy suspected he had been off with another woman, and a bitter argument would follow. They would stop seeing each other for a short while until both decided to give it another try.

During one separation Judy met Alec Wilder for lunch at the Algonquin, where he made his home. They were in the dining room and Judy was about to describe her latest fight with Gerry when she noticed several tourists at the next table hanging on her every word. She turned to them and in a polite matter-of-fact tone told them, "You really better go. It's gonna get really fucking rough."

After another breakup she called Yetta and tearfully announced, "I'm not attractive anymore."

"Of course you are," Yetta insisted. "You're good-looking, you're bright."

To illustrate her point, Judy said she had been to a party the previous night. She met a handsome stranger and took him home to the Dakota, but neglected to mention her mastectomy. The encounter was a disaster.

Yetta could hardly believe what she heard. "Judy, you don't do things like this. You don't pick up a stranger and not tell him. Of course it's not going to work."

With yet another split Yetta got a phone call at two in the morning. Judy was crying on the other end, explaining she had just thrown Gerry out but wanted him back.

"For God's sake, call him up."

"I can't do that."

"You want me to call him up?"

"Yes."

Yetta called Gerry, who had an apartment just around the corner from the Dakota. "Judy's very unhappy. Why don't you go see her. She's waiting for you."

"You sure?" Gerry asked.

"Yes, I'm sure."

The two of them made up, but the identical scene was replayed several times. Gerry had reached the end of his rope. He knew Judy had been to the hospital for tests recently, but the results had been cheering. She had held up admirably through the travail of *Hot Spot* and there was every reason to think she would soon be employed again. Her weight was down, she looked good, she seemed strong psychologically. Gerry decided to end the relationship at the first opportunity.

Arnold was well aware of the trouble between Gerry and Judy. In many and serious ways he knew more about Judy than she knew about herself. Arnold was a protector, a trouble-shooter. He could anticipate crisis and knew how to spare Judy the brunt of the impact. Arnold realized that Gerry was getting ready to leave Judy. He called him and arranged to have drinks. They met and made talk for a few minutes, and then with some difficulty Arnold got to the point. "Gerry, I want you to be good to Judy. She's dying."

20

~~~~~~~~~~~~~~~~~~

*I*t had become a ritual. Yetta would drive Judy up to Columbia Presbyterian Hospital for periodic tests. Judy would go in for X rays around 11:30 and a half-hour or so later the doctor would come out and personally tell her that there was no sign of cancer. Yetta and Judy would head off for a favorite café and eat too much lunch and drink too much wine.

During one visit, however, the routine changed slightly. Judy went in for X rays and thirty minutes later the nurse came out and said. "The doctor's sorry he had to leave on other business. But he wanted me to tell you everything is fine." Yetta and Judy left for their customary celebratory lunch. But it struck Yetta as odd that the nurse and not the doctor had come down to announce the results.

Two months later Judy was experiencing some mild pain in her right breast. She arranged to have another series of X rays but told Yetta, "I don't want you to go this time. Maybe you're a hex." Judy went instead with their mutual friend, a pretty young woman named Cam. Afterward the nurse again emerged, made apologies for the doctor, said the pain in the right breast was due to a slight bruise, and told Judy that there was still no indication of spread. Judy and Cam met Yetta for another lunch and it was agreed that in future Cam would escort her for tests.

Judy was pleased with the reports of her continued good health and she was delighted that she and Gerry were suddenly able to resolve their differences. Sometime after Yetta's last visit to Columbia Presbyterian, Gerry came to Judy and apologized for his infidelity and assured her that he would be faithful in the future. Their relationship was soon better than ever. They spent most of the summer up in Washingtonville; Gerry planted more trees and Judy did more gardening, at which she was becoming increasingly expert. They even got the notoriously leaky swimming pool to hold water.

Judy had her agents scouting new properties for her. She was rather annoyed at the sudden spate of Doris Day films. Judy respected her as a band singer but said that as a comic actress she left a lot to be desired. These films were precisely the sort of light romantic comedies that had been Judy's specialty, and it distressed her that none of the offers were coming her way. Still, she figured it was only a matter of time before she was back on screen, and then she would be flooded with scripts again.

All things considered, life was going well. As far as Judy knew, the tax hassle was yet in abeyance and Arnold appeared to be managing her finances without undue difficulty. The only emotional setback came in early October, when a good friend died unexpectedly. His name was Nick Travis and he had known Gerry since both played in big bands at separate high schools outside of Philadelphia. Nick was a superb trumpet player and he went on to become one of the top session men in New York. It was at his suggestion that Gerry formed his own big band in 1960. Nick joined as lead trumpet, and he and Judy became quite close.

Nick was in the middle of a messy divorce when he died suddenly of a perforated ulcer. His wife whisked him away before his friends could pay their last respects. Gerry got in touch with several musician friends and planned a fitting send-off at St. Peters Church, whose priest was a well-known supporter of jazz. They organized something of a jazz wake and Gerry told Judy about it. Without saying why, she said she would not be able to attend. Gerry was surprised by the reaction but knew better than to try to talk Judy out of something once her mind was made up.

It was a rainy early-autumn afternoon when the service was held. It was a touching tribute; the musicians played tunes associated with Nick, and some read words. When it was over Gerry walked to the church vestibule and found Judy in a scarf and raincoat. She had been there the entire time, pacing and peeking in through the door. Later that night Judy told Gerry, "When I die, that's how I'd like to go." It seemed more than just a passing notion; it was like some chilling prescience.

The pain returned. Judy told Arnold, and he arranged for her to see a Park Avenue specialist. This time Yetta went along, and Judy was in and out of the examination room in five minutes. The doctor told her that the pain was not cancer-related but the result of a rare affliction of the sternum that was chronic but not terminal. Judy was told not to leave town and to continue the medication she had been taking. She was immensely relieved at the news.

The entire visit was a charade. As far back as the first peculiar trip to Columbia Presbyterian, Arnold had known the truth of her condition. Rather than face Judy, the physician had phoned Arnold and told him that the cancer had metastasized and was inoperable. He explained she still had a year or more to live, and Arnold asked whether or not she should be told. The doctor replied that some individuals upon learning they are terminally ill get over the shock and experience a kind of positive, productive reaction. Others become emotionally paralyzed and the realization actually shortens their life. Given Judy's history of depression, the doctor recommended she be shielded from the truth. Arnold agreed, and he resolved to tell no one else. But when he saw the rumblings in Judy's relationship, he decided to confide in Gerry. It went no further than the two of them. Arnold knew if he told Yetta it would somehow change her behavior, and Judy, whose powers of perception sometimes bordered on the clairvoyant, would know the truth. The last person he'd tell would be Helen, who was hopelessly transparent and might heedlessly add to Judy's misery. In times of crisis, Helen herself often preferred fantasy to fact.

This was not the only information Arnold kept from Judy. She had lost the IRS tax appeal and the government placed a lien against her house in Washingtonville. He explained her medical condition to the agent assigned to her case and implored him to delay action until after she had died. In an astounding show of compassion, the agent consented. Judy's mounting medical expenses used up what little money she had left. Arnold let on that things were tight and that she should do what she could to curtail her spending. He told no one that he was paying her rent and sundry other bills.

Judy was not entirely oblivious of her financial straits. At one point she looked for a less costly place in which to live but had to give up the search because of her weakened condition. Nor were her friends entirely in the dark. Lennie Bernstein approached Arnold and offered to arrange a benefit concert. Arnold said that would break Judy's heart and, according to some, said that if he heard any more talk of a benefit, he would break Lennie's nose.

Although Judy continued to write songs and read scripts, she gradually walled herself off from friends. It was an instinctive, defensive process. She was self-conscious about her visibly declining health, she was afraid of being let down, and she was determined to spend time only with those who meant most to her. Judy occasionally saw the Buffingtons and another couple to whom she'd become close, Shirley and Willis Conover. The rest of her time she spent with Gerry, Yetta, Arnold, Helen, and Jonathan. David stopped by daily. Betty and Adolph stopped by hardly at all.

The pain was persistent, and it aged her. Her eyes looked weary, her smile careworn. There was no color in her cheeks, her skin became rough to the touch. Toward the end of the year she began to lose her hair. All of this she attributed to the diagnosis of the Park Avenue specialist, but that did not erase the ravages of which she was only too aware. She wore a wig and heavy makeup when she went out, if she went out at all.

One afternoon Yetta took Judy shopping at Saks. Judy picked out a few odds and ends and charged the merchandise. The salesgirl asked for identification, and Judy almost wept on the spot. She hadn't realized that the change was as obvious to others. For so long she had avoided day-to-day recognition. Now, when she most needed it, it wasn't there.

Judy became very involved in Gerry's work. She accompanied him when he opened at Birdland with Dizzy Gillespie. Between sets Dizzy came over to the table and Judy said hello. He did a double-take and quickly tried to hide his surprise. Judy said nothing about it but could see herself mirrored in his reaction. A short while before, Gerry had had a gig at the Village Vanguard. Max Gordon was watching from the wings when he felt a light kiss and heard a soft voice say, "Hi, Max." He turned to see Judy and gave her a warm greeting. They got together for dinner and laughed about the old days of the Revuers. It seemed so long ago.

As the holiday season approached, Judy was feeling somewhat better and she decided to throw a small New Year's Eve party at her place. People came and went over the course of the evening; there were familiar faces and some not so familiar. The next day, when she went to get her mink coat—her one concession to fame—she found it had been stolen. She turned to Gerry and said, "Boy, when things go bad . . ." The insurance company settled the claim for $1000 and that went immediately to Arnold who turned it over to the government.

Judy's strength started to fade. She spent more time at home in her bedroom. On good days Yetta talked her into shopping just to get some fresh air. One morning they went to Lord &

Taylor and were riding the elevator up to the dress department. The doors opened on the third floor, and a plump little Jewish lady stepped in. The doors closed and the lady looked at Judy as though she were a long-lost niece. "Judy, how are you?"

Judy studied the lady for some sign of familiarity, then as courteously as possible said, "I'm terribly sorry, but do I know you?"

The lady smiled and took Judy's hand. "No. But you're our Judy."

Judy smiled back.

A few days later she drove with Gerry to the plant district in lower Manhattan. They went from shop to shop and she purchased hundreds of flower bulbs of every description. She said she intended to surround the house in Washingtonville with flowers that summer, and Gerry told her he thought it was a wonderful idea. On the cab ride back uptown he seemed to know she would never see them in bloom.

The pain became acute and Judy took to her bed. She was prescribed painkillers, but they were only fitfully effective. In recent weeks her eyesight had begun to fail. She wore glasses, but the daylight hurt her eyes and she drew the shades. Those few friends who visited her bedroom were greeted by an almost sepulchral half-light. When the Conovers came to see her, she sat in bed wearing the wig she had worn in *Hot Spot*. At one point in the conversation she told them, "You're old friends. I'm not going to put up with this anymore." She removed the wig, and her head was wreathed in baby-fine golden curls, not unlike the way Jonathan had looked at birth.

Helen endured mightily. She waited on Judy and looked after Jonathan. David came by every day. Judy said nothing about her worsening health, but saw to it that David and Jonathan spent more time together. A nurse was hired to look after Judy, and she was an enormous help. But when the pain was most severe, there was nothing anyone could do. Judy woke up screaming late one night and Helen called Yetta who rushed over at once. The next day Yetta called a number of doctors, each of whom first consulted with Judy's physician, then refused to see her. Yetta suspected the worst. She hoped Judy was still abiding by the Park Avenue diagnosis, but that hope was soon shattered. The phone rang and it was Judy. The alcoholic wife of a friend had come to Judy for advice and comfort for years. The woman had recently burst into the bedroom drunk and hysterical. She threw herself across the bed and begged, "You must help me." Yetta commiserated at the insensitivity. Judy moaned, "What does she want from me? I'm dying. What does she want?"

Judy talked no more about death. She was frightened and depressed, withdrawn. Her near-blindness denied her the diversion of reading or television. Gerry was with her constantly. There were nights when her head would grow cold. He sat in a chair by her bed, stroking her head, warming her till dawn.

Earlier that year, before discovering the true extent of Judy's illness, Yetta had purchased a restaurant near New London, Connecticut. She hated the idea of being away from Judy, but she had to open that spring or risk financial ruin. Around the first of May, Yetta was in her apartment packing late into the night for her planned departure the next morning. It was after two when she got a call from David. He said he had asked his own physician to go see Judy. The physician in turn spoke with Judy's surgeon at Columbia Presbyterian, who admitted the truth of her condition. As gently as he could, David said to Yetta, "I have to tell you that Judy is dying." Yetta shrieked, then wept. She had known intuitively but had not let herself face it. Yetta explained she had to leave for Connecticut the next morning. David said he had to travel to Russia in order to record a Stravinsky concert. He would do what he could to prepare Jonathan for the inevitable. At least Gerry and Arnold would be there to look after Judy.

Yetta telephoned each day, even though the combination of medication and painkillers often left Judy somewhat punchy and confused. One morning Judy called Yetta and announced she was feeling better and wanted to make the hundred-mile trip to the restaurant in Connecticut. Yetta said fine, knowing the doctors would forbid it.

The next day Judy became semicomatose. When she was conscious, she realized the burden had become too much for Helen. She treasured Jonathan above all else and she did not want him to see her like this. After consulting with her physician, Judy had Gerry take her to Mount Sinai Hospital on May 26.

Arnold left strict instructions with the head nurse that only a few people were to be admitted to Judy's room. The list expressly included Gerry, Arnold, Yetta, David, Harry, Maude, and Helen. Yetta traveled in from Connecticut several times. Helen could not bring herself to go to the hospital.

For weeks Gerry and Arnold took turns keeping vigil. Judy slipped further into a coma, with only fits of consciousness between eight and ten hours of unconsciousness. During one of her lucid moments, Gerry showed her the results of their latest attempt at songwriting. A few years earlier Judy had gone to see the Broadway comedy *A Thousand Clowns*. She enjoyed the play, and the image of the title became fixed in her mind. A few days later she wrote a poem using that title. Gerry had intended to put it to music for some time, and came up with the melody just after Judy entered the hospital. He sang it for her:

> A thousand clowns I'll bring you
> Just to make you laugh.
> A blue baboon
> And a red raccoon
> A lavender giraffe.
>
> A thousand stars I'll string you
> To weave into a crown,
> And pale perfume
> From a rose's loom
> And a peacock-feather coat.

A thousand songs I'll sing you
To help you with your dreams
Of rainbow's ends
And loving friends
And sparkling silver streams.

A thousand years I'll love you
Our love will never die
And when a thousand years from now,
They're looking at the sky

They'll see two stars together
As close as they could be;
One star will be you my love,
The other will be me.

Judy smiled faintly and tried to say she liked the song, but she had difficulty talking. A few days later, on Friday June 4, Arnold visited and told her he had taken Jonathan to a night baseball game at Yankee Stadium. She smiled again and squeezed his hand, unable to speak. She closed her eyes and did not regain consciousness.

At five A.M. on Monday, June 7, 1965, just two weeks shy of her forty-third birthday, Judy died.

21

~~~~~~~~~~~~~~~~~~~~~~

Yetta arrived at the Dakota late Monday morning. The place was filled with people. Yetta approached Gerry, and the two of them cried in each other's arms. She then noticed Betty and Adolph at the telephone. They were busy trying to reach Adlai Stevenson. They wanted him to deliver the eulogy they planned to write about what a great actress Judy had been.

Yetta walked over to Arnold with Gerry and nodded in the direction of Betty and Adolph. "Who the hell are they? Where the hell have they been the past year? I'm not going to let them talk about what a great actress Judy was. She was a great person. Arnold, I don't want them writing the eulogy."

Gerry and Yetta walked down Central Park West to the Ethical Culture Society and met with its president, Algernon Black. He agreed to deliver the eulogy, and Yetta gave him notes about what he might say. Certainly Judy had been a unique and stunning actress. She had probably done more than any other actress to pioneer the postglamour modern age of realistic, down-to-earth roles. Her whole approach to her art was one of professionalism and unpretentiousness. She embodied a decency of spirit. She found a style and humor and grace in the ordinary, and this was what her public had responded to so strongly over the years. With time she might even have realized her ambitions to write and direct. But that was secondary. What distinguished Judy was her humanity, her unfailing generosity to friends, her support of unpopular causes at a tremendous price to her career. This was Judy's true legacy, not just the memory of a handful of plays and films.

The funeral service was held at Frank E. Campbell's on Madison Avenue. Outside, thousands of people crowded the street to pay their last respects to a woman they had always seen as one of them. Inside, the Guarneri String Quartet played Mendelssohn and Mozart. There were more than five hundred mourners, many of them standing. The casket was surrounded by flowers from Katharine Hepburn and Spencer Tracy, Shelley Winters, Sydney and others. Algernon Black stepped to the pulpit and spoke.

"Every once in a while a human being lives among us who for intelligence, aliveness, charm, dignity, and grace seems to be of the gods.

"It isn't just a matter of popularity, it's an affection—not sentimental or superficial. She respected people. She never played down to people, but always respected their intelligence. To have the courage to love, to enjoy the differences among men, this was all in her comedy.

"No words can possibly say what we mean. And you can't say it in a moment, either. It will take time to appraise what she meant to us and our generation."

There was a graveside service for family and a few close friends. They returned to the Dakota for drinks. There had been an almost haunting sense of déjà vu about the day. All the old faces were there: Yetta, Betty and Adolph, the Buffingtons, the Conovers, Arnold, Gerry, Jonathan, Helen, Harry, Maude, David. Everything was in place; only, there was no Judy. She had been the unique center of this multiform little world. With her gone, everyone would drift; it would never be the same again.

People drank and talked, and talked about Judy. Later somebody asked Jim Buffington how he thought Judy would like to be remembered. He paused a moment, then said, "As a serious actress and a good person." Then his face betrayed a grin and in a warm imitation of Judy's Billie Dawn voice he added, "I'd like to be remembered as the most beautiful, skinny, long-legged woman you ever met."

People started leaving toward evening. Jonathan had gone home with David, and soon only Helen and Yetta remained. Helen was holding up bravely, but she was dazed and Yetta decided she should not be left alone. Helen went to her room and was soon asleep. Yetta could not bring herself to step inside Judy's bedroom. Instead she stretched out on a living-room couch, drew a blanket over her shoulders, and hoped to dream of Judy.

Willis Conover had been keeping an eye on Gerry throughout the day, and when they left the Dakota he suggested they walk over to Broadway for a couple of drinks at a neighborhood bar. Gerry was bearing up as best he could under the strain. During the last weeks of Judy's life, he had started to see actress Sandy Dennis, and that helped alleviate some of the pain and loneliness. He sat at the bar looking straight ahead almost in a trance. Just then a stranger stepped over to the jukebox and played "The Party's Over." Judy's voice filled the room, as though she were returning Gerry's bedside song to her.

> The party's over,
> It's time to call it a day.
> No matter how you pretend
> You knew it would end this way.
>
> It's time to wind up
> The masquerade.

Just make your mind up
The piper must be paid.

The party's over
The candles flicker and dim.
You danced and dreamed through the night
It seemed to be right
Just being with him.

Now you must wake up,
All dreams must end.
Take off your makeup,
The party's over, it's all over,
My friend.

Gerry cried for Judy.

Index